IIAS Series: Governance and Public Management

International Institute of Administrative Sciences (IIAS)

The International Institute of Administrative Sciences is an international association with scientific purpose based in Brussels. As a non-governmental international organization its activities are centred on the study of public administration and on providing a forum in which comparative studies – including both practical experiences and theoretical analyses of experts in public administration from all cultures – are presented and discussed. The Institute is interested in all questions related to contemporary public administration at national and international levels.
Website: http://www.iias-iisa.org

Governance and Public Management Series

Series edited by:

Gérard Timsit, Emeritus Professor, University of Paris 1 Panthéon Sorbonne;
Wim van de Donk, Tilburg University, The Netherlands

Series Editorial Committee:

Gérard Timsit, IIAS Publications Director
Rolet Loretan, IIAS Director General
Wim van de Donk, Member and Series Editor
Michiel De Vries, Member
Christopher Pollitt, Member, IRAS Editor in Chief
Fabienne Maron, IIAS Scientific Administrator and Publications Coordinator

The *Governance and Public Management* series, published in conjunction with the International Institute of Administrative Sciences (IIAS), brings the best research in public administration and management to a global audience. Encouraging a diversity of approaches and perspectives, the series reflects the Institute's commitment to a neutral and objective voice, grounded in the exigency of fact. How is governance conducted *now*? How could it be done better? What defines the law of administration and the management of public affairs, and can their implementation be enhanced? Such questions lie behind the Institute's core value of *accountability*: those who exercise authority must account for its use – to those on whose behalf they act.

Governance and Public Management Series
Series Standing Order ISBN 978–0230–50655–8 (hardback)
978–0230–50656–5 (paperback)
(*outside North America only*)

You can receive future titles in this series as they are published by placing a standing order. Please contact your bookseller or, in case of difficulty, write to us at the address below with your name and address, the title of the series and the ISBN quoted above.

Customer Services Department, Macmillan Distribution Ltd, Houndmills, Basingstoke, Hampshire RG21 6XS, England

Innovation in the Public Sector

Linking Capacity and Leadership

Edited by

Victor Bekkers, Jurian Edelenbos and Bram Steijn

Professors of Public Administration, Department of Public Administration, Erasmus University Rotterdam, the Netherlands

First published 2011 by
PALGRAVE MACMILLAN

Palgrave Macmillan in the UK is an imprint of Macmillan Publishers Limited,
registered in England, company number 785998, of Houndmills, Basingstoke,
Hampshire RG21 6XS.

Palgrave Macmillan in the US is a division of St Martin's Press LLC,
175 Fifth Avenue, New York, NY 10010.

Palgrave Macmillan is the global academic imprint of the above companies
and has companies and representatives throughout the world.

Palgrave® and Macmillan® are registered trademarks in the United States,
the United Kingdom, Europe and other countries.

ISBN 978–0–230–28452–4 hardback

This book is printed on paper suitable for recycling and made from fully
managed and sustained forest sources. Logging, pulping and manufacturing
processes are expected to conform to the environmental regulations of the
country of origin.

A catalogue record for this book is available from the British Library.

Library of Congress Cataloging-in-Publication Data
Innovation in the public sector : linking capacity and leadership /
    edited by Victor Bekkers, Jurian Edelenbos, Bram Steijn.
        p.   cm.
    Includes index.
    ISBN 978–0–230–28452–4 (hardback)
    1. Organizational change.   2. Administrative agencies—
Management.   I. Bekkers, V. J. J. M.   II. Edelenbos, Jurian.
III. Steijn, Abraham Jan, 1959–
JF1525.O73I57 2011
352.3'67—dc22   2011004357

Printed and bound in Great Britain by
CPI Antony Rowe, Chippenham and Eastbourne

Contents

Part IV Discussion

List of Figures and Tables

Figures

Tables

Notes on the Contributors

Damon Alexander is a research fellow in the School of Social and Political Sciences, University of Melbourne.

Victor Bekkers is Professor of Public Policy at the Department of Public Administration, Erasmus University Rotterdam and Director of the Center for Public Innovation, the Netherlands.

Mark Considine is Professor and Director at the Centre for Public Policy, Department of Political Science, University of Melbourne, Australia.

Jurian Edelenbos is Professor of Water Governance at the Department of Public Administration, Erasmus University Rotterdam, the Netherlands.

Lars Fuglsang is Associate Professor in Social Sciences at the Department of Communication, Business and Information Technologies, Roskilde University, Denmark.

Ernst Ten Heuvelhof is Professor of Public Administration at Delft University of Technology and the Erasmus University Rotterdam, the Netherlands.

Tarmo Kalvet is Senior Research Fellow of Technology Governance at the Department of Public Administration, Tallinn University of Technology, Estonia.

Rainer Kattel is Professor of Innovation Policy and Technology Governance at Tallinn University of Technology, Estonia.

Joop Koppenjan is Professor of Public Administration at the Faculty of Social Sciences, Erasmus University of Rotterdam, the Netherlands.

Martijn Leijten is Assistant Professor of Organization and Management at the Faculty of Technology, Policy and Management, Delft University of Technology, the Netherlands.

Veiko Lember is a research fellow at the Department of Public Administration, Tallinn University of Technology, Estonia.

Jenny M. Lewis is Professor of Public Administration and Public Policy at the Department of Society and Globalization, Roskilde University,

Denmark, and the School of Social and Political Sciences, University of Melbourne, Australia.

Pauline Meurs is Professor of Health Care Governance at the Institute of Health Policy and Management, Erasmus University Rotterdam, the Netherlands.

Mirko Noordegraaf is Professor of Public Management at the Utrecht School of Governance (USG), Utrecht University, the Netherlands.

John Storm Pedersen is Associate Professor at the Department of Society and Globalization, Roskilde University, Denmark.

Christopher Pollitt is BOF/ZAP Research Professor of Public Management at the Public Management Institute, Katholieke Universiteit Leuven. He is also Editor-in-Chief of the *International Review of Administrative Sciences*.

Tiina Randma-Liiv is Professor of Public Management and Policy at Tallinn University of Technology, Estonia.

Filip De Rynck is Professor of Public Administration at the Faculty of Business Administration and Public Administration, University College Ghent, Belgium.

Wilma van der Scheer is a researcher at the Institute of Health Policy and Management, Erasmus University Rotterdam, the Netherlands.

Bram Steijn is Professor of Human Resource Management in the Public Sector at the Department of Public Administration, Erasmus University Rotterdam, the Netherlands.

Wijnand Veeneman is Associate Professor of Organization and Management at Delft University of Technology, the Netherlands.

Joris Voets is Senior Researcher at the Public Management Institute at K.U. Leuven and Programme Coordinator of the Policy Research Centre on Governmental Organization in Flanders, Belgium.

Haiko van der Voort is a teaching professor at the Department of Policy, Organization, Law and Gaming, Faculty Technology, Policy and Management of Delft University of Technology, the Netherlands.

Part I
Introduction

1
Linking Innovation to the Public Sector: Contexts, Concepts and Challenges

Victor Bekkers, Jurian Edelenbos and Bram Steijn

The innovation challenge of the public sector

In March 2000, when the European Council met in Lisbon, it set out the Lisbon Strategy, also known as the Lisbon Agenda. This strategy is an action and development plan for the European Union (EU). Its aim is to make the EU 'the most dynamic and competitive knowledge-based economy in the world capable of sustainable economic growth with more and better jobs and greater social cohesion, and respect for the environment by 2010' (European Union, 2000). The assumption behind this strategy is that innovation is the main driver of economic change. It is often perceived that more innovation is required when relatively low productivity and slow economic growth in the EU are detected, and certainly when comparisons are made between the EU's economic performance and that of other countries such as China and India. The idea is also that innovation is a necessary condition for creating a competitive economy that will have a positive influence on environmental and social renewal. However, innovation itself presupposes an institutional environment in which companies, non-governmental organizations and governments are able to learn, develop and share advanced knowledge, which is also free to flow. The philosopher's stone is the knowledge economy, where innovation leads to an economy in which new knowledge, products and services can be developed. At the same time, the emergence of this knowledge economy is necessary in order to become an innovative economy.

The innovation challenge of public administration is twofold. First, governments play an important role in establishing the conditions that will enable a knowledge- and innovation-driven economy to prosper.

In order to realize the actions of the Lisbon Agenda, policy programmes have been drafted and implemented for this purpose. An example is the withdrawal of all kinds of administrative burdens so that young and talented scholars and scientists from outside Europe will consider European knowledge and research and development institutions as interesting prospective employers. Another example is the subsidizing of specific research and development projects in small and medium enterprises. A third example is the liberalization of (state-dominated) markets like telecommunications, water and energy supplies, as well as public transport systems. Through increased competition within these markets and the entry of new competitors, policy-makers expect new products and services to emerge. In particular, the innovation policies of the EU, in relation to the completion of the internal market, were grounded on the supposed benefits that liberalization and privatization would generate.

Secondly, innovative economies can only prosper if the public sector is also able to develop into an innovative sector that is able to deal with a number of vital societal challenges, such as the quality of the education system, the fight against crime, the regeneration of socially and economically deprived cities and regions, the development of a sustainable economy or of traffic infrastructure that lacks congestion. In meeting these challenges, governments are forced to reflect on their governance strategy. What kinds of interventions are needed to deal with these challenges? What policy instruments can be used effectively? With whom should government organizations cooperate, knowing that the resources (such as information, knowledge, competencies and money) that are needed to deal with these issues are scarce and limited? In meeting these challenges, governments are forced to reflect on their own internal organization and management structure. For instance, it may be worth looking at the rather fragmented and multi-layered structure of government, the rather bureaucratic culture of many governmental organizations or the quality of the human resources that are available. Hence, a competitive economic European sector also presupposes an innovative public sector, because the two sectors are interdependent.

It is clear that many western government organizations are wrestling with their role and position in society. This process is connected to uncertainties regarding the responsiveness of governmental organizations to societal challenges, which very often have a 'wicked' character, such as the fight against crime, traffic congestion, water management, air pollution, economic and social decline, and segregation. The ways in which governments are handling these problems not only affect their effectiveness but also influence the legitimacy of the governments themselves. Thus, it seems that governments and governmental institutions are being confronted with a substantial crisis of authority, a crisis to do with the legitimacy of the position of the government in contemporary society as well as to do with the process of acquiring legitimacy (Beetham, 1991; Morris, 1998). This process depends on a process of identification, taking place in the actual interactions between governments and citizens, companies, societal groups and societal organizations. These interactions are manifold: they include the delivery of public services, the development of a specific policy, the assessment of taxes, elections or the reconstruction of a neighbourhood (Adriaansens, 1985). The transformation of society, as a result of a number of autonomous economic, sociological and technological developments (e.g. individualization, globalization, increased interdependency and the penetration of network technology; see Castells, 1996) as well as government policies themselves (e.g. liberalization), has not only substantially influenced the role and position of government in society but has also influenced the ways in which citizens (or groups of citizens), companies and societal organizations have been able to identify themselves with the multiple (and often contradictory and ambiguous) roles, positions and functions of government in contemporary society. At the same time, governments are confronted with rising expectations from citizens, citizens' groups and companies to meet their demands, wishes and interests. For citizens, it has become increasingly difficult to establish the nature and identity of government. This has led to a number of uncertainties and ambiguities. Why do government interventions make sense? Why should they be perceived as being meaningful? What is the role of politics in dealing with different collective challenges, such as the creation of sufficient economic growth, safe neighbourhoods or a sustainable environment (Stone, 2003)? How to deal with actors who take up their own role in organizing collective action? Hence, it can be argued that there is a growing alienation in characterizing the relationship between government and society. This undermines the effectiveness and legitimacy of government, which forces governmental organizations to embark on an 'innovation journey' (cf. van de Ven et al., 1999).

The aim of this chapter

This chapter addresses a number of backgrounds, concepts and issues that are relevant to achieving an understanding of the nature of the innovation journeys on which public organizations have embarked. The need to innovate, as will be argued, does not only reflect a desire to create a more efficient and effective government, which is to some extent the dominant view in the new public management literature and which is often focused on the modernization of public service processes (Osborne and Brown, 2005; Bekkers et al., 2007; Windrum and Koch, 2008). It will be argued that an innovative public sector is required to create a legitimate public sector that is able to meet a number of 'wicked' societal challenges – challenges for which innovative approaches have to be developed and implemented that reconcile different and very often contrasting values, of which efficiency and effectiveness are just two, in a trustworthy and appropriate manner (March and Olsen, 1989; Korteland and Bekkers, 2008). This also has implications for the assessment of public sector innovations. Furthermore, it will be argued that in order to create an innovative public sector, one of the challenges for government organizations is to invest in their linking capacities. The development of these linking capacities can be perceived as a necessary condition for public sector innovation, while the need to innovate can be understood from the need to restore the lost connections between government and society. What are the relevant mechanisms that play an important role in the creation of the new linkages? Is the specific nature of the public sector itself (in terms of, for example, the lack of competition and its bureaucratic nature) a handicap in the creation of these linkages? Does the public sector have its own incentives (in contrast to the private sector) that stimulate innovation? In addition, if public innovation is defined as being a necessary condition for establishing meaningful interactions between the government and society (in terms of lost connections and linking capacities), what are the relevant issues that may explain successful processes and forms of public innovation? The next few sections address these issues.

Lost connections and linking capacities

The need for public innovation can be defined as the search for new ideas and concepts, technologies, techniques and methods, forms, systems and procedures to create meaningful interactions between the government and society in order to deal with a number of societal challenges. In investigating the potential of the public sector to be innovative, it is interesting to see what kinds of developments have contributed to the notion that these interactions have become more meaningless and have contributed to the loosening of the connections between the government and society. As the authors themselves have witnessed numerous attempts to reconnect the government with society, which also exhibits the willingness of governments to innovate, it may be helpful to have a closer look at a number of modernization and innovation programmes.

Lost connections: Disconnecting government

Over the course of the last few decades, several developments (that are partly autonomous and partly emerging as intended and unintended outcomes of political decision-making) have contributed to the creation of a growing distance between the government and society. This increasing gap has raised questions about the effectiveness, legitimacy and responsiveness of the government in such a way that they may be framed as lost connections. Without pretending to be able to provide an extensive list, the following developments can be mentioned.

Societal and organizational fragmentation

The continuous process of societal and organizational specialization, differentiation and fragmentation has contributed to a 'scattered society' (Frissen, 1999) and, as a consequence, to a scattered public sector. This development has led to a rather narrowly defined, self-referential, partial, one-dimensional, mono-rational approach towards complex societal problems and citizens' needs. This narrow approach fails to appreciate the problems and needs, where different but interdependent aspects and factors as well as multiple rationalities do play an important role (Luhmann, 1984; Mayntz, 1987; Willke, 1991). The emerging process of alienation between the government and society could therefore, according to Habermas (1987) and Mannheim (1980), also be understood in terms of a growing functional rationalization of society in which the substantial rationality of the 'living world' of citizens is colonized by the 'system world' of public administration.

The alleged crisis of representative democracy

Furthermore, there is an alleged crisis of representative democracy and its institutions (e.g. Barber, 1984). These institutions fulfil a role in the binding allocation of political values for society as a whole (cf. Easton, 1965). This crisis can be described as a situation of lost connections as well. Some scholars (e.g. Barber, 1984) argue that there is a division between citizens and politics, where elected representatives do not represent the 'will of the people' and are prone to elitism.

On a more fundamental level, the crisis of representative democracy can be understood as a consequence of a number of other developments, such as the process of individualization, the collapse of the 'great ideologies' of the nineteenth century, the growing emancipation and empowerment of citizens (especially as consumers of public services and as engaged citizens with rising expectations) and the emergence of single-issue movements. These developments have eroded the legitimacy of the claims and arguments put forward by governments and politics on behalf of the citizen. The citizen himself, his individual interests, needs and beliefs have moved into the centre of the political and administrative system, and so far governments have not reacted appropriately (Bekkers et al., 2006).

Globalization

Another relevant development that contributes to a disconnected government is the globalization of economic, social and cultural life. Industrial society has transformed itself into a network society in which, based on the pervasiveness of modern information and communication technology (ICT) in our economic, social and cultural life, a new economic and political order has emerged. This is an order in which the role of the state or government has fundamentally been hollowed out (Castells, 1996). These processes of transformation already existed, but with their speed and impact they reached new dimensions. It has forced governments to undergo major changes, such as the establishment of international competitive welfare states, supporting a strong knowledge- and service-based economy, and the management of all kinds of migration flows.

Europeanization

Partly as a result of the previously discussed development, the process of European integration and the increased Europeanization of policy-making and implementation have led to a shift in governance from the nation state towards European institutions in order to effectively coordinate the economic, social and safety issues with which European countries are being confronted and that can no longer be solved nationally. Besides this shift towards European institutions, there has also been a shift towards other international and supranational organizations. This change has contributed to the 'hollowing out' of the traditional role of the state, based on clear geographical boundaries and jurisdictions, and thereby contributes to alienation mentioned earlier (van Kersbergen and van Waarden, 2004). At the same time, the democratic legitimacy of a number of these international institutions appears to be at a rather low level. The relatively low turnout at the European elections in 2009 can be seen as an indicator of the low level of trust that many people in Europe currently have in European political institutions.

The market-based revolution in public administration

One final development that may have contributed to the disconnection between the government and society is the transfer of the rather classical functions of the state and the public sector on the delivery of (semi-)public goods and services towards the private sector, and the introduction of a stronger market orientation, such as the liberalization of the health care sector and the energy market. The assumption underlying this development is that citizens should act as proactive rational consumers. There is, however, some doubt on the necessity of such a shift in roles and the frame of reference. For instance, do citizens want to act as rational consumers? How transparent are liberalized markets? As a result of this shift, public and political concerns have emerged regarding the way in which public interests have to be safeguarded in these new, liberalized sectors (WRR, 2001). Furthermore, the introduction of private sector-based frames of reference in the public sector has also stimulated the use of market-based management techniques, new governance and organizational concepts and instruments, such as performance management, outsourcing, privatization, agency formation, quality management and e-government (Pollitt and Bouckaert, 2000).

Linking capacity: Reconnecting government

In the current practice of public administration, there is a permanent quest to restore these 'lost links' and to establish new meaningful connections and interactions, which also influence the content of many public innovation programmes and processes (e.g. Bekkers et al., 2007). This quest certainly appeals to the linking capacity of public administration. Hence, one of the central challenges of public administration is to develop their own linking capabilities or to mobilize the connective capability of society and societal groups themselves. The popularity of a number of temporary ideas, concepts and instruments in public administration may also be interpreted as expressions of the desire to create new links, to adjust the current links or to re-establish the old links between society and government. For instance, the call for integrated policy-making and service delivery, the plea for vision and leadership, the discussion about norms and values, the emergence of network steering but also of re-centralization, discussions about electronic government and about citizenship, the importance of accountability and the emphasis on e-government can all be defined as ways to connect government to society in a meaningful way or to establish meaningful interactions between the two.

During the last two decades, three major reform programmes have been formulated and are being embraced by many governments in order to meet a number of internal and external challenges.

New public management

The rather permanent discussion about fundamental flaws in the functioning of public administration has led to a counter-movement with reform ambitions. Established in the late 1980s, 'New Public Management' (NPM) has evolved into a highly popular label for a wide variety of reforms in the public sector (Hood, 1995). Pollitt (2003, pp. 27–28) identifies the following eight key elements of 'New Public Management':

- A shift in values and priorities away from universalism, equity, security and resilience towards efficiency and individualism, defining the role of a citizen as a 'homo economicus'
- A shift in the focus of management systems from inputs and processes towards results and outputs
- A shift towards measurement and quantification, especially through the development of performance indicators and benchmarking systems
- A preference for more specialized, 'lean', 'flat' and autonomous organizational structures
- A substitution of formal, hierarchical relationships between or within organizations by contracts or contract-like relationships
- A much wider deployment of markets or market-type mechanisms for the delivery of public services
- An emphasis on service quality and a consumer orientation
- A broadening and blurring of the frontiers between the public sector, the market sector and the so-called third or non-profit sector.

As NPM has been embraced by politicians, policy-makers and scholars of public administration over the course of the last ten years, the result has been that 'the so-called public sector is becoming more business-like, with the introduction of competition, output measures and corporate management styles' (Lawton, 2005, p. 231). This has also influenced the innovation agenda of public administration and the use of ICT in order to achieve these specific modernization goals. From an NPM perspective, public innovations should be focused on creating a business-like public sector (Lawton, 2005).

Governance

An important conceptual change within public administration has been the shift from 'government to governance' (Kickert et al., 1997; Rhodes, 1997; van Kersbergen and van Waarden, 2004; Frederickson, 2005). Although governance is a popular concept that acts as a container for many reform programmes, it can be argued that all applications of the governance concept have three elements in common (van Kersbergen and van Waarden, 2004). First, the governance concept refers to pluricentric rather than unicentric systems. The governance approach assumes that the actions of a wide variety of public, private and semi-public actors affect social problems like organized crime and socially deprived neighbourhoods in large cities. Successful interventions in these problems require the organized, concerted actions of all of these actors, thereby overcoming the problems of collective action that this variety of actors implies. This presupposes that the actors are able and willing to define their interdependency (Rhodes, 1997; Koppenjan and Klijn, 2004). Secondly, networks, whether inter- or intra-organizational, play an important role. These networks organize relations between relatively autonomous, but interdependent actors. In these networks, hierarchy or monocratic leadership is less important or even absent. The formal government may be involved, but not necessarily so, and if it is, it is merely one – albeit an important – actor among many others. Thirdly, the focus is on the processes of governing instead of the structures of government. These processes concern negotiation, concentration and cooperation rather than the traditional processes of coercion, command and control (van Kersbergen and van Waarden, 2004, p. 152).

The innovation agenda that is based on the idea of governance tries to set out the conditions under which cooperation between different public, semi-public and private actors can become successful as well as to develop all kinds of network-like arrangements that are required in order to pick up all kinds of 'wicked policy problems'.

E-government

Since the emergence and massive penetration of ICT in our daily lives at the beginning of the 1990s, governments have embraced the innovation potential of the Internet in particular to rearrange their relationship with society. Related innovation programmes have been labelled as 'electronic government', or e-government. The OECD (2003) definition of e-government is the use of ICT, particularly the Internet, as a tool to achieve better government. Central to this is the promise that ICT will result in a better government which is more open, more accessible, more responsive, more collaborative and more demand-oriented than government in the pre-Internet era. ICT has the potential to break down all kinds of barriers that clients face. If it is used properly, a seamless and integrated government that operates as a whole becomes reality. E-government is described here as the use of modern ICT, especially the Internet and Web technology, by a public organization to support or redefine the existing and/or future (information, communication and transaction) relations with external and internal 'stakeholders', in order to create added value (Moon, 2002; Bekkers and Homburg, 2005). The relevant stakeholders include citizens, companies, societal organizations, other government organizations and civil servants. Added value can be found in the following goals: increasing the access to government; facilitating the quality of service delivery; stimulating internal efficiency; supporting public and political accountability; increasing the political participation of citizens; and improving inter-organizational cooperation and relations.

Reinventing the state?

At the same time, the three major reform movements and the innovation programmes that have been developed in their slipstream have not produced only blessings. Some negative side effects of these movements should also be taken into consideration because they can be perceived as contributing to the 'lost connections' mentioned earlier. For instance, although NPM has led to a substantial modernization of contemporary public administration (OECD, 2005), some scholars have pointed to the fact that as a consequence, economic and more instrumental values, such as efficiency and effectiveness, have become more important in relation to more political and substantial values, such as freedom, equity and security. Some even talk about the emergence of a 'managerial state' (Clark and Newman, 1997) in which the perverse effects of a managerial approach towards societal problems contribute to the alleged process of alienation, in which values and problem definitions other than efficiency and effectiveness are suppressed (Ringeling, 1993). In addition, the paradigm shift from 'government to governance' raises new questions. In order to create new, meaningful interactions between governmental and other actors, new authority structures and arrangements must emerge that go beyond the traditional jurisdiction of a state (for instance, international and supranational cooperation). Alternatively, within a state, new cooperative arrangements can develop that cross the traditional jurisdictions of intra-state public organizations (for instance, public–private partnerships and regional cooperation structures between municipalities), very often in order to improve the effectiveness of collective efforts, such as the desire to improve public safety or the sustainable development of urban and rural regions. However, within these emergent governance arrangements, binding collective decisions are being made and power is being exercised. The consequence is that governance arrangements can be seen as a political order, but what is the legitimacy of this new political order that goes beyond the traditional political order that is represented by the classical institutions of the state (Bekkers et al., 2007)?

The financial crisis of 2008 and 2009, in which the globalized banking system collapsed and governments were forced to intervene on a massive scale, has illustrated the added value of governments to ensure financial, economic and social stability. At the same time, it forces governments to impose impressive cut-back programmes on society and on themselves in order to finance the massive expenditures that have been made to soften this financial crisis. Hence, it could be argued that politics and society are 'bringing the state back in' (cf. Evans et al., 1985). This implies that, at the end of the first decade of the twenty-first century, a new innovation agenda for the public sector will emerge, which will embrace the necessity of the goals that have been formulated in the Lisbon Agenda even more (see Section 1).

A number of developments and reform ideas have now been discussed that illustrate the nature of the past and present innovation agendas of the public sector. However, the notion of innovation, and of public innovation in particular, has been taken for granted. Hence, it is important to discuss the nature of public innovation.

The concept of public innovation

This section discusses the idea of innovation, by looking at the nature of innovation as well as exploring a number of innovations.

Innovation as change and learning

Innovation can be defined as being a necessary condition for the modernization of government in order to meet new societal challenges. One of the founding fathers of modern innovation theory, Joseph Schumpeter (1942), defined innovation as a process of creative destruction in which 'new combinations of existing resources' are achieved. However, in his view, innovation cannot be separated from entrepreneurship. They are two sides of the same coin. He defines entrepreneurship as 'Die Durchsetzung neuer Kombinationen'; that is, as the will and ability to achieve new combinations that have to compete with established combinations. An innovation itself has been mostly defined as 'an idea, practice or object that is perceived as new by an individual or unit of adoption' (Rogers, 2003; Fagerberg et al., 2005).

Innovation requires change and the willingness to learn, but change is not always necessarily innovative, while a learning process does not always lead to new ideas, practices and so on (Rogers, 2003; Osborn and Brown, 2005; Veenswijk, 2006). The important factor is how radical the innovation is; what is the 'newness' of the change that has occurred and what is the nature of the learning process that has led to the willingness to change? A distinction can be made between (a) incremental innovations, which can be defined as minor changes in existing services and processes; (b) radical innovations, which fundamentally change the existing ways of organizing or delivering services as well as produce new products and services; and (c) systematic or transformative innovations, which are defined as major transformations that emerge, for instance, from the introduction of new technologies (like the steam engine or the Internet) (Mulgan and Albery, 2003). According to McDaniel (2002), it is also important to make a distinction between evolutionary and revolutionary innovations. Evolutionary innovations occur within an organization rather incrementally, allowing an organization to adjust to small changes in its internal and external environment. Revolutionary innovations are not part of the normal process of adaption and change, but create major upheavals within an industry or policy sector. They represent major breakthroughs and create major changes. However, what is essential is that innovations make a difference, in such a way that the actors involved perceive the innovations as discontinuity with the past (Osborn and Brown, 2005).

However, the need to break with the past and the willingness to change presupposes a learning process within governments. What is the nature of this learning process? Does this process focus on the fine-tuning of the output and the outcomes of specific policy programmes, as well as the instruments and resources that are used to produce specific policy outcomes? Or does this (implicit or explicit) learning process focus on the (conceptual) assumptions that lie behind the management and organization of specific policy programmes (Argyris and Schön, 1978; Hall, 1993)? How is feedback organized so that knowledge, information and experiences are used to improve existing programmes or to develop new programmes, also in relation to changing societal and political circumstances (Baumgartner and Jones, 2002)? In the first case, the nature of the learning and change process that occurs resembles the idea of incremental and evolutionary innovations. In the second case, the outcomes of the learning and change process can be defined as radical, transformative or more revolutionary innovations. Hence, it is important to investigate not just the nature of these processes but also the conditions under which these processes can take place. A related question is whether the specific institutional context of the public sector is an innovative context that supports renewal and modernization.

Categorizing innovations

Several attempts have been made in the literature to classify innovations. These classifications vary to some extent, but are rather similar in other ways (Schumpeter, 1942; McDaniel, 2002; Mulgan and Albury, 2003; Fagerberg et al., 2005; Moore and Hartley, 2008; Windrum, 2008). By drawing inspiration from these different classifications and translating them to the realm of the public sector, the following classification of public innovations is proposed here:

- Product or service innovations, focused on the creation of new public services or products. A Dutch example is the Integrated Environmental Licence, or the 'Omgevingsvergunning'. Different environmental permits, which deal with different legal obligations, based on different laws and regulations that have to be taken into consideration if a citizen or a company wants to build a new residence for its company (a shop, a plant or a farm) or wants to change a home, have been integrated into one umbrella-like permit
- Technological innovations that emerge through the creation and use of new technologies, such as the use of text messaging devices and cell broadcasting to warn citizens in case of an emergency
- Process innovations, focused on the improvement of the quality and efficiency of internal and external business processes, such as the

redesign of service delivery processes (e.g. the digital assessment of taxes)

- Organizational and management innovations, focused on the creation of new organizational forms, the introduction of new management methods and techniques, and new working methods. One example is the creation of performance management systems to monitor the outcomes of policy programmes or programmes that are aimed at increasing the mobility of public servants. Another example of organizational innovation is the one-stop shops that should prevent citizens and companies from being sent from pillar to post, when for instance they apply for a social benefit, a permit or other forms of government assistance
- Conceptual innovations. These innovations occur in relation to the introduction of new concepts, frames of reference or even new paradigms that help to reframe the nature of specific problems as well as their possible solutions. For instance, an innovative idea in water management is not the desire to control the flow of water as such – through dikes or the deepening of rivers and canals – but to create reservoirs that help to store abundant water
- Governance innovations, which are directed at the development of new forms and processes of governance in order to address specific societal problems, such as the governance practices that attempt to enhance the self-regulating and self-organizing capacities of policy networks
- Institutional innovations, which are fundamental transformations in the institutional relations between organizations, institutions and other actors in the public sector, and more specifically in public administration. Examples include the introduction of elements of direct democracy through referenda and the election of public officials, such as mayors, in a representative democracy in which some officials have been appointed by the queen, which is the case in the Netherlands (Bekkers et al., 2006, pp. 11–12).

However, it is important to note that these innovation types are not exclusive. In practice, the different types correlate with each other. For instance, the introduction of the Internet as a form of technological innovation enables governments to redesign the information and transaction relations and processes with citizens and companies in order to optimize working practices and information-processing (in terms of process innovation).

The two logics and the context of public innovation

Innovations in the public sector differ in two ways from innovations in the private sector. First, it is argued that the ultimate goal of innovation in the public sector is to achieve legitimacy. This goes beyond the development of new products and services, the exploitation of new markets and the invention of new production processes in order to meet the changing needs of consumers. This also goes further than fulfilling needs at an acceptable price that is set by the balance between the demand and supply of these new innovative products and services. Secondly, public sector innovations differ from private sector innovations when taking into account the specific institutional context in which they emerge. How decisive is this context? Although competition is viewed as a necessary condition for innovation which, according to some scholars, leads to a hardly innovative public sector, it is argued here that the public sector can also be perceived as an innovative sector.

Innovation caught between consequentiality and appropriateness

How should innovations in the public sector and the sector's innovative capacities be valued? Public sector activities are organized around two logics, from which specific values, norms and criteria can be derived in order to judge the innovative nature of public administration (March and Olsen, 1989). The first is the logic of consequence. Innovations can be judged from the perspective of the consequences they have and the preferences and expectations that precede them. Efficiency and effectiveness play an important role in the logic of consequence. Does the innovation work? What are the costs and the benefits, and how are they balanced? For instance, the storage of personal biometric data can be used in the fight against crime or terrorism. When assessing this innovation from the logic of consequence, the following questions would be asked. How reliable are the technologies that are used? What are the costs of a central database, and how accessible is this database? Furthermore, the reform movement described earlier that embraced the blessings of 'new public management' as well as e-government legitimized the changes that they advocated, by pointing at all kinds of efficiency and efficacy gains.

However, innovations in the public sector are also judged on their appropriateness, which, according to March and Olsen, means taking into account the specific political and societal context in which governments have to operate. It also refers to the specific identity of public administration (March and Olsen, 1989, p. 160). This identity is shaped in and by politics, which can be defined as the binding allocation of values for society as a whole (Easton, 1965). In this binding allocation, values and norms have to be balanced, given a specific situation and context. Hence, in the example of assessing biometric data, not only should costs and benefits be taken into account, but also the effects that this innovation has on other values such as privacy. Furthermore, in establishing the appropriateness of such an innovation, it is important to take into account the specific situation: the specific conditions in which the storage and use of biometric data are acceptable. This suggests the need to take into account the balancing between more economic and other values that lie behind innovations, while trying to meet the needs and challenges of specific groups or of society as a whole (in terms of responsiveness). The ability of government to achieve appropriateness through the introduction of specific 'rules' can be seen as the necessary condition for creating a legitimate government. By rules, March and Olsen (1989, p. 22) mean 'the routines, procedures, conventions, roles, strategies, organizational forms and technologies around which political activity is constructed'.

An innovative public sector. Contradictory terms?

The political character of the public sector also affects its ability to innovate. As mentioned earlier, innovations in the public sector should be judged not only on their consequentiality but also on their appropriateness. In order to achieve the right level of appropriateness, governments have developed all kinds of rules to safeguard the lawfulness, rightness and justness of their decision-making processes (Morris, 1998). Some scholars believe that these rules and the specific political setting of public administration lead to a situation in which innovation is hardly possible. Other scholars have put forward arguments that innovation in the public sector does take place. These arguments are now explored (Bekkers et al., 2006, pp. 12–13).

Arguments against

Some have stated that innovation in the public sector is a contradiction in terms. In comparison with the private sector, the public sector may hardly be perceived as being innovative. Several arguments are put forward to support this statement. The most important one is that the public sector lacks competition, which is defined as a necessary condition for innovation. According to Schumpeter, innovation (as a process of creative destruction) is the cornerstone of any capitalist system. Companies can only survive if they are able to create new combinations: new products, new markets, new production methods, new organizations and so on (Schumpeter, 1942). The public sector is a sector in which there is no competition. Governments have a monopoly on the production of specific public and quasi-public goods and services. In some cases there has been a good reason for this, namely the failure of the market to provide public goods.

Moreover, the public sector is dominated by a bureaucratic culture in which standardization and formalization are important values; values that also refer to the 'Rechtsstaat' in which the rule of law, providing legal security and equality before the law, is an important asset. On the one hand, standardization and formalization foster these values, because they add to stability and predictability; on the other hand, they discourage individual initiative and risk-taking (Schumpeter, 1942, p. 207). Standardization and formalization can, therefore, hardly be defined as fruitful conditions for innovation. They can, however, be seen as important characteristics of mechanistic organizations. In a classical study, Burns and Stalker (1961) compared the characteristics of mechanistic organizational structures with organic ones. They concluded that there is a strong positive relationship between the organic nature of organizations and the capacity to adapt and to innovate. The characteristics of organic structures are a dynamic and complex organizational environment, horizontal coordination and a communication mechanism, and less standardization and formalization, thereby creating more variety and competition between ideas. Variety has also been considered a necessary condition for innovation. Through variety, it is possible to search for 'new combinations'. Scott (1998) has even declared that the state and state organizations in general do not like variety, which they perceive as a threat to their control, deliberately destroying the variety of locally developed solutions for wicked problems as well as the local and contextual intelligence and wisdom that have been used to develop these solutions.

Furthermore, the political nature of public administration, rooted in representative democracy, has been perceived to be a handicap for innovation. Three reasons have been given for this. First, the democratic and political nature of public administration is in many cases a culture of compromise, in which different political values and different rationalities should be reconciled. These compromises can hardly be defined as being innovative, because they have a rather incremental character, thereby referring to Lindblom's (1959) notion of policy-making as the 'science of muddling through'. The second reason is the negative perception and assessment of risk and risk-taking. Bureaucratic and political cultures are perceived as risk-avoiding cultures. They are rather dynamic in their conservatism (Van Gunsteren, 1976). Moreover, in a bureaucratic and political culture in which political and public accountability has become a very sensitive and risky issue (also in combination with the 'hyper' attention of mass media to following the actions of politicians and public managers), there are fewer natural incentives left to take specific risks by looking for 'new combinations'. The third reason is the short-term orientation of politics (Van Gunsteren, 1976). Drucker (1985) has stressed the importance of 'systematic innovation and entrepreneurship', which implies that organizations should develop a long-term, goal-oriented and systematic perspective on how to mobilize internal and external resources – such as knowledge, people and funds – in order to look for 'new combinations', thereby creating fruitful conditions for innovation. Investments in research and development and the setting up of research and development departments are examples of systematic innovation. However, in public administration, this long-term orientation does not exist. Politics is characterized by a short-term orientation, focused on winning the hearts of (possible) voters and interest groups through 'quick wins'. This is the reason why Schumpeter (1942, p. 93) was rather sceptical about the innovative nature of the public sector and the role of democracy in it.

Arguments in favour

However, in observing the practice of public administration, a large number of innovations can actually be seen. In observing the different and new perspectives on the role and position of government with regard to the steering of societal developments (in terms of modes of governance), the way in which the government has organized itself during the last five decades, the way in which public administration has introduced all kinds of quality, budgeting and performance management systems, the way in which citizens participate in policy-making processes, the way in which public administration attempts to improve its service delivery process, and the way in which ICT has been used, a process of creative destruction is discernable. However, in order to see these changes, it is perhaps important to use another perspective on innovation. It is important to switch from a rather dominant revolutionary perspective on innovation to a more evolutionary and incremental perspective, in which a long-lasting series of smaller steps have resulted in fundamental changes in the end (Zouridis and Termeer, 2006). These fundamental changes can only be seen if observed after some time has passed.

There are other arguments that support the idea that it is in the nature of the public sector to be an innovative sector (Zouridis and Termeer, 2006). Developments in the environment of public administration – such as globalization, individualization, fragmentation and computerization (see e.g. Osborne and Brown, 2005) – as well as the political and public problems that emerge from them can hardly be described as being stable and simple. They generate enough complexity and dynamism to force the government to search for new answers and approaches. Ecological problems, problems regarding the social quality in cities, the fight against crime and terrorism, the economic development of regions, the increasing ageing of the population in relation to the provision of social benefits, and the social and economic integration of ethnic minorities are all examples of 'wicked problems'. The way in which these social problems are translated into political and public problems, combined with the way in which solutions are formulated and measures are taken, creates permanent pressure on government organizations. The emerging turbulence is in many cases an important incentive to look for new combinations in order to be innovative, because it could, in the end, lead to changes in electoral voting, to changing political coalitions. Elections, mass media attention and the growing empowerment of citizens to raise their voices and to take action, if their interests are really at stake, all put the government under pressure to innovate.

The pressure to innovate and to look for new combinations is also being stimulated by the multi-rationality of public administration. Policy problems can be understood in terms of a permanent struggle between different rationalities (Snellen, 1987). A distinction can be made between political rationality (focusing on the question 'who gets what, how and when?'), legal rationality (stressing the importance of the 'rule of law'), economic rationality (stressing the importance of an efficient allocation of costs and benefits) and professional/scientific/ technological rationality (putting forward the values that relate to professional and scientifically acquired knowledge, based on e.g. professional standards and professional theories of action). The tensions that emerge from the confrontation of values can create a kind of dialectical process, in which compromises between these values are reached on a higher level, thereby creating new combinations of problem definitions and problem-solving strategies.

Innovation also refers to new ways of 'framing and naming', thereby creating new discourses, introducing new sensitizing concepts and opening the way to look for innovative solutions in order to overcome conflicts between these rationalities. Verbal and rhetorical innovation can be regarded as an important innovation strategy within public administration, because language and rhetoric are very important and powerful instruments in public administration for creating new coalitions that advocate new frames of reference (van Twist, 1994; Stone, 2003). One example of this kind of conceptual innovation is the notion of sustainability, which tries to combine economic and ecological values.

Another factor that adds to the innovative nature of public administration is the convergence between the public and private sectors, which stimulates a more intensive copying of private sector management, organization and technology concepts on the part of public sector organizations. Moreover, public sector organizations are more eager to learn from one another, which can be derived from the popularity of benchmarking and best practice studies. Therefore, learning by copying or mimicking best practices from the private sector and from other public sector organizations can also be seen as a potentially effective innovation practice (Pollitt and Bouckart, 2000).

Public innovation as linking capacity: Some relevant issues

Innovation in the public sector is influenced by a number of factors, several of which have been discussed in the previous sections. For a more managerial overview, in which for instance the influence of the environment, the structure and culture of organizations are discussed, Osborne and Brown (2005) are referred to. This section references a number of issues that have recently been discussed that are also valuable in providing relevant background information when reading the rest of the chapters in this book. However, a complete overview cannot be provided here. At the same time, the issues addressed here refer in one way or another to the idea that many public innovation attempts deal with the issue of establishing new linkages or restoring lost linkages, and the willingness and capability to do so.

Milieux of innovation

In the private sector, the idea of local seedbeds of (primarily technological) innovation is a well-known concept that has also been referred to as 'milieux of innovation' (Castells, 1996, p. 36). The empirical insight is that technological innovation is not made up of an isolated instance. It reflects a given state of knowledge, a particular institutional and

industrial environment, a certain availability of skills in order to determine problems and to solve them, an economic mentality to make
specific applications cost efficient, and a network of producers and
users who can communicate their experience cumulatively, learning by
using and by doing. The ability and willingness of the relevant actors
to cooperate and to link and share ideas, knowledge, experience and
information beyond traditional organizational borders, as well as to
exchange vital resources such as staff, is essential in these 'innovation
milieux'.

This insight is relevant to the innovation agendas of governments in
three ways. First, when policy-makers and managers within government
organizations embrace innovation as an important societal value, they
should ask themselves how they can create the conditions so that these
'milieux of innovation' can emerge and be fostered. Their role is more of
an infrastructural one, thereby providing the economic, social, cultural,
educational, physical, technological and environmental infrastructure
for the establishment of these 'milieux' – alone and in cooperation with
other relevant stakeholders. Secondly, in order to meet a number of
societal challenges, it is important to understand that these 'milieux'
emerge through the creation of policy networks. Policy networks can
be described as loosely coupled forms of cooperation between rather
autonomous but interdependent public, private and semi-public stakeholders that aim to create a shared innovative definition and approach
towards specific policy problems (Koppenjan and Klijn, 2004). Thirdly, it
is interesting to see how the characteristics of these 'milieux of innovation' match with the characteristics and factors that have been described
in the previous section on whether an innovative public sector is a
contradiction in terms, or if it is alive and kicking. Where in public
administration are these 'milieux' located? Are the necessary resources
available, and are they being shared? Is there an open attitude towards
'trial and error'?

Openness and variety

In relation to these 'milieux of innovation', it is important to look at
the process of innovation that occurs in these settings. In the private
sector literature, this process has been recently framed in terms of 'open
innovation'. A typical idea of 'open innovation' is that innovation is not
something that can be attributed to a person (the entrepreneur), or to a
research and development organization or department, but to the free
and interactive exchanges of knowledge, information and experience,

in which new ideas and concepts are discussed, tested and proven in intra- and inter-organizational networks, which are often intertwined (von Hippel, 1988; Chesbrough, 2003).

Openness refers to the absence of boundaries and the free flow of ideas, knowledge, information and experiences. Moreover, it involves the existence of an open culture and a safe context in which 'trial and error', 'reflection' and 'learning' can take place without penalization for making 'mistakes' or for not realizing results at once. Openness also refers to the availability of a variety of different perspectives and different bodies of knowledge that can be used and challenged. It refers to a free and informal space or network, in which there are not too many restrictions for developing new and creative ideas and concepts. Innovation often takes place in the 'grey, informal' area between formal organizations (Nooteboom, 2006). However, the organization of the embeddedness of these 'free spaces' is important for the follow-through or adoption of innovation in existing, formal organizations and institutions (Edelenbos, 2005). This adoption and diffusion of innovation often involves ensuring that there is a careful balance between exploration and exploitation (March, 1999). Exploration is the search, discovery, novelty and innovation. It involves variation, risk-taking and experimentation. It occasionally leads to important new directions and discoveries. Exploitation refers to the refinement, routinization, production and implementation of knowledge. It involves choice, efficiency, selection and reliability. It usually leads to improvements but is often blind to major redirections. Innovation means finding a good balance between exploration and exploitation: 'Both exploration and exploitation are needed (...). Exploration cannot realize its occasional gains without exploitation of discoveries. Exploitation becomes obsolescent without exploration of new directions' (March, 1999, p. 5).

Variety is also relevant from another perspective. Variety also refers to the closeness or openness of policy networks, when looking at the number and intensity of the relations that are maintained within these 'innovation milieux'. This is based on Granovetter's (1973) idea of 'the strength of weak ties'. The idea is that new, innovative ideas come from actors who are not in the centre of the network. Relative outsiders, who are loosely connected with the key players in the network, are more often a source of innovation than the actors who are closely and intensively linked with one another. Actors who know one another quite well are not surprised by their ideas and insights. These have been shared and are known. Actors who do not know one another well, either because they scarcely meet or because they have not met one another, more often represent new insights, ideas and perspectives. However, the meeting of people at the periphery and in the centre of a network does not automatically occur. Often, active management (boundary-spanning activities, see discussion below) is required in order to organize these interconnections (Edelenbos and Klijn, 2006).

Trust and social capital

Due to the emphasis on the networked character of all kinds of inter-organizational or intra-organizational 'public innovation milieux', another issue is the quality of the relationships between the actors involved. A free flow of ideas, knowledge and experiences will not occur if actors are afraid that the knowledge and information that they provide will be used against them in such a way that their interests are harmed. Hence, special attention is paid to the trustworthiness of the relationships between the actors involved and to the social capital that is present in these networks (Putnam, 1993, 2000; Fukuyama, 1995; Nooteboom, 2002). Fukuyama (1995, p. 26) has defined trust as 'the expectation that arises within a community of regular, honest, and co-operative behavior based on commonly shared norms, on the part of other members of the community (...) these communities do not require extensive contractual and legal regulation of their relationships because prior moral consensus gives members of the group (...) a basis of mutual trust.'

Hence, numerous studies have identified strong and stable relationships of inter-organizational coordination and cooperation as the solution to the somewhat puzzling question of product innovation (Maskell, 2000, p. 113). The emerging conclusion is that the process of innovation and learning is fuelled by interactions between distinct bodies of knowledge developed in independent organizations pursuing objectives of competiveness. However, if these interactions are purely market-driven interactions, then it can be observed that they have proved incapable of transmitting the qualitative information needed in developing new products in interaction between firms due to the asymmetrical distribution between the seller and the buyer regarding the main characteristics of what is offered for sale (Maskell, 2000, p. 113). These, but also other market failures, form the exchange of knowledge between firms that can only be overcome if and when open market relations are superseded by stable and reciprocal exchange arrangements based on some elements of trust (Maskell, 2000, p. 113). Trust thus characterizes relationships between organizations when each is confident that the other's present value of all foreseeable exchanges exceeds the possible benefits of ending the relationship (Maskell, 2000, p. 114).

These days, more and more empirical evidence is being provided that trust leads to better outcomes in complex decision-making processes (Edelenbos and Klijn, 2007). Much of today's information is specialist information and is not always easy to trade in. It is tacit information, which rests on the expertise of persons or organizations (parts). However, learning about and creating new solutions for complex problems requires that organizations exchange these specialist information and capabilities. In situations where there is trust, there will be greater levels of confidence in other actors and the flow of information and willingness to exchange information is likely to be greater as well. As a result, the problem-solving capacity is enlarged (see Zand, 1972; Deutsch, 1973; Lundvall, 1993). The same reasoning can be applied to stimulating innovation. From an economic point of view, involvement in innovation is a risky and uncertain activity (Lundvall, 1993). No one knows what the outcome will be or if efforts to create innovative products or solutions to problems will be successful. It is also next to impossible to create adequate control mechanisms against the opportunistic behaviour of other actors because nobody can know beforehand what kind of opportunistic behaviour they will need to protect themselves against. Trust can facilitate innovation because uncertainty about opportunistic behaviour is reduced, and the feeling that other actors will exercise their goodwill in the search for innovative solutions is increased (Zand, 1972; Nooteboom, 2002). By proving continued trustworthiness, a local climate of trust is produced that fosters the exchange of vital information in order to innovate (Maskell, 2000, pp. 114–115).

Leadership and boundary-spanning

In Schumpeter's (1942) definition of innovation as 'Durchsetzung neuer Kombinationen', special attention is paid to the idea of 'Durchsetzung' as the will and power to create and implement innovations. In Schumpeter's vision, the entrepreneur was the embodiment of this will to succeed. Leadership has been perceived as one of the cornerstones of innovation, because it plays an important role in changing the status quo, in breaking away. Hence, it can be seen that there is a strong relationship between innovation and transformational leadership (Burns, 1978; Bass and Avolio, 1994). The characteristics of this type of leadership are that leaders should be able to create and communicate a clear vision that inspires and unites, thereby changing the perceptions and values of others, that leaders should be able to cope with resistance and scepticism, thereby overcoming all kinds of hurdles, that they should be able to create a coalition of the willing, and that they should be able to create a context for change.

More recently, also in relation to the importance of networks or 'milieux of innovation', more attention is being paid to another type of leadership, which can be understood in terms of 'boundary-spanning' and 'brokerage'. Leifer and Delbecq (1978, pp. 40–41) have defined boundary-spanners as 'people who operate at the periphery or boundary of an organization, performing organizational relevant tasks, relating the organization with elements outside it'. These managers stimulate interactions between people at the intersections of different organizations in an informal area where (diverging) perspectives, values and information meet, leading to innovation. Boundary objects can be helpful in finding an initial common ground. Boundary objects provide a shared language that allows for a representation of domain-specific knowledge in a structure and format that are known on the other side of the boundary (Carlile, 2002). They provide a concrete means for specifying and learning about differences and dependencies across a boundary as rich representations of their own perspective (Carlile, 2002). These objects become 'tangible artefacts (...) like forms of communication that inhabit several intersecting social worlds and satisfy the information requirements of each of them' (Star and Griesemer, 1989, p. 393). These boundary objects, like visions as with transformational leadership, have different meanings in different social worlds, but their structure is common enough to more than one world to make them recognizable. The creation and management of boundary objects is considered a key process in developing and maintaining divergence and coherence in intersecting social worlds (Star and Griesemer, 1989, p. 393). This bringing together of different and new perspectives can also be called the 'structural hole argument' (Burt, 1992), which refers to the bringing in of new information, new knowledge and thus new actors between an existing network of actors and actors (or even networks) that have been separated from the activities in the specific network, thereby enhancing variety in the network, which has been earlier identified as an important condition for innovation (Schuller et al., 2000).

In studying public administration, these insights are revealed especially in agenda-setting theory, where innovation can be defined as the ability to open the policy window. The successful launch of a policy change (in this study's terms – an innovation) is the result of opening a window in the interplay between different streams: solutions that have been floating around become attached and coupled to a problem, while policy entrepreneurs seize the opportunity to change the decision-making agenda due to an increased political receptivity to discussing alternative problem definitions and solutions (Kingdon, 1995). Kingdon (1995, p. 179) has described policy entrepreneurs as advocates who are willing to invest their resources – time, energy, reputation and money – into promoting a position in return for anticipated future gains in the form of material, purposive or solidarity benefits. What are his qualities? He has expertise, he has the ability to speak for others, he is known for his connections or for his negotiating skills, which enables him to act as a broker while reaching out to other and new contacts and networks, and he is persistent (Kingdon, 1995, pp. 180–181). However, what is essential is his ability to couple not only actors and interest but also when the time is right.

The divergence and convergence of innovations

Another relevant issue is the diffusion and adoption of innovations within the public sector. Although there is quite a bit of literature on diffusion and adoption in the private sector (for an overview, see Rogers, 2003), little attention is paid to diffusion in the public sector (Korteland and Bekkers, 2008), with an exception in the literature on the transfer of policy concepts (Dolewitz and Marsh, 2000). Hence, it is important to identify which factors account for the diffusion of innovations in the public sector and to identify the specific factors that relate to the political context of these innovations. Korteland and Bekkers (2007) have shown that besides the functional characteristics of an innovation (in terms of, for example, relative advantage, observability, compatibility, trialability and reinvention), timing (with reference to the existence of policy windows and focusing on events that create new opportunities) as well as mimicking aspects are important.

Knowledge about the diffusion patterns of innovations is also interesting in relation to two convergence hypotheses. Is there convergence in the way in which different organizations within the national public administration as well as between different national administrative systems adopt innovations (e.g. Pollit and Bouckaert, 2000)? Also, is there convergence between the public and private sectors, when looking at the adoption of private management concepts and techniques in the public sector? In addition, how can this process of convergence, if it exists, be understood? Does the tendency of isomorphism to which DiMaggio and Powell (1991) refer really exist? Isomorphism refers to a constraining pattern in which more and more organizations adopt an innovation – either through coercion, group and peer pressure or imitation – which leads to a situation in which an innovation becomes a legitimate mode of operation. However, from the literature on 'policy innovation and transfer', the possibility of 'polydiffusion' is stressed, indicating an interpretation of the policy innovation and making it suitable in one's own context leading to differentiations of the same innovation (Mossberger, 2000).

The rationale of this book: Vision and overview

This introductory chapter has attempted to argue that the innovation challenge of the public sector in relation to the needs of public sector organizations is to engage in meaningful interactions with all kinds of actors in society, including citizens, companies, interest and issue groups, and non-governmental organizations. These interactions take place in the context of a number of societal challenges that have a rather 'wicked' character, such as the fight against crime, the social quality of urban regions or the ageing of the population. These meaningful interactions are not given, but they have to be established. However, the tragedy is that a number of societal developments (such as globalization and individualization) and several political developments (such as liberalization and Europeanization) have undermined the possibility of establishing these meaningful interactions. This has been described in terms of lost connections. Hence, the innovation challenge of the public sector is to restore the lost connections or to establish new connections. This implies that the linking capacities of public sector organizations are an important asset for developing and implementing public innovations. Hence, the first research question that this book deals with is:

How can public innovations be understood in terms of the need for linking capacities in order to create meaningful interactions between the government, the market and society?

A number of issues have been discussed that play an important role in the possibility of developing, fostering and implementing these linking capacities, such as the importance of 'public innovation milieux', the emergence of policy networks of collaboration, the openness of the networks and the variety of resources (knowledge, experiences, people, information and contacts) and actors in these networks, the social capital in these 'innovation milieux', the boundary-spanning role of leadership within and across these networks as well as the diffusion and adoption of new practices across organizational borders. Furthermore, when assessing the process and outcomes of public innovations it is important to re-conceptualize the factors that are normally put forward in the private sector innovation literature as being relevant for innovation. It has been argued that the nature of public sector innovation has a more evolutionary than revolutionary character. It has also been argued that although the bureaucratic character of the public sector frustrates innovations, the dynamic and complex character of the public sector in which different rationalities and values have to be balanced can stimulate innovation. Hence, the second research question is:

> *What role do 'milieux of innovation' play in the development and implementation of innovations in the public sector, what are the relevant mechanisms, and how does the specific institutional setting of the public sector influence the functioning of these milieux?*

When the outcomes of these linking capacities are assessed, it is important to take into account the specific nature of the public sector, which is 'the binding allocation of public values for society as a whole' (Easton, 1965). Public innovations – in terms of new products, processes, concepts and techniques that imply a discontinuity with the past – are always driven by an attempt to reconcile different values that go beyond sheer economic values such as efficiency and efficacy. Hence, in the assessment of public innovations, it is important not only to focus on the logic of consequence (stressing the efficient and effective consequences of these new products, services, processes, concepts and techniques) but also to look at the appropriateness of these public innovations, thereby contributing to a legitimate and trustworthy public sector (March and Olsen, 1989). Hence, the third research question is:

> *How can the process and outcomes of innovation in the public sector be assessed, given the need for government to act efficiently and appropriately?*

A number of the issues discussed above are returned to in the following chapters of this book. First, a number of the contributions deal with the specific context of innovation in the public sector. The institutional characteristics of the public sector itself should be taken into consideration as relevant characteristics of the 'milieux of innovation' in which public innovations occur, especially in comparing these characteristics to the private sector. This is the second part of this book: 'milieux of public innovation' (after a specific perspective on public innovation is introduced in the first part of the book).

What do these questions suggest for the planning of the chapters in this book? Christopher Pollitt addresses the question of how innovative the public sector is, as well as how a public sector that is involved in a continuous battle for innovation should be appreciated. Does the public sector have its own 'milieux of innovation', with its own characteristics and logics? The discussion about the innovativeness of the public sector is always mirrored through a look at the private sector. In comparing some empirical findings regarding the innovative nature of the Danish private sector with the public sector, is there a striking resemblance or are there distinctive patterns of innovativeness in both sectors? What does this tell us about the influence of the institutional context on the nature and degree of innovation in both sectors? Lars Fuglsang and John Storm Pedersen focus on this question in their contribution to this book. The institutional context may also be interesting from another perspective. The specific institutional setting of a country also refers to the availability of resources, which influence the degree and nature of innovation that takes place in a country and the innovation policies that are formulated. In their contribution, Rainer Kattel, Tiina Randma-Liiv and Tarmo Kalvet address the issue that smaller states have the administrative capacity to develop effective innovation policies that strengthen the economic positions of smaller states in an increasingly globalized and interdependent competitive environment. Lember, Kalvet and Kattel focus on the relationship between public procurement and public sector innovation in their chapter. The idea behind many policy programmes is that more competition will lead not only to lower prices but also to the development of new innovative services. Is this the case, when looking at the experiences of a number of Nordic Sea and Baltic cities? This is a relevant question as policy-makers define competition very often (also inspired by NPM) as a relevant condition to create 'milieux of innovation'.

The next part of the book (Part III) deals with the relationship between networks (as 'milieux of innovation') and the management of innovation within these networks that can be located within the government or along the boundary of the private and public sectors. Leadership is a relevant aspect of the management of these networks. Jenny Lewis, Mark Considine and Damon Alexander discuss how the nature of networks influences the management of innovation processes *within* the government. The chapter authored by Van der Voort, Koppenjan, Ten Heuvelhoff, Martijn Leijten and Wijnand Veeneman (Chapter 7) demonstrates how competing values and logics (as a source of variety) refer to different bodies of knowledge and rationalities within a policy network – regarding the construction of an innovative railway project, influence the management of such a project. This also affects the assessment of the outcomes of the project. Joris Voets and Filip De Rynck explore the innovative capacities of inter-governmental network managers as they operate along the boundaries of various organizations and networks with the Flemish government, and the different values and rationalities that they have to reconcile. Wilma van der Scheer, Mirko Noordegraaf and Pauline Meurs focus on leadership in the Dutch health care sector, in which entrepreneurship and competition have been introduced. How do health care executives perceive the necessary innovation and how do they retain legitimacy, when confronted with the balance between economic and societal values?

In the final part of this book (Part IV), Bekkers, Edelenbos and Steijn discuss and compare the findings of the previous chapters. The findings are positioned in the theoretical framework, which is set out in Chapter 1.

Part II

Contexts, Processes and Aspects of Innovation

2
Innovation in the Public Sector: An Introductory Overview

Christopher Pollitt

Introduction

This short introductory chapter attempts to do two things. First, it offers a few general observations that are designed to put innovation into some kind of conceptual and historical perspective. Secondly, it draws, from the observations, some guidelines – or at the very least, pointers – for the kind of research that is more likely to yield a better understanding of public sector innovation. This exercise is intended to set the scene for the more detailed, expert and nuanced contributions that follow. It also lays out some markers that can be taken up again towards the end of the book.

Putting innovation into perspective

To begin with, consider six observations.

One: Innovation is not a concrete object; it is a concept, or rather, a word that labels a concept. Even well-informed people can have quite strong disagreements about whether a particular development should or should not be 'awarded' this label – in other words, it is not always clear what is and what is not to be counted as 'innovatory' (see e.g. Moore and Hartley, 2008; Osborne et al., 2008). As the UK National Audit Office discovered: 'There is no widely accepted or common definition of what counts as an "innovation" ' (National Audit Office, 2006b, p. 4). To take one of many examples, Hartley (2005) acknowledges the definitional variety and then goes on to distinguish between:

- Product innovation
- Service innovation

- Position innovation
- Strategic innovation
- Governance innovation
- Rhetorical innovation.

At the same time, she excludes:

- Continuous improvement.

One can imagine, therefore, the huge problems of operationalization that are involved in research that attempts to compare rates of innovation among different organizations or during different time periods by *counting* innovations. There is also the meta-problem that those who wish to review the literature and conduct meta-analyses may well be comparing studies that do not use the same units of analysis.

This is slightly worrying because it means that the academic field of public administration has adopted yet another key concept that is difficult to define, operationalize or measure. In the last 15 years, for example, a lot of ink and paper has been spent on trying to stabilize and operationalize other key concepts, which include 'network', 'leadership', 'governance' and 'trust', among others. Thus, 'innovation' now joins the 'Vital but Vague' club. It is perhaps not a healthy sign for this field that so many of its key concepts are contested and vague.

Two: Innovation is not *just* a concept, although it is currently a very fashionable concept, with a strongly positive normative overtone. It is perpetually on the lips of politicians and management gurus. Innovation units of one kind or another have blossomed among governments, industry and academia. Among other things, innovation is supposed to be the magic that will preserve Western European and North American economic competitiveness against the emerging Asian challenge. It is also supposed to be the magic that will allow us to continue to improve public services while constantly driving their costs down. Barry provides an interesting historical perspective on this fashionable concept:

> In the nineteenth century, a measure of population was often used as an indicator of national well-being. By contrast, today, measures of research and development activity, innovation and intellectual capital have been turned into one of the clearest indicators of the health and creative productivity of the economy. The failure to be innovative, and hence the failure to modernize, is a moral one.

Measurement of innovative activity serves to reveal the failure, and establish a basis for its solution.

(Barry, 2001, p. 104)

Surely, then, no one can actually be *against* innovation? Yet, academics should always be somewhat suspicious of such seemingly magical concepts, especially when they seem to be so difficult to measure and pin down (Pollitt and Hupe, 2009). 'Destroy the old, create the new' was a saying of Chairman Mao's Red Guard during the Cultural Revolution, and the outcome measurements of that particular project were not exactly positive. The sad truth is that many of today's management seminars on innovation are littered with buzz words and woolly concepts while being almost entirely bereft of any specific, empirically grounded propositions.

Three: Innovation is nothing new. It may not always have been called innovation, but ever since the advent of, *inter alia*, waterscrews, writing and gunpowder, public authorities have been promoting, adapting to, regulating and sometimes commandeering innovations. Thus, the study of public sector innovation should not be imagined to be something that has only recently made an appearance. The early work of Rogers, which is now reported in the fifth edition of his classic text, *Diffusion of Innovations*, was carried out 50 years ago and included public as well as private sector cases (Rogers, 2003). There is much to be learnt from casting the net even wider, and further back in history, than some contemporary writers on the subject have so far been able to do (Pollitt, 2008). This is not to say that we are not facing new forms and trends in innovation. One recent trend, which should be of great interest to public administrators, is the way in which the public regulation of innovation and intellectual property has become an increasingly international endeavour, often mediated through various kinds of international organizations. 'Certainly, policing intellectual property rights has become a major concern for developing organizations of international governance' (Barry, 2001, p. 105). Some of these influential organizations are fairly bereft of democratic control, and may fall prey to well-organized corporate or professional interests, as Brunsson and Jacobsson's provocative work on technical standards has shown (Brunsson and Jacobsson, 2002).

Four: The common assumption that innovation occurs mainly or exclusively in the private sector, and that therefore we must turn to the private sector to find out how to do this, needs to be discarded

(Moore and Hartley, 2008, p. 6). Historically, the public sector has been a major source of innovations in organization, technology and ideas themselves. Consider just three examples. First is the novel planning and technology – including the floating, prefabricated harbours assembled in just a few days that were involved in the D-Day landings on the Normandy coast (Ferrand, 1997; Compagnon, 2001). The second example is the invention and progressive refinement of techniques for vaccinating entire populations, thus saving many millions of lives and avoiding countless morbidities (and one could add sparking hundreds, if not thousands, of other innovations in public education and health care, where professional teachers, doctors and nurses see it as part of their mandate to improve their services). Third is the Internet and the World Wide Web, which came out of two public organizations, DARPA and CERN, respectively (Mulgan, 2007, p. 4). This is not to say that the study of private sector innovations is irrelevant – far from it – but it is important to qualify the unrestrained priority some studies give to commercial contexts and to the false belief that only competitive markets can fuel innovation. There is no reason for public servants to feel any sense of inferiority when considering the record of public sector innovation. On a more positive note, it might make sense to look back at some of the major public sector innovations of the past and see if it is possible to identify any reasonable common denominator conditions that appear to be conducive to organizational and individual creativity.

Five: Innovation is risky business. 'Innovations often require departments to take well-managed risks' (National Audit Office, 2006a, p. 4). Many innovations do not work very well, and even some of those that do work turn out to have additional, undesirable and unforeseen consequences – such as the motor car, the hamburger, performance-related pay or – to make a 'sore point' – innovative financial derivatives that bundle up, *inter alia*, shaky home loans. '[I]nnovation does not necessarily lead to improvement' (Moore and Hartley, 2008, p. 9). It is quite rational to anticipate that a substantial proportion of innovations will fail, at least to some degree. Yet this must be considered in a context where:

> People in government fear nothing more than newsworthy failure ... When new initiatives fail – and inevitably a large proportion do – they become highly newsworthy, with a focus on who is to blame.
>
> (Altshuler, 1997, p. 39; see also
> National Audit Office, 2006b, pp. 5–6)

It may be worthwhile for public administrators who are interested in innovation to ask themselves the questions posed by Mulgan: 'What's a reasonable success rate to aim for in radical innovations: one in two or one in ten? Should civil servants rely on politicians for new ideas – or vice versa?' (Mulgan, 2007, p. 5). What would the range of answers among innovation experts look like, and if one believes such questions cannot be answered, why is that and where does it leave the experts as advisors to political and managerial decision-makers? Further – and possibly most difficult of all – how can politicians and other public office holders persuade the media and the public that it is acceptable, in certain contexts and under certain conditions, to spend public money on things that turn out to be failures?

For practitioners, the danger is that they will be instructed to innovate, be congratulated when their first innovation goes well, and then be denigrated when the next one fails. After this, new bureaucratic regulations will be imposed to prevent this kind of failure from being repeated. Such cycles or alternations from tight to loose to tight controls again are well-known occurrences in public management (Pollitt, 2008).

Six: The process of establishing intellectual property rights for innovations does not only concern the invention of the devices and procedures themselves. It frequently also entails the invention (or, at least, redefinition) of roles and subjects. 'Who or what the social subject of invention is may itself be up for grabs' (Barry, 2001, p. 106). For example, should writing innovative computer software be considered an act of authorship, where the individual author is awarded the rights of exploitation as a private person, or is it an act of design or invention, where the intellectual property can be bought and sold between corporations? Alternatively, what should be the policy towards potentially profitable innovations that happen to emerge from governmental organizations (be they ministries, agencies, laboratories, etc.)? *Pro bono publico* is an ambivalent guideline here. Is it in the public interest to give these innovations away for free, so that they can be quickly exploited by the market and civil society? Or is it more in the interest of citizens for the public authorities themselves to retain the property rights, and use any financial rewards to offset public expenditure and reduce the taxpayer's burden? Real world examples of both lines of logic are not hard to come by, but which should apply in which kinds of circumstances? What kinds of laws, both national and international, are needed to guide and frame these decisions? These are matters that should surely concern public administrators, since they are inseparable from the classic scholarly concerns with the distinctions between public and private, and with the application of the law to delineate and police that ever-shifting border.

Pointers for research on innovation

Since the social sciences in general and public administration in particular are ridden with deep epistemological differences, there can be no one, unified set of recommendations for future research. To simplify – almost certainly to *over*simplify – this chapter borrows from research in policy studies by using Kay's idea of a continuum from a nomothetic to an ideographic pole. Those closer to the nomothetic end believe in the possibility of general theory, favour hypothetical-deductive approaches and enjoy model-building and testing, if possible through the use of quantitative techniques (Kay, 2006, chapter 2). Those closer to the ideographic end are more pessimistic concerning the likelihood of broad, law-like generalizations and instead tend to emphasize the subtleties of context and interpretation. Among historical institutionalists, many currently favour the narrative as a form of synthetic sense-making and explanation provision. This may permit limited generalizations about context-specific mechanisms and processes, but not the general theories pursued by the other camp (Pollitt and Bouckaert, 2009, chapter 9). The two camps differ on many basic issues, including on the nature of causation and explanation (see e.g. Kurki, 2008). Certainly public administration, which has always been a multi-disciplinary field of scholarship, is part of the battleground on which these warring paradigms compete (Ferlie et al., 2005; Luton, 2008; Lynn et al., 2008).

Borins' recent book *Innovations in Government* (2008) gives us a good taste of the research agenda of those in the nomothetic camp. In the future, they would like to look more at populations of innovations than at individual cases. In keeping with this search for representative generalizations, they want to include failed innovations as well as successful ones. All this implies that there is a need to standardize the meaning of 'innovation' itself, so as to be able to count and compare. Further, the nomotheists want 'to know more about the impacts, in different kinds of task situations, of different organizational design and leadership practices on performance and innovation' (Kelman, 2008, p. 49). They want to sharpen their quantitative methods, relying less on simple cross-sectional surveys that cannot easily yield an understanding of evolutionary dynamics over time. Also:

Too much regression-based work on public management has used survey respondent self-reports of some aspects of the organization's performance as the dependent variable, while gathering information about predictor variables using self-reports from the same survey – creating the problem of common-method bias....

(Kelman, 2008, p. 50)

This all makes good sense, within this particular paradigm. However, it is not the only paradigm.

The approach taken by those closer to the ideographic pole is very different. To begin with, there is a deep suspicion of the 'variables paradigm' that continues to dominate not only the Kennedy School but also most of the American and much of the European social sciences. Andrew Abbott, in looking back at the Chicago School of sociologists, has put it forcefully thus:

[N]ot only do variables not exist in reality, they are misleading even as a nominalist convention. For the idea of a variable is the idea of a scale that has the same causal meaning whatever its context: the idea, for example, that 'education' can have 'an effect' on 'occupation' irrespective of the other qualities of an individual, whether those qualities be other past experiences, other personal characteristics, or friends, acquaintances, and connections...The Chicago view was that the concept of net effect was social scientific nonsense. Nothing that ever occurs in the social world occurs 'net of other variables'. All social facts are located in contexts. So why bother to pretend that they are not?

(Abbott, 1997, p. 1152).

Similarly, it may be argued that all public sector innovations occur in particular contexts, and therefore looking for general, de-contextualized models of how to increase innovations – for example, by 'leadership' or 'dedicated inter-disciplinary teams' – is likely to prove either fruitless or positively misleading. The conditions that lead to high rates of innovation in Japanese social care are quite unlikely to be the same combination that generates innovation in Dutch telecommunications regulation.

One obvious area for ideographic research is the idea of innovation itself. How has it risen to its current prominence? Which groups have promoted its growing popularity, and which benefit from its fashionability? What rhetorical strategies have been used to persuade us that it is so important? How has its meaning shifted from one period to the next and from one place to another? How does its career as a concept compare with that of other concepts that have risen to the top of governmental agendas in recent times, such as 'quality', 'leadership' and 'partnership'? How is its definition adjusted and manipulated to fit current preoccupations – why, for example, is incremental improvement frequently defined *outside* of the category of innovation, and what are the consequences of this in terms of organizational recognition and motivation? Why, for instance, did the UK central government's definition of innovation change from one of radical, discontinuous change to one of continuous improvement (Osborne et al., 2008, pp. 63–64)?

Secondly, what about public administrations that do *not* give innovation the rhetorical prominence it has received in northwestern Europe and in North America? Are they simply static and stodgy, or do they experience their own forms of change and improvement without the hype surrounding innovation? If so, what forms do they take?

Thirdly, what happens to innovations in the longer term? So much of the research on innovation has, understandably, focused on the early days – on the moment of innovation itself, what leads up to it, and what makes some innovations 'catch on' by attracting the right kind of 'early adopters'? However, what about the later stages of its development? Public management reforms are known to have dwindled and faded as fast they first appeared (Pollitt, 2007). What proportion of administrative innovations is short-lived, and is there any pattern to those that become perennials rather than fade after the first bloom? What are the basic plots of innovation narratives (Booker, 2004)?

Final reflections

Finally, perhaps some self-reflexivity is in order. After all, one of the stereotypical images of the innovator has been that of the tangle-haired mad professor. Universities are supposed to be one of the prime social sources of new ideas. Yet at the same time, as Kuhn has pointed out, most academics spend most of their time within a paradigm of 'normal science', which means that their ideas are cushioned within a dense framework of definitions and citations of previous work. Scholarly reputations are protected by fitting in ever so carefully with all the ideas that have come before. The ever more influential journal citation indices do not measure how innovative our articles have been; instead they measure how many of our peers have read them and wish to cite them. Some highly innovative papers receive low citation statistics, precisely because the academic peer group does not know quite where or how to fit them into the currently received orthodoxy. At our annual appraisal interviews we may be asked what we have published, but we are seldom asked what new ideas we have had over the course of the past year. If we do happen to have had a good idea, we may not receive much help or advice from within the university about how to spread it and implement it, or perhaps that advice is there but we do not know where to look for it.

In short, not only are we supposed to study innovation, as academics we are also supposed to *do* it. Books like this one are meant to be a way of generating new ideas through debate and interaction. It may be appropriate to conclude with the advice of the Nobel Prize-winning physicist, Linus Pauling. 'The way to get good ideas', he said 'is to get lots of ideas and throw the bad ones away.'[1] So let us begin the getting and the throwing away!

Note

1. (www.firstscience.com/home/poems-and-quotes/quotes/linus-pauling-quote_2399).

3
How Common Is Public Sector Innovation and How Similar Is It to Private Sector Innovation?

Lars Fuglsang and John Storm Pedersen

Introduction

This is a first attempt to compare innovation in public institutions with innovation in private firms in Denmark. Public institutions are often believed to be less innovative than private firms. However, innovations may, in fact, have always existed within the public sector – in forms similar to those found in the private sector. Innovations performed by employees in their daily work may even be critical to the reliability and overall stability of these institutions. This chapter argues that it is important to examine how innovation takes place in public sector institutions. While most of the discussions around New Public Management (NPM) and other government reforms have centred on their economic effects, much more attention could be devoted to innovation as a critical aspect of public sector change. Based on a comparison of two surveys to Danish public institutions and private firms, this chapter examines how frequently innovation does occur in public institutions, and compares similarities and differences between public and private sector innovation.

The problem context

It is a widely held belief that public sector institutions innovate less than private companies. Nevertheless, research has never been able to prove this (see e.g. Earl, 2002; Earl, 2004; Koch et al., 2005; National Audit Office, 2006a, 2006b). For example, in a Canadian study, Louise Earl (2002) found that in some critical areas of change, Canadian public sector organizations are almost twice as innovative as private firms.

In addition, Koch et al. (2005) found numerous examples of innovations in the public sector.

Furthermore, some studies that recognize public innovation have found that such innovation is often organized in a different way (see e.g. National Audit Office, 2006a). Private sector innovations are assumed to be more employee-based and responsive to users' needs. Public sector innovations are linked to the initiative of policy and senior managers, and they are organized in a top-down manner. Case studies indicate, however, that this is not always the case (see e.g. Fuglsang, 2008). Practice-based innovations or 'bricolage' integrated with daily routines do also exist. Innovations are sometimes hidden in the daily work of employees. Deviations from routine can be critical to making sure that public sector services work properly.

The issue of innovation is timely also in relation to NPM and government reform. NPM seems to be on the retreat at least in some aspects (Pollitt, 2003; Dunleavy et al., 2006). Perhaps it is better to say that NPM is an ongoing phenomenon that is defined and redefined several times. However, discussions around NPM have mostly been spurred by the economic effects it is believed to have. There is reason to investigate how NPM or government reform can respond to the need for bricolage and innovation in public sector daily activities.

Before this is done, more thorough investigations into how innovations already take place in different ways in public sector institutions as a response to various problems should be conducted. Public service research is needed to look at public sector innovation in a more systematic way. This could eventually lead to improvements in reliability, productivity, innovation and regulatory compliance in public service development (Spohrer et al., 2008, p. 10).

This chapter is a contribution to these efforts. Based on the Danish case, the authors seek to answer the following questions: (1) How common is public sector innovation in Denmark? (2) How similar or different are public and private sector innovation?

What innovation means

Innovation is not a very precise term. The UK's National Audit Office has pointed out that 'There is no widely accepted or common definition of what counts as "innovation"' (National Audit Office, 2006b, p. 4). However, as is also stated in the report, there is agreement in the literature that innovation involves at least two related activities, namely (1) doing something new and (2) developing this new thing to work in a given context. Innovation is a concept that fleshes out the two intertwined activities of capturing new ideas and making these ideas work in a given context.

Innovation can thus be seen as 'new ideas that work' (Young Foundation, 2006, p. 9) or 'the effort to develop an element that has already been invented, so that it has a practical-commercial use, and to gain the acceptance of this element' (Sundbo, 1998, p. 12). The National Audit Office defines innovation in a similar way, as: 'Having new ideas, developing the best ones, and implementing them in such a way that there is (at least) a good chance that they will improve the ways in which your organization operates and performs' (National Audit Office, 2006a, p. 8).

There is agreement that innovation does not have to be new to the world, but just new to the firm or the organization in order to count as innovation. It is also generally accepted practice to include incremental (small-step) innovations into the definition of innovation – not just radical innovation. Furthermore, innovation does not just refer to technological innovation, but also to service innovation, organizational innovation, marketing innovation, process innovation, conceptual innovation and so on. Innovation occurs in different types and forms depending on the context.

Some authors argue that innovation must be intentional or deliberate in order to count as innovation (Koch et al., 2005, p. 1). It is also argued, however, that innovations can sometimes be understood as being unconscious or accidental (Toivonen et al., 2007), and strongly integrated with practice. Some argue that innovations must be repeated in order to count as an innovation (Toivonen et al., 2007), but others believe that it is also pertinent to include ad hoc innovations within the definition of innovation, that is innovations in relation to specific problems posed by clients (Gallouj and Weinstein, 1997). The latter may be typical for service innovation, where the provider–client relationship is a critical one.

These difficulties in defining innovation pose problems for the study of innovation at the aggregate level. In the Community Innovation Survey (CIS) as it was carried out in the UK in 2002–2004 (CIS4) for example, the following brief definition of innovation was provided:

> Innovation is defined as major changes aimed at enhancing your competitive position, your performance, your know-how or your capabilities for future enhancements. These can be new or significantly improved goods, services or processes for making or providing

them. It includes spending on innovation activities, for example on machinery and equipment, R&D, training, goods and service design or marketing.

Given this definition, respondents must then judge for themselves whether a given change they can think about in their organization should count as an innovation or not. In this way, innovation can take many forms, depending on respondents' interpretations. This may, in fact, be a good research strategy, because it can be argued that it requires specific knowledge and experiences to recognize an innovation and its relevance.

The same research strategy has been applied as the basis for this chapter. Attempts were made not to provide a very narrow definition of innovation as a basis for data collection (see below). It is recognized that innovations can take many forms and evolve in many different ways in different sectors. However, it is important to stress that innovation is more than just new creative ideas. Innovation must include specific and important changes in order to count as innovation.

In the literature on innovation in private enterprises, a distinction is sometimes made between three historical models of innovation, called Schumpeter I, II and III (see e.g. Phillips, 1971; Sundbo and Fuglsang, 2002; Fuglsang, 2008). Which of these models are relevant to the public sector in the context of government reform and NPM?

In Schumpeter I, innovation is organized around an entrepreneur, who is understood as a dedicated type who gets things done and is capable of going against the mainstream and the 'circular flow' of everyday life. This model of innovation was relevant at the beginning of the twentieth century, when economic development was dependent on entrepreneurial individuals. The entrepreneur and his role in economic development were described by Schumpeter in his pioneering work from 1911, *Theorie der wirtschaftlichen Entwicklung: Eine Untersuchung über Unternehmergewinn, Kapital, Kredit, Zins und den Konjunkturzyklus* (Schumpeter, 1969).

In Schumpeter II (Schumpeter, 1947), innovation is seen as being organized around research and development (R&D) laboratories in large enterprises or within the state, or in close cooperation between the state and large enterprises. Innovation has become a routine that is taken care of by trained specialists: researchers, engineers and so on. This model became important during the period around the Second World War, when the state started to invest in R&D on a larger scale and when enterprises began to invest more systematically in research laboratories.

In Schumpeter III (Lundvall, 1988; Bessant, 2003; Chesbrough, 2003; von Hippel, 2005), innovation is an open and interactive process that involves many internal and external sources and ideas from various types of actors. Internally in the enterprises, employees are more broadly involved in idea-generation and development processes. At the strategic level, it is the enterprise and its employees that bind the different activities together. Innovations are driven and catalysed at a decentralized level in the enterprises. This model has become more relevant in later years when innovative resources have become more distributed across society.

In the context of government reform and NPM, Schumpeter III may imply a move away from top-down and closed innovation towards more interactive and situated innovation. In the public sector, this move is attractive for many reasons. It appeals to requests for a more situated public sector that listens more attentively to citizens' demands. However, this model is also controversial and problematic: it moves a step away from the principles of universalism and political control.

Another point of view is that this model already exists in the public sector. Public institutions are dependent on employee-based, interactive and open innovations in order to remain reliable and trustworthy. Employees must be able to respond to concrete problems in their daily work in order for services to be delivered in a proper manner. If this is the case, the key role for NPM is not to stimulate this model, but rather to respond to it. This chapter argues, however, that it is important to examine how innovation takes place in public sector institutions before a new wave of NPM initiatives is launched to promote more situated innovation.

The data on innovation

Two different sets of data on public and private sector innovation in Denmark are analysed in this chapter.

Public innovation

The data concerning public innovation come from a recent Web-based survey (Pedersen, 2007). The population for the survey was top leaders in kindergartens, schools, after-school institutions, institutions specializing in treating disabled persons and homes for the elderly. These are welfare institutions run by Danish municipalities.[1] More than 11,000 of these institutions exist. The survey was sent to a representative sample of the leaders of 1502 institutions. The 1502 institutions were selected on the basis of a two-step stratified cluster sampling.

A total of 759 leaders from these institutions responded to the questionnaire, which means that the response rate was 51 per cent. The leaders in the sample were sent an email with a description of the survey and a link to the questionnaire.[2]

In accordance with the research strategy presented earlier, innovation was defined as the respondent's perception of 'An important change in the way in which the institution carries out its function within the past 5 years'. This is a broad definition that allowed respondents to form their own interpretations of the situation. Furthermore, this definition stresses that innovation refers to specific and important changes.

A wastage analysis shows no significant differences between the final sample (the group of institutions that responded to the questionnaire) and the whole population (the whole group of institutions). However, special institutions for the disabled and residential homes are underrepresented in the survey due to problems in finding the email addresses of these institutions. With the exception of this source of error, the investigation is representative of over 11,000 welfare institutions that were the targets of the survey.

Private innovation

The data on the Danish private companies are taken from the CIS (see CIS4, CFA, 2006a). This survey is conducted once every four years in the 27 EU countries, three European Free Trade Association (EFTA) countries and the EU candidate countries. The population of the Danish CIS4 analysis is described as being representative of Danish business innovation (CFA, 2006b).

In the questionnaire, innovation is defined in the following way (own translation):

An innovation is the introduction of a new or significantly improved product (good or service), a new or significantly improved process or marketing method or a significant organizational innovation. An innovation is the result of activities that intentionally are directed towards improving the enterprise's products, processes, marketing and/or business procedures. Notice that R&D activities in the enterprise always must be counted as part of the innovation activities.

In other words, and also applicable in this case, innovation is understood quite broadly as something that can take place in four different areas. Innovation is also defined as something that must lead to specific and important changes.

How common is public sector innovation?

According to the results of the survey, 64 per cent of public sector institutions said that they had innovated within a five-year period from 2002 to 2006. This figure is somewhat lower than the figure for private sector innovation. In the private sector, 72 per cent of Danish companies said that they had innovated in a two-year period from 2002 to 2004 (CFA, 2006a).

Other things being equal, the level of innovation in public institutions, therefore, clearly seems to be lower than that in the private sector. The level of innovation is nevertheless high. The majority of the public sector's welfare institutions stated that they had innovated. Furthermore, in the CIS survey to private firms, four different questions were asked regarding innovation (product innovation, process innovation, organizational innovation and innovation in marketing). In the survey to the Danish public institutions, only one question was asked about innovation. This gives the private companies more opportunities to state that they were innovative. On the other hand, this may be counterbalanced by the longer time span studied in the public survey (five versus two years).

No significant variations in the level of public innovation were found across the various types of institutions, the size of the institutions as measured by the number of employees, the activities conducted by the institutions (education, care-taking, etc.) or across the core staff employed.

Only the size of the municipality and the governance structure had effects on the level of innovation. The probability of finding innovative institutions is more than twice as high in municipalities with more than 100,000 inhabitants compared to municipalities with fewer than 100,000 inhabitants. The probability of finding innovative institutions is 1.6 times higher if the institutions are managed on the basis of a contract between the municipality and the institution compared to when there is no contract.

This seems to indicate that contractualization has a positive impact on innovation. Contractualization can be seen as one classical NPM strategy (see Pollitt, 2003). Contracts could potentially lead to a more decentralized approach to public sector innovation, with a greater involvement of employees, which could explain the higher level of innovation.

However, according to Greve (2008), between 2003 and 2007 there was an increase in the number of municipalities that applied contracts, from 42 per cent to 67 per cent. The introduction of contracts could, in itself, be interpreted as innovation. The increase in the number of municipalities that apply contracts could, therefore, partly explain the higher level of innovation in these municipalities.

It seems reasonable to conclude that innovation is a common phenomenon in public sector institutions. Almost two out of three welfare institutions are innovative and all categories of institutions are innovative. Therefore, innovation in the public sector is not a contradiction in terms (Earl, 2002). Furthermore, there are some signs that contractualization may be positively correlated with innovation.

If this is true, it should be explored in more detail how this works in practice. Does contractualization put pressure on institutions to innovate? Does it imply a more decentralized framework which makes it easier for leaders to respond to ideas developed by employees, as indicated in a new survey (KREVI, 2008)? These are very complex issues that are probably manifested very differently in the different municipalities.

How similar are public and private sector innovations?

Public sector welfare institutions operate in the context of politics and public rules. Private companies operate in the context of the market economy. For this reason, public and private innovations are sometimes believed to be very different. Public innovation is seen as being dominated by top-down approaches. Private innovation is seen as being more employee-based and customer-sensitive.

Some of the major sources of public sector innovation are presented in Figure 3.1. These sources can be divided into three categories, namely: (a) very important, (b) important and (c) not important.

Very important

According to the respondents (the top managers), employees are the most important source of innovation. Seventy-eight per cent of public managers said that employees were important 'to a high degree' as a source of innovation, while 18 per cent of the managers said the employees were important 'to some degree'. Hence, for 96 per cent of the managers, employees were an important source of innovation. In comparison, only 58 per cent of Danish private firms stated that

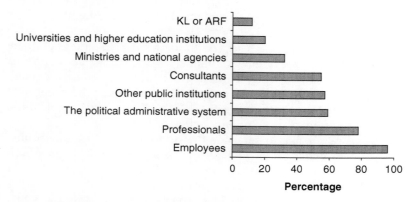

Figure 3.1   Sources of innovation 'to a high degree' and 'to some degree'

internal sources within the enterprise or the enterprise group are information sources with a great impact on innovation. Information sources for innovation that do have a great impact on private firms include users (32 per cent) and other market sources (34 per cent).

Thus, it can be seen that innovation in public institutions seems to be at least as much employee-based as in the private sector. This includes the professionals as a special group (teachers, pedagogues, nurses, etc.). Most employees in the Danish public sector welfare institutions are professionals. There is no evidence to show that innovation in the public sector is a top-down process dominated by politicians and senior managers.

Important

Important sources of innovation include the political-administrative organizations,[3] other public sector welfare institutions and consultants.

The political-administrative organizations

Some 20 per cent and 38 per cent of the managers said that the political-administrative organizations were important sources of innovation 'to a high degree' and 'to some degree', respectively. Seen from the perspective of the public institutions, the political-administrative organizations set up the basic success criteria for services and service delivery. They also change and set up new success criteria (Pedersen, 2008). For this reason, these organizations are regarded by the institutions as an external and important source of innovation.

Other public sector welfare institutions

Five per cent and 49 per cent of the managers said that other public sector institutions were an important source of innovation 'to a high degree' and 'to some degree', respectively. This is understandable, as other public sector institutions are important elements in the institutions' context regarding learning, informal knowledge-sharing and so on. Almost one out of every four managers (23 per cent) said that the institutions had innovated 'mostly on the basis of cooperation with other public sector welfare institutions' (Pedersen, 2007, p. 173).

Consultants

Consultants play an important role for private and also for public institutions. Twelve per cent and 43 per cent of the public managers said that consultants were an important source of innovation 'to a high degree' and 'to some degree', respectively. Unfortunately, the survey did not show which type of consultants the institutions cooperate with and about what. However, the survey did show that by using consultants, the institutions became relatively good at meeting external success criteria which, over time, is linked to the capacity of innovation. In other words: consultants helped the institutions to innovate in order to fulfil regulatory requirements.

Private firms

For the private firms, the political-administrative organizations are not as important as a source of innovation. For example, only 4 per cent of the firms stated that public cooperation partners have a great impact as a source of innovation. However, the picture is not very clear. Of those firms that said they had innovation cooperation with other firms and institutions, public cooperation partners had a share of 16 per cent. Furthermore, 17 per cent of the private firms said that meeting regulatory requirements had a great impact as an effect of product innovation. The figure was 18 per cent for process innovation. Therefore, regulatory requirements also have an impact on private innovation, though to a lesser extent.

Forty-five per cent of the private firms stated that they have innovation cooperation partners. Of those who have innovation cooperation partners, other firms have a share of 40 per cent. These are competitors and other companies from the industry, consultants, commercial laboratories and private institutes, as well as suppliers of equipment, materials, components and software. There is a considerable external orientation in private firms.

Thus, in many ways, there appear to be similar patterns in public and private innovation. Internal sources are decisive. Regulatory mechanisms play an important role in both sectors. Finally, there is a considerable external orientation towards similar institutions, firms as well as consultants.

Not important

As shown in Figure 3.1, some actors are not seen as important sources of innovation. This is the case for (1) ministries and national agencies, (2) universities and higher education institutions and (3) KL (Local Government Denmark – the national association of the municipalities) and ARF (the National Association of Danish County Councils, which is today the Danish Regions).

One might wonder why ministries and national agencies are not regarded by managers as important sources of innovation. The ministries and national agencies make many decisions that directly or indirectly oblige the institutions to innovate. The reason why ministries and national agencies are not regarded as important sources of innovation is most likely that they are seen as 'far away' governance institutions compared to the municipalities, which are regarded as being 'very close'. In other words, the ministries and national agencies might objectively be more important to the welfare institutions' innovation than the municipalities. However, the municipalities are perceived by the top managers as being more important for the institutions' innovation.

One might wonder the same of universities and higher education institutions. As a matter of fact, they seem to play almost the same role for public and private organizations. Furthermore, in Denmark, almost all professionals are educated not in universities or other higher education institutions, but rather in special institutions for the education of teachers, nurses, pedagogues and so on located around the country. The managers, who are mostly professionals themselves, therefore have stronger relationships with these institutions than with the universities and higher education institutions.

Another issue is why KL and ARF are not regarded by managers as important sources of innovation. KL and ARF play a key role in almost all major agreements between the government and the municipalities and regions. For this reason, these associations have been involved in many major initiatives to promote innovation. Unfortunately, the survey does not indicate any major reason why KL and ARF are not regarded as important sources of innovation by the managers of the welfare institutions.

The main conclusion regarding the sources of innovation is that employees are the most important source – just like in the private sector. After the employees come the political-administrative organizations, other public sector welfare institutions and consultants. As in the private sector, public innovation is based on a mix of internal and external sources.

The main effects of innovation

In the following section, some of the main effects of innovation in the public and the private sector are described to see if there are any major differences. It is interesting also to find out which elements of NPM and government reforms are satisfied through innovation (efficiency, quality etc.).

The effects of innovation on public institutions are typically as follows:

1. The quality of welfare services improves.
2. The production and delivery of services is improved because the internal resources in the welfare institutions are better utilized.
3. The external success criteria set up by the political-administrative organizations for the production and delivery of welfare services are better fulfilled.

Increased quality of welfare services

Seven out of ten top managers said that the quality of services improved as a result of innovation. Only one out of ten managers (9 per cent) felt that the quality of the services went down because of innovation.

Improved flexibility and capacity

Six out of ten managers (64 per cent) felt that the flexibility of the institutions' production and delivery of services improved as a consequence of innovation. Only one out of seven managers (13 per cent) felt that the flexibility decreased.

Four out of ten managers (43 per cent) said that the institutions' capacity regarding the production and delivery of welfare services increased because of innovation. Only one out of seven managers (14 per cent) said that the institution experienced a decrease in capacity regarding the production and delivery of welfare services because of innovation.

Increased fulfilment of the external success criteria

One out of two managers (49 per cent) felt that the external success criteria for the institutions' production and delivery of welfare services set up by the political-administrative organizations were better able to be fulfilled because of innovation. Only one out of ten managers said that the opposite was the case.

The effects of innovation in the private sector are similar in many ways. In the CIS survey, a distinction was made between the effects of product innovation and the effects of process innovation.

Table 3.1 shows that the most important effects of product innovation are more products, improved quality and new markets or increased market share. Regulatory requirements, environmental concerns, and health and safety also play an important role.

From Table 3.2 it can be seen that increased flexibility, capacity and reduced costs are the most important effects of process innovation. Regulatory requirements again all play an important role in innovation, as measured by the effects.

Table 3.1   Effects of product innovation, great impact, 2002–2004

Increased range of goods or services	Entered new markets or increased market share	Improved quality of goods or services	Reduced environmental impact or improved health and safety	Met regulatory requirements
33%	27%	34%	9%	17%

Source: CIS4, CFA (2006a).

Table 3.2   Effects of process innovation, great impact, 2002–2004

Improved flexibility of production or service provision	Increased capacity for production or service provision	Reduced cost per unit produced or provided	Reduced material or energy consumption per unit produced or provided	Reduced environmental impact or improved health and safety	Met regulatory requirements
31%	27%	24%	11%	12%	18%

Source: CIS4, CFA (2006a).

Improved quality, flexibility, capacity and regulatory requirements are important effects of innovation in both the private and public sectors. This shows that there is not just a focus on economic benefits (see also below). Innovation is not just about efficiency, but also about generating new value in terms of quality. In this way, innovation is broader than the conventional dominant targets of efficiency and control in NPM.

To conclude, it has been found that innovation already exists in the public sector to a large extent. Innovation is employee-based. Public innovation is open to input from the environment to a high degree and has a strong emphasis on quality and flexibility.

This means that public innovation is not, as often understood, a rare phenomenon. It is not dominated by politicians and senior managers alone. Compared to private innovation, public innovation is not any less employee-based, or any less exposed to input from other institutions or companies. Furthermore, it is not targeted towards classical NPM goals to become more effective and efficient alone.

Differences between public and private innovation

Some differences between public and private innovation were found, however. One important difference is that economic benefits are more important for private than for public innovation.

Only one out of seven top managers (15 per cent) said that innovation had a positive impact on the welfare institutions' economy. In other words, most institutions do not improve their economic situation because of innovation. Thirty-two per cent of the managers said that innovation had a negative impact on the economic situation. Finally, 52 per cent of the managers said that innovation had been neutral in affecting the institutions' economic situation.

In contrast to this, according to the CIS survey, innovation has a positive effect on the economic situation of private companies. In the CIS4 investigation, there were at least two ways to measure the economic importance of innovation. First, a measure of the intensity of innovation was suggested. The intensity of innovation is defined by expenditures on innovation in relation to turnover. According to the CIS4 (see CFA, 2006b), the innovation intensity is greatest in small companies (with a small turnover) and, divided by industry, within knowledge services. The question then becomes whether or not this measure of investment can be coupled to income.

A measure that tells us how important innovation is to income distributes turnover of product innovative firms on different types of

Table 3.3   The distribution of turnover between product types in product innovative companies, 2004

Unchanged or only marginally modified products (%)	Products that were new to the enterprise (%)	Products that were new to the market of the enterprise (%)
78	11	10

Source: CIS4, CFA (2006a).

products. Table 3.3 shows that, in 2004, 21 per cent of the turnover in product-innovative firms came from products that were new to the company or new to the company's market.

Table 3.3 indicates that innovation activities are relatively important for turnover in product-innovative Danish enterprises. In other words, there is a considerable economic incentive to innovate.

From this, it can be concluded that the link between innovation and economic benefit is much stronger in the private sector than in the public sector. In the public sector, innovation seems to be driven by a concern for quality rather than efficiency or other economic benefits.

Discussion

How can it be explained that public innovation is linked more to quality than to efficiency? One explanation could be the absence of real markets in the public sector. The survey showed that only 2 per cent of welfare institutions operate under conditions similar to those of a market economy. Furthermore, only 5 per cent of the institutions said they would do this in 2011. On the basis of this, it could be said that the welfare institutions do not operate under market pressures. Hence, they are not forced to innovate with a strong focus on economic efficiency. This adds more room to adopt a quality-oriented approach to innovation.

Another explanation could be the increase in the rights of citizens as users. Since 2001, a whole series of public sector reforms – 16 major reforms in all – have been implemented in Denmark by the present liberal-right government (Pedersen, 2009). These include a structural reform of the public sector, a quality reform of public services, a tax reform and many other reforms. These reforms have, among other things, given the citizens more rights in terms of the production and delivery of services. In a way, government reforms have driven up citizens' requests for quality. Innovation is one way in which the institutions can respond to the requests. In this way, innovation becomes linked to a quest for quality rather than efficiency.

This link between innovation and quality may also be supported by employees in the public sector. Employees respond to concrete needs to improve quality and delivery. They pursue strategies of bricolage and tinkering in order to ensure that services are delivered in a proper manner. NPM initiatives leading to increased control and standardization could have reduced the room for bricolage. However, there is no evidence that employees comply completely with this: employee-based innovation is significant in the public sector, as it has been pointed out in this chapter, and case studies have also shown that tinkering and bricolage are important activities, even in areas where NPM seems very strong, such as elderly care (cf. Fuglsang, 2008). New alliances are formed between employees and citizens, which lead to more innovation and a focus on quality. This may in turn lead to less legitimacy for the more 'cruel' aspects of NPM.

In the policy context of NPM and other government reforms, there is therefore a need to modify NPM towards an approach that stresses quality and innovation. This could imply a more situated and responsive approach to innovation and citizens' needs. Therefore, in this policy context, there is a request for interactive, employee-based and open innovation – in other words, for Schumpeter III.

However, as discussed above, perhaps the problem is not to create this approach, since it may already exist in the public sector. Employee-based innovation seems to be the rule rather than the exception. Perhaps the real challenge is the ability to respond in an adequate way to existing forms of quality-oriented, interactive, employee-based and open innovation in the public sector. A more systematic approach to situated innovation as it already exists could have the double purpose of improving innovation (or quality) and regulatory compliance.

Conclusion

Public innovation is often seen as being different from private innovation. Public innovation is believed to be much rarer, more top-down, closed and less employee-based than private innovation. While private innovation has moved from planned and closed innovation (so-called Schumpeter II) to interactive, employee-based and open innovation (Schumpeter III), public innovation is seen as being locked into the planned and closed model.

However, as has been pointed out in this chapter, it has never been proven that public innovation is rare, top-down, closed and less employee-based. It has not been possible to prove this hypothesis here. Rather, it appears as if there are already many similarities between private and public innovation – with some exceptions, including the economic effects of innovation.

According to several commentators, NPM ideas seem to be on the retreat in some areas, or are at least being reformulated. The issue of quality-oriented innovation becomes one new focal point in NPM. Rather than providing economic efficiency, standardization and more control as a main focus, NPM could seek to stimulate innovation and improve on quality. In this context, the Schumpeter III model becomes attractive. It seems appropriate to develop a public sector that is more situated and responsive to users' needs.

It has been argued here that before new NPM initiatives are launched to promote innovation and forge the link between NPM, quality and innovation, the ways in which innovation already takes place in the public sector should be examined. As argued above, it may turn out that much of what is desired in fact already exists. If this is so, as it does seem to be, judging from the data discussed in this chapter, the key role of NPM in this case will not be to stimulate interactive innovation, but rather to respond to it in an adequate and systematic manner.

Notes

1. Hospitals were not included in the survey. The reason for this is that hospitals are very different from kindergartens, schools and so on in terms of staff, number of staff, budget/turnover, core services and so on. A number of other welfare institutions that do not produce core welfare services for citizens were also not included in the survey. Examples are public sector institutions that take care of waste water treatment, the maintenance of parks, renovations and so on.
2. Institutions from the following municipalities took part in the investigation: Aabenraa, Aalborg, Århus, Brøndby, Esbjerg, Frederiksberg, Frederikshavn, Greve, Guldborgsund, Hedensted, Herning, Hjørring, Holbæk, Hvidovre, Kalundborg, Kolding, København, Mariagerfjord, Norddjurs, Odense, Roskilde, Slagelse, Thisted, Tønder, Viborg.
3. The political-administrative organizations are first and foremost ministries, national agencies and the Mayor's office in the municipalities and regions.

4
Small States, Innovation and Administrative Capacity

Rainer Kattel, Tiina Randma-Liiv and Tarmo Kalvet

Introduction

'What distinguishes the small nations from the large', writes Milan Kundera (2007, p. 28), 'is not the quantitative criterion of the number of their inhabitants; it is something deeper. For small nations, existence is not self-evident certainty but always a question, a wager, a risk; they are on the defensive against History, that force which is bigger than they, which does not take them into account, which does not even notice them.' Kundera expresses the rational and reasonable fear felt by small nations and states of 'going under' and succumbing to history; that fear also explains why there is a specific research interest in small states and their unique challenges.

However, the concept of small states, as well as that of innovation and administrative capacity, is subject to a relatively wide range of definitions and usage. Before describing the aim of this chapter, we briefly discuss how small states, innovation and administrative capacity can be defined and how these terms are used here.

Definitions

The most widespread definition of innovation originates with Joseph Schumpeter and with slight modification is used by international organizations such as the Organisation for Economic Co-operation and Development (OECD) and the European Union (EU). Perhaps the best-known formulation of this definition is as follows:

An innovation is the implementation of a new or significantly improved product (good or service), or process, a new marketing method, or a new organizational method in business practices, workplace organization or external relations.

(OECD and Eurostat, 2005, p. 46)

Innovation is the means by which entrepreneurs seek to overcome competition in order to earn profits. Innovations are usually based on some type or form of skills and knowledge (not necessarily in a codified form; for instance, experience, networks, etc., often involve uncodified knowledge) that are used to gain a competitive advantage. Innovations are often associated with a steep learning curve and quick growth in productivity that, in turn, often lead to strong and sustained economic growth (Reinert, 2007). Innovation-based productivity explosions create enormous competitive advantages through agglomeration, clustering, positive externalities and economies of scale and scope that, as cumulative dynamics, engender virtuous cycles of growth and rapidly rising living standards. At the root of such complex interactions is deeply embedded policy-making of increasing coordination, dialogue and cooperation managed by a highly capable public administration (Evans and Rauch, 1999; Wade, 2004). By 'policy-making' and 'administrative capacity' we mean 'a model of capacity as a set of relationships that determine governance rather than as a set of attributes attached to instruments of government' (Jayasuriya, 2005, p. 21). This understanding allows administrative capacity, policy design, analysis, implementation, coordination and evaluation to play key roles instead of being limited to a formal set of rules and chain of command.

This chapter is based on the relational understanding of small states that has been used widely in recent small-states literature. According to this definition, 'being a small state is tied to a specific spatio-temporal context, not a general characteristic of the state. A small state is not defined by indicators such as its absolute population size or size of GDP relative to other states. Instead, a small state is defined by being the weak part in an asymmetric relationship'[1] (Thorallsson and Wivel, 2006; Steinmetz et al., 2009). Smallness indicates a power deficit. In addition, smallness or size is a dynamic characteristic of a country; its impact changes over time. It is best understood as a relatively important determinant in the welfare of that particular country.[2]

Aim of the chapter

Innovation, and economic development for that matter, was born in small states and, even by today's standards, in microstates like Renaissance city states. Cities such as Venice, Florence, Delft and others were extraordinarily successful at innovation – using knowledge to create economic gains – and in outcompeting nations much larger in terms of geography, demographics or other measures of size (Hall, 1999; Landes, 1999, pp. 45–59; Reinert, 2007). It can be argued that in these cities, 'smallness' was one of the key factors that contributed to an institutionally embedded and yet diversified economy – both concepts then already seen as pivotal ingredients for sustained growth. Indeed, early key political economists such as Giovanni Botero (1590) and Antonio Serra (1613) juxtaposed small city states with great economic and often military power to natural resource-rich large areas that were economically backward. Today's wisdom seems, instead, to regard smallness as a source of multiple constraints on innovation and economic development in general (e.g. Armstrong and Read, 2003; contrast with Easterly and Kraay, 2000). These constraints can be summarized as follows:[3]

(1) Almost by definition, small states (particularly the less developed ones) have small home markets that limit the possibilities for economies of scale and geographical agglomerations.
(2) Small home markets and dependence on exports threaten small states with overspecialization, lock-in and low diversification of the economic structure.
(3) Small states do not have the financial capabilities or human resources to invest in cutting-edge science, research and development (R&D), which makes prioritization, selectivity and adaptability key to policy design.
(4) The latter presupposes high administrative capacity and a professional public administration that, again, many small states with a lower level of development seem to lack almost by definition.
(5) Rent-seeking and vested interests make the development of Weberian civil service and professional policy design, often seen as being key for sustained economic development, difficult if not impossible for small states.

However, the last significant attempt to deal with small states and innovation is already over 20 years old. *Small Countries Facing the Technological Revolution,* edited by Freeman and Lundvall, appeared in 1988. Still, despite the title, the authors do not in reality deal so much with the issue of smallness as with the issue of innovation systems in general, as this concept was in its infancy at the time and was mainly developed by the same authors. Edquist and Hommen's (2008) work, while entitled *Small Economy Innovation Systems,* suffers from the exact same problems: it actually only deals with innovation systems issues relevant to highly developed countries from Finland to South Korea. The book does not, in fact, discuss almost any size-specific issues as far as innovation and innovation policy are concerned. In essence, innovation literature is seemingly aware of the issue of size, while in reality it tends to gloss over size. Small-states literature, on the contrary, tends to assume that size is a constraint on economic development and innovation.

Just as important, while the role of public administration in development is increasingly drawing attention to itself in development studies (Evans and Rauch, 1999; Wade, 2004), this fundamental relationship between public administration and development has received only incidental attention in small-states literature (e.g. Ó Riain, 2004).

A number of new challenges and risks have emerged in the international economy during recent decades that re-emphasize the issue of size and the need to address administrative capacity. Prevailing theoretical solutions to these challenges, both in innovation and administrative sciences (the innovation systems approach and [neo-] Weberian state, respectively), have clear flaws when applied to small states, that is, these concepts actually do not help to overcome the constraints created by new challenges.

Unlike for much of the twentieth century, it is argued that today, state size is again one of the key determinants of how and why companies innovate (state size has an impact on company-level innovation, although the impact changes somewhat with the level of development). Successful small economies have learned to overcome issues arising from size. New challenges in the global economy transform size into one of the key tempo-spatial dynamic characteristics of a polity. Administrative capacity is among the most crucial factors required in order to overcome these challenges.

New challenges and risks

While innovations and technological changes are often seen as the key drivers of economic growth and development, it is seldom recognized that many innovations can bring significant adverse side effects as well for two key reasons:

(1) Innovations and technological changes often work through a process that Schumpeter (1912, 1942) described as creative destruction, where new products, activities, jobs and industries are created and old ones evaporate.

(2) Many innovations create dynamics, such as economies of scale, that become, as Arthur (1994) and others have shown, powerful enforcers of learning mechanisms and of various feedback linkages among value-chain actors that all lead up to strong path dependencies and barriers of entry for competitors (companies, regions, countries) (also Nelson and Winter, 1982).

These aspects of innovation necessitate a public sector-led process that can be called creative destruction management (following the original Schumpeterian idea), where public policies support the creation of new knowledge, companies and jobs and alleviate the destructive effects (Drechsler et al., 2006; Kregel and Burlamaqui, 2006). During much of the twentieth century, successful instances of creative destruction management were greatly helped by the particular nature of the then prevailing techno-economic paradigm (detailed in the next subsection).

Mass production, or the Fordist system of production, used huge hierarchical organizations and long-term planning that were directed at creating stability in production and reaping economies of scale and scope (Chandler, 1990). Increasing real wages and living standards that guaranteed stable consumption patterns effectively became part of that production and planning system. While first realized probably by Henry Ford when he more than doubled his workers' salaries, this system was perfected by the small Nordic welfare states during the 1960s and 1970s (Katzenstein, 1985; Mjoset, 2000). The rise of the East Asian economies can also be understood as an exemplary case of using the mass-production paradigm. The then small economies of Asia developed via strong state-led industrialization efforts that were based on creating strong government-owned enterprises and networks of enterprises in order to create economies of scale (e.g. Amsden, 1989; Wade, 2004). Essentially, the Nordic welfare states and the Asian tigers showed that size did not matter as long as one was able to capture the logic of the paradigm: mass production assumes mass consumption that in turn feeds on mass employment that is not interrupted by sickness, old age or any other similar circumstance (i.e., welfare state regulations, other forms of regulation or customs such as long-term employment that socialize unemployment risks).

The Fordist paradigm was thus 'naturally' prone to agglomeration effects (as integration into large hierarchies was its fundamental principle) that in turn created middle-income jobs (significantly helped by the welfare state-type regulations), not only in developed countries but also increasingly in the developing world (for instance, Mexico's real wages were continuously increasing precisely until the end of the Fordist paradigm in the mid-1970s; see Palma, 2005). The Fordist paradigm worked similarly for regions as economic agglomerations, and the welfare state also carried the fruits of innovation to geographically remote areas.

The breakdown of this system has been mitigated by three developments: (1) a change in the techno-economic paradigm following the new technological revolution based on information and communication technology (ICT) coming to full force during the 1990s; (2) the adoption of the Washington Consensus economic policies; and (3) the administrative reforms of the last 30 years. The question that is posed for European small states is the following: How does membership in the EU influence the above-mentioned challenges and the states' ability to deal with them? Indeed, the EU's impact on small states offers a glimpse into how administrative capacity in small states is changing or even needs to change in order to benefit innovation in these states. Each development and how it influences innovation in small states is briefly discussed.

Techno-economic paradigm shift

The term techno-economic paradigm was coined by Carlota Perez (1983, 2002, 2006) and goes back to the theory of long waves of economic development originally described in 1924 and 1926 by Nikolai Kondratiev (1998a, 1998b). According to Perez, the paradigm lasts somewhere for around half a century and consists of a 'common sense' about how the capitalism of that particular period works and develops. The paradigm also describes how technological change and innovation in a given period are most likely to take place: what organizational forms and finances are conducive to innovations; what technological capabilities, skills and infrastructure are needed; what policy changes potentially enhance innovation; and what kinds of best practices of business development emerge and thrive. Note that paradigms always form around a set of key innovations and technologies that then encompass and transform the whole economy.

The current ICT-based techno-economic paradigm goes back to key innovations in the 1970s and has engendered fundamental changes in production processes in almost all industries (including many services and agriculture). Perhaps the most profound feature of the ICT paradigm is the growing use of outsourcing and the breaking up of various production functions that have, in turn, created strong de-agglomeration pressures, both in highly industrialized as well as in developing countries (for discussion, Samuelson, 2004; Krugman, 2008). Gains from techno-logical change and innovation no longer 'travel' easily within regional or national geographic boundaries. Large production units and mass employment are substituted by highly specialized networks that operate and source production and knowledge, often supra-regionally or even globally – creating a vicious cycle of increasing competition, increasing pressure to cut costs and lower wages, and, with extensive concessions (in taxes, etc.), luring foreign investors who often bring few fruits to the specific location. As a result, enclave economies and de-linkaging effects emerge (Gallagher and Zarsky, 2007). At the same time, the ICT-led paradigm also enables the creation of niche production with the poten-tial to become supra-regional or even global (for instance, hospitals specializing in a specific type of heart surgery) (Prahalad, 2006).

The ICT-led paradigm increases pressures for de-agglomeration, de-linkaging and de-diversifying. This has become the key challenge for many smaller or peripheral nations/areas where such pressures are already quite strong. It is not so much the issue of size as such (e.g., scarcity in human capital) that has become important but, rather, a combination of geographic location and economic specialization patterns – summarized as the position a nation holds in international value chains. For instance, while Finland is both geographically periph-eral and demographically relatively small (c. 5 million inhabitants), its place in the international mobile electronics production value chain is very high. Finland is also seeing a growing outflow of R&D activities into regions with lower costs and larger agglomeration effects, such as India.

Finland's position, however, has little if any positive bearing on Finland's neighbouring country, Estonia (80 km to the south, c. 1.4 mil-lion inhabitants). In the mass-production paradigm, Estonia could have devised relatively simple strategies to reap benefits from its proximity to highly developed markets by specializing in lower-end products/markets and moving up the value ladder. National policy-making could have created successful catching-up strategies. Instead, Estonia's electronics industry specializes in simple production and assembly of products, resulting in low wages and substantial de-linkaging effects (Kalvet, 2004; Högselius, 2005). The ICT-led global-production paradigm makes such strategies highly temporary and largely futile as there is growing evidence that upgrading in such sectors does not happen very often (Giuliani et al., 2005).

While the ICT-led paradigm significantly amplifies de-agglomeration, larger nations/regions are somewhat more hedged against risks imminent in the current paradigm. First, this means that smaller (and especially developing) countries have a growing dependency on international markets, production networks and finance. Secondly, it can be argued that for smaller nations, the policy space needs to be redefined. If local and foreign companies have growing incentives to de-link production, R&D and so on, from a given geographic position, then investing more in education, creating more cultural possibilities and devising better social programmes only seem to delay the inevitable (also Cimoli et al., 2005). Small-state policy-making needs to become supra-regional (for instance, within the EU). Size, in terms of political influence and power – of having the human resources needed to negotiate supra-regional policies – is becoming key to the economic success of small states. While it can be argued that this concept is generally known in small-states literature (see e.g. Ingebritsen et al., 2006 for a collection of useful discussions), the key new understanding here is that this concept also affects innovation. Indeed, when mass production innovation policy is local (creating local technological capabilities and markets and then moving to exports), the ICT paradigm innovation policy of small states has to be supra-regional from the start. In fact, hardly any small country in Europe or anywhere else in the world is capable of or is practising such policies yet.

It has been argued that the logic of dispersion of global production networks that creates de-agglomeration and de-linkaging effects is not necessarily inevitable to the ICT paradigm (Perez, 2006). Still, the global macroeconomic environment – namely, Washington Consensus policies – creates significant incentives to instate policies that enable the adverse effects of the ICT paradigm and innovations. While these policies might seem to be precisely supra-national in nature, in many areas such policies have expanded rather than reduced de-agglomeration effects. While for many small countries economic openness has become the key economic policy mantra, it is argued here that this situation might in fact increase the global competition challenges that these countries face.

The Washington Consensus

Initially a list of '10 policy instruments about whose proper deployment Washington can muster a reasonable degree of consensus' (Williamson, 1990), the Washington Consensus may have failed in light of the mainly negative experience many developing countries have had with these policies (World Bank, 2006; Rodrik, 2007), with some calling it the 'Washington Confusion' instead (Rodrik, 2007). On the level of actual policy-making, however, the Washington Consensus still seems to be in full force, appearing in many new disguises. While the simple battle cry of the 1990s – stabilize, privatize, liberalize – has given way to more intricate phrases and policy advice, they still boil down to the same core ideas.

Two observations are crucial. First, whatever its intellectual roots and its current health, the Washington Consensus essentially became the vehicle delivering the techno-economic paradigm change globally as it enabled a growing geographical dispersion of production in the form of foreign direct investment. Secondly, the main policy vehicles of the consensus, such as financial globalization and foreign direct investments-based growth policies, have failed to deliver growth (Rodrik and Subramanian, 2008) and, instead, have magnified the negative effects of the ICT paradigm. In combination, both effects have had a huge impact on the way in which innovation takes place in many companies, especially in developing countries and poorer regions, and the way in which most countries see and define the policy space available to them. Indeed, one of the most fundamental characteristics of industrial change in developing countries, such as those in Central and Eastern Europe during the 1990s, has been that a majority of companies have actually engaged in process innovation (e.g. in the form of the acquisition of new machinery) in seeking to become more cost effective in the new marketplace.

Since the main emphasis of the Washington Consensus policies is on both macroeconomic stability (low inflation, low government deficits, and stable exchange and interest rates) and open markets (low if any trade barriers, common technical standards, etc.), these policies have two main assumptions. First, that increased foreign direct investments (that should thrive in stable economic environments) bring foreign competencies, know-how, linkages and increased competition for domestic producers that, secondly, create more pressures to innovate in the form of better and cheaper products and services. If these assumptions are coupled with the real changes taking place in production networks due to the changing paradigm, however, we get highly dynamic forces engendering structural change in more vulnerable areas. Indeed, these changes were largely the reason for the consensus policies in the first place (Kregel, 2008a, 2008b). Yet, as the economic performance of the 1990s shows, dynamic changes in (developing) countries following Washington Consensus policies have been highly surprising, not to say disappointing (World Bank, 2006; Amsden, 2007; Chang, 2007). The policies were highly effective in destroying admittedly outdated industrial capacities in the developing world, yet they were also similarly spectacularly ineffective in creating new capabilities and opportunities. With increasing dependence on international markets, production networks and finance, small states also face growing financial fragility (see further, Kregel, 2004).

In sum, without counterbalancing by international policy initiatives, the created international policy environment is highly fertile ground for the negative effects of the techno-economic paradigm change. For small states, this situation significantly increases the challenges brought on by ICT-led globalization of production networks. While there are clear gains from trade, economic specialization and trade patterns become key determinants in the way a small country integrates into the world economy (e.g. the clear difference in the way Finland's and Estonia's electronics sectors are integrated into world markets). Small developing countries have to keep in mind that waving the flag of rather simple liberalization and openness might just as easily undermine their own competitiveness in the long run because of de-industrialization and de-agglomeration. Under these circumstances, smallness becomes a crucial factor in designing innovation policies. How can the combined, potentially negative impact of the ICT paradigm and the global environment, as defined by Washington Consensus policies, be counteracted? Innovation and industrial policy measures that have been accepted during the last 500 years, such as infant industry protection (also included in Willamson's 1990 article but not enforced under the Washington Consensus), are not only discredited and politically hardly acceptable (for instance within the EU), but are also unlikely to work, for instance in the case of Estonia's electronics industry. Existing specialization patterns and global dynamics are simply too strong for such measures to gain any significant traction. Yet, the global financial meltdown of 2008 and 2009 raises questions about the conventional wisdom of having a very open trading policy. A much more active role for the state seems very likely in the next decade. Small states in particular, both highly developed and developing, should reconsider their innovation, industrial, fiscal and monetary policies in order to counterbalance the potential negative dynamics. This concept presupposes high levels of policy and administrative capacity and, specifically, capacity that can deal with widening international influences and networks.

Administrative reforms and the changing nature of administrative capacity

Administrative capacity is one of the key preconditions for creating policies and programmes conducive to innovation and sustained economic development. However, the Washington Consensus and its underlying neo-liberal ideology have had great impact on administrative reforms and the ways in which many policy-makers and also scholars understand administrative capacity. Since the early 1980s, most countries have been influenced by New Public Management (NPM) ideas and reform trajectories, with their economic rationalism and managerialism. NPM reform ideas have also had an impact on state-building efforts in a number of new democratic countries where the early years of transition coincided with NPM popularity in the West. NPM ideology sat well with countries that were abolishing their one-sector economies, carrying out large-scale privatization and contracting out government services. Additionally, a number of international organizations (e.g. the World Bank, OECD) promoted NPM reforms with no critical or context-related assessment in the 1990s. Although NPM reforms already started to draw severe criticism in the second half of the 1990s, some of NPM's core ideas are still alive in public administration reform practices. As documented by many researchers (for an excellent summary, Pollitt and Bouckaert, 2004), neo-liberal administrative reforms have hollowed out the state at a time when the state's capacity to steer the economy is critically needed.

In addition, administrative capacity is something that small states have problems with almost by definition. NPM reforms, although they partly originated in small states such as New Zealand, have posed particular challenges to small societies. By creating private monopolies instead of public monopolies, especially in microstates, market-driven reforms (privatization, contracting out public services) have had questionable outcomes due to the limitations of small markets (e.g. lack of competition). Public–private partnerships have been difficult to develop on a merit basis because of the personalism and interrelatedness within small societies (Lowenthal, 1987), which, in turn, may easily give way to problems with control and accountability, corruption and nepotism. Finally, two important mantras of NPM – decentralization and deregulation – pose an essential human capital requirement by assuming the presence of a critical mass of professional leaders. This can be questionable even in large countries and is extremely difficult to develop in small states. At a time when small states are increasingly challenged to step up their policy-making efforts on the international level, a wave of NPM-based administrative reforms or reform tendencies may easily undermine these very efforts.

NPM is not suitable medicine for the problems of small states. Moreover, elements of traditional (Weberian) bureaucracies are also not well suited to the context of small societies. Bureaucracy presupposes depersonalization: the exercise of state functions and roles must be separated from any particular individual in order to exercise rational power (Weber et al., 1978, p. 959). However, small societies are more inclined towards personalism since individuals can be more influential and informal networks are densely interwoven (Parsons, 1951, p. 191). In a small society, individuals may be more important than structures, procedures or institutions. The high personalization of institutions in small states contributes to the instability of organizations and policies (Randma, 2001), whereas stability is seen as a cornerstone of Weberian administration. Organizations, situations and decisions tend to be more personalized in societies where 'everyone knows everyone else'. Rationality requires consistency, which may be missing in the structures and decisions in small public administration that can be largely based on the knowledge and skills of particular individuals (Randma-Liiv, 2002). The problems of implementing bureaucratic principles in small societies may not stem so much from the design of rational–legal bureaucracy itself as from the inappropriate application and circumvention of its norms and procedures in small administrations. A fundamental issue in small public administration appears to be the modification of a Weberian bureaucratic model in which large size is a critical variable. If small states operate with bureaucratic models inherited from larger states and comprehension of desirable adjustments remains limited, small states may face severe problems in matching bureaucratic rules with their predominantly particularistic societies. Where traditional bureaucratic models of civil service do not suit small states, they can discover their own approaches to public administration. Consequently, both in designing administrative systems as well as in managing public organizations, the key is to find an optimal compromise between classical bureaucratic principles and flexibility. Small states may not merely represent, to paraphrase Richards (1982), a hybrid or halfway house between primitive and modern systems of administration. The form of administration in which the personal factor is so important is well recognized. The question remains whether and how different countries accommodate, exploit and regulate personal relationships in a way that facilitates 'good government' and whether common patterns can be identified. First, it is important to note, as Katzenstein

(1985) argued, that the post-war success of European small states is at least partially due to prolonged political stability and that, secondly, Asian tigers also tend to have highly stable political and administrative environments because of their limited liberal democracies. Small and new democracies fall into neither category and, as we have seen above, NPM reforms within the mass production paradigm have hollowed the administrative stability characteristic of small successful European economies.

The challenges described above (The sections, Techno-economic paradigm shift and The Washington Consensus) point towards yet another tendency: the concept of administrative capacity itself is changing and particularly so for small states. Jayasuriya (2005, p. 22) offers an excellent summary of the changing nature of administrative capacity:

- Public intervention or regulation is dependent on regulatory and governance structures that are widely dispersed; for example, they might be in civil society or located in global policy networks.
- The location of these regulatory resources falls outside the traditional Weberian and Westphalian boundaries of the state.
- Governance is transformed into a type of meta-governance that consists of the enrolment, legitimization and monitoring of the various governance and regulatory resources. In essence, meta-governance entails organizing a set of relations that delimit a particular field of governance. This relational capacity is central to the effectiveness of public action or regulation in the new regulatory state.

Global challenges make the need for change in the nature of administrative capacity especially clear for small states. However, it is important to note that characteristics of capacity that lie outside the Weberian boundaries necessitate different skills from policy-makers and in particular from civil servants. The Weberian bureaucracy is characterized by legal domination, that is, having a legal basis for a bureaucrat's actions. Activities that fall outside a strict legal environment and that have to do, for instance, with national or international networking fall under what Weber called charismatic domination, characterized by different personal skills and which often take place in much less-regulated legal environments. Networking can be more easily accomplished in small states, and it is actually part of everyday life. Small states are also characterized by more informal communication networks and an interwoven elite (Lowenthal, 1987), which may result in an efficient coordination process between government and non-government actors.

Consequently, small states may offer a useful glimpse into how such an evolving idea of administrative capacity can be accomplished and, moreover, how smallness itself – if intelligently and systematically used – can become an asset for the broader meaning of governance.

The role of the European Union in small states, innovation and administrative capacity

The EU has become one of the most important policy factors for small states within the union (Thorallsson and Wivel, 2006). However, the influence of the EU on small states and their economic development and innovation differs quite greatly according to each state's level of development. Significantly, though, for both 'old' and 'new' European small states, the integration into and membership in the EU has turned out to be an ambivalent affair.

First, the impact of accession into the EU for the Eastern European small economies has been pivotal for their innovation policies in the 2000s. Since joining the EU in 2004, and already during the accession talks, a strong but barely publicly discussed change towards a much more active state role occurred in innovation policies in most Eastern European countries. The EU's structural funding played a clear and strong role in this change, particularly during negotiations and the planning that comes with it. These changes come with two specific problems: (1) the over-emphasis in emerging Eastern European innovation policies on linear innovation (from laboratory to market) that is based on the assumption that there is a growing demand from industry for R&D (Radoševic and Reid, 2006; also INNO-Policy TrendChart Country Reports, 2006–2007) and (2) the increasing use of independent agencies in an already weak administrative-capacity environment lacking policy skills for networking and long-term planning. Such Europeanization of innovation policy in Eastern European small states, while highly positive in directing these countries to reorient economic policies towards more sustainable growth, in its implementation often only deepens and intensifies the existing problems of networking, clustering and coordination. In other words, Eastern European small states have grave difficulties adjusting their administrative capacity to changing inner-EU and global conditions. These problems have become particularly vivid during the financial troubles that these countries have faced since late 2008. The countries seem shell-shocked and paralysed by the global crises to such an extent that they are incapable of organizing any coherent response to quickly contracting economies.

Secondly, for 'old' small European states, enlargement of the union has brought, on the one hand, clear advantages in terms of significantly larger markets and access to wider pools of human and technological resources. In some cases, and foremost for Ireland, European structural funding has also played a crucial role in building up technological capacities and enhancing economic development in general. On the other hand, particularly for those small economies belonging to the common currency area, the euro has also brought unique challenges. Up to 2008, most euro-area countries suffered from real exchange rate appreciation, as they could not compete with Germany's productivity and export growth. They were faced with growing downward pressures on their wages and difficulties with export competitiveness (Finland and Ireland are exceptions here; see further Pisani-Ferry et al., 2008). The loss of independent monetary policy and restrictions on fiscal policy are clearly quite serious challenges for many European small states. These challenges have only intensified in the aftermath of the global financial woes: in the absence of independent monetary policies, countries such as Ireland face strong deflationary pressures and are equally unable to respond to the crises.

New global challenges and risks for small states necessitate regional collaboration in policy-making for innovation. Although to this day no serious initiatives can be detected here, it is clear that because of the policy-making mechanisms in the EU, small states are bound to work more closely together (Thorallsson and Wivel, 2006). The EU may involuntarily push small states towards more collaboration in various policy areas, including innovation policy. The EU has certainly enforced the strengthening of administrative capacity in European small states, and this influence will only grow in the coming years. In particular, small Eastern European countries need to increase their efforts to upgrade their administrative capacity.

Theoretical and practical developments

While numerous fundamental changes in the international economy and in technological development pose new challenges to small states, there is no clear theoretical understanding of how to deal with these risks. Perhaps the most developed and influential approach in innovation studies is the one that emerged in the mid-1980s: the concept of national innovation systems (NIS), defined as 'the network of institutions in the public and private sectors whose activities and interactions initiate, import, modify and diffuse new technologies' (Freeman,

1987, p. 1). The approach emerged to meet a growing need to understand competitiveness better at the country level and to know how to influence it. The existing theories were felt to be partial. Since then, the NIS approach has strongly influenced national governments and international organizations all over the world (Sharif, 2006). Indeed, it can be argued that the NIS approach is the theoretical framework most often used in academic and policy analysis literature.

NIS literature, however, does not deal with issues specific to small states or with the risks described above. Research on (mainly national) innovation systems has focused on activities related to the production and use of codified scientific and technical knowledge: '... when one turns to policy analysis and prescription, as well as to the quantitative survey-based studies that support and justify policy, we would contend there is a bias to consider innovation processes largely as aspects connected to formal scientific and technical knowledge and to formal processes of R&D' (Jensen et al., 2007, p. 684). For smaller countries, and especially for smaller developing countries, other sources of innovation, especially those related to process and organizational innovations, are more relevant. Innovation policy discussions have also been dominated by discussion of 'high-technology elements' (such as an emphasis on venture capital funds, support of patenting, technology transfer) that often assume the existence of relatively large home markets. Although much research is being done on ICT sector innovation systems, discussion of the current ICT-led paradigm and its increasing pressures for de-agglomeration, de-linkaging and de-diversifying effects is only just emerging (also Edquist and Hommen, 2008). Further, the systems-of-innovation literature rarely deals with the effects of macroeconomic policies on innovative activities at a company level (i.e. how the liberalization of markets or exchange rate fluctuations impact company-level innovation; Cimoli, 2000 is a rare exception). The same holds for financial fragility.

Finally, while the state is generally considered an important factor that influences how concrete innovation systems develop, discussion of policy-making itself, administrative capacities and constraints associated with small size is practically missing in innovation and systems-of-innovation studies.

Consequently, while new challenges and risks in the international economy re-emphasize size-specific issues, it is argued here that no coherent theoretical framework captures all of these issues. Indeed, few empirical studies detail how small states cope with the challenges and risks.

While there are no clear theoretical tools for dealing with the above-mentioned challenges, attempts can be made to discern how successful small states have coped with these challenges so far and whether theoretically relevant conclusions may be drawn from this. A taxonomy has been developed that shows how small states have in recent years coped with a drastically changed international environment and how successful ones have been able to promote innovation under the challenges. This chapter looks, on the one hand, at how small states deal with issues of competitiveness, which is understood as a combination of two dynamic trends: the state's competitiveness improves when there is an increasing number of economic activities along with growing productivity and strong spillovers (increasing diversity), while real incomes and social cohesion grow at the same time. On the other hand, this chapter looks at political–administrative regimes and reforms as a third dimension (with colours) and as a proxy for administrative capacity in order to connect the changes taking place in these spheres with changes in competitiveness and innovation performance. Figure 4.1 summarizes this tentative and ideal-typical taxonomy.

While it is clear that no real-life state fits exactly into such taxonomy, it is still heuristically useful. Such taxonomies help to highlight the numerous ways in which small states can enhance or lose their competitiveness; they clarify how the ICT-led paradigm, the macroeconomic environment built around Washington Consensus ideas and the impact of administrative reforms have created deeply diverging ways in which innovation impacts on small economies and their competitiveness.

The taxonomy allows us to draw the following conclusions about successful innovation policies in small states in recent years.

First, successful states have been able to gain oversized international policy influence that is combined with their very high position in one or more important global economic value chains (Finland and electronics is a prime example). However, such branding and even marketing have also been important for satellite states such as the Baltics. Seeking an oversized international presence (with clear economic undertones such as being innovative, open, etc.) has become part of a successful small state's economic policy and capacity.

Secondly, successful capacity-building does not have clear NPM or Weberian tendencies but, rather, has neo-mercantilistic characteristics of corporatism and tolerated rent-seeking in fields deemed as priority areas (e.g. finance, technology and other areas with

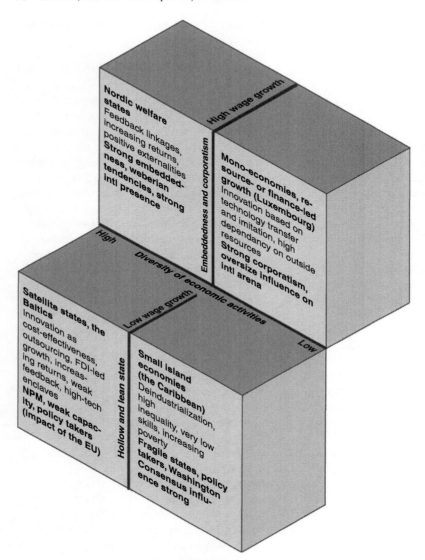

Figure 4.1   Taxonomy of small-states development

strong innovation and high barriers of entry). As size creates limits and international/national dependency grows under the ICT-led paradigm, building on sectors with strong spillovers is a key feature of successful innovation policies.

Thirdly, all four types of small-state development are characterized by rather specific ways that companies innovate in their respective economies. Each type is characterized by a set of prevailing incentives for private sector innovations; however, it is important to note that for all four types, country size has become a key determinant of innovation incentives, albeit in highly differing ways. While large states accommodate all four types of development (as different regions or cities, for instance), small states tend to get locked into path-dependent development trajectories.

Fourthly, successful small states have found a policy mix that enhances their domestic home-market expansion (e.g. by using procurement policies) and export orientation via their own brands or distinct international standing (especially in technologically advanced industries and services). Successful small states are not necessarily card-carrying members of economic openness but, rather, of economic uniqueness, both in terms of home markets and in terms of exports. Indeed, it can be argued that the economies of scale prevalent under the mass-production paradigm have been replaced with highly specialized economies of scope that can be scaled up to global markets.

Such a mix of domestic markets and strong economies of scope in exports enables the creation of agglomeration effects that act as natural barriers of entry, helping domestic producers grow while keeping competition at bay. Such barriers of entry are, in fact, key to keeping activities and jobs. Losing them is particularly easy under today's form of ICT-led globalization and Washington Consensus-dominated development thinking.

Conclusion: Death of distance, rebirth of size?

The ICT revolution, and the enormous reshaping of industries it enables, has been called the 'death of distance'. It is argued that the same revolution, along with the impact of Washington Consensus policies and NPM administrative reforms, has led to a rebirth of size as a key factor that geopolitical units must take into account while devising innovation and economic policies for growth and development.

Indeed, size matters enormously to innovation. While the logic of the previous mass-production paradigm was in itself highly conducive to the emergence of agglomeration and linkaging effects – key factors driving innovation and sustained economic growth – under the paradigm amplified by Washington Consensus globalization, these effects were reversed for many countries. The mass-production paradigm thrived under a top-down policy-making framework: welfare state policies and/or state-led industrialization policies could carry the positive spillovers of innovation and technological change to remote areas of distinct geopolitical entities. Today this seems to be increasingly difficult.

Country size also matters as it is a key determinant of company-level innovations, of the kind prevailing in the private sector.

Innovation policies should be built from the bottom up – creating local networks and scaling them up into wider networks – essentially the opposite of the mass-production paradigm, where the creation of national or supra-regional economies of scale was key.

However, creating the administrative capacity that is required for such policy development assumes an administrative stability that is difficult to create in small states per se and has become even more difficult during the last few decades because of NPM reforms and constraints on small administrations.

In the deeply interlinked fields of innovation and administration, it is found that size matters for small states facing new challenges that are not satisfactorily addressed in the theoretical literature (neither innovation systems nor Weberian state theories, respectively, do justice to small-states issues). There is an urgent need for theoretical work that addresses problems specific to small states. Such research is needed in order to understand how small states need to develop their innovation policy under the new ICT-led paradigm, which perhaps poses the biggest challenge to them.

Notes

1. However, based on small-states literature (e.g. Sutton, 1987; Bray and Packer, 1993), administrative capacity is considered more size-sensitive than other areas because it depends directly on factors such as interrelatedness and the particularity of small societies. Distinguishing between small states and small societies is particularly valuable for small administration studies. Benedict (1966) noted that the main criteria of size for 'territories' ('states') are area and population; whereas the criteria of size for 'societies' are the number and quality of role relationships. The study of public administration has more implications from the notion of small societies where 'everyone knows everybody else', and where the cut-off line between small and large states is usually set at 1–2 million inhabitants.
2. As a note of caution, the specific characteristics of small states can be easily confused with the problems of development. For example, Benedict

(1966, p. 32) claims that less-developed countries, even large ones, are socially characterized by personal role relationships – a finding that has been claimed to be a specific feature of small societies. Montgomery (1986) argues that a paradox of administration in developing countries is the great reluctance to make decisions and to take action. This finding is similar to what others have claimed about small states, including Lowenthal (1987, p. 35) and Sutton (1987, p. 19). Consequently, issues of development should not be underestimated when studying small states (also Montgomery, 1986; Warrington, 1997).

3. Classic summary of the first three arguments are Walsh (1988) and Freeman and Lundvall (1988); also earlier, Robinson (1963).

5
Public Sector Innovation at the Urban Level: The Case of Public Procurement

Veiko Lember, Tarmo Kalvet and Rainer Kattel

Introduction

Public procurement for innovation has been an important national innovation policy tool since World War II (European Commission Working Group, 2006 [hereafter ECWG]). Sometimes referred to as 'technology procurement' (Edquist et al., 2000) or 'innovation oriented procurement' (Rothwell, 1984), public procurement for innovation represents a special form of public procurement that:

> Occurs when a public agency places an order for a product or system which does not yet exist at the time, but which could (probably) be developed within a reasonable period. Additional or new technological development work is required to fulfil the demands of the buyer.
>
> (Edquist and Hommen, 2000, p. 5)

Unlike in regular procurement, where governments place orders for ready-made or 'off-the-shelf' products, procurement for innovation involves procuring products that need additional research and development (R&D) work and thereby influences the innovative capacity of providers. Such procurements are used to solve existing as well as emerging economic and social challenges. The Internet, GPS technology, the semi-conductor industry and passenger jets are perhaps the most prominent examples that resulted from government innovation-oriented procurement having major economic and social impacts (Cabral et al., 2006).

So far, the European Union (EU) has taken very limited advantage of procurement for R&D and innovation. This is especially the case when the EU is compared with its global competitors such as the United States, Japan, China and other Asian countries. In fact, public procurement for innovation has been regarded as marginal in total public procurement. Consider the following comparisons between the EU and the United States:

- In 2004, less than 1 per cent of the total EU-wide tendered procurement budget was allotted for R&D procurement. The US equivalent was 15 per cent.
- The EU spends four times less on civilian R&D procurement and 20 times less on defence R&D procurement than the United States.
- Low procurement of R&D by – and not financial assistance from – public authorities is the main reason for the existing R&D investment gap between the United States and the EU (ECWG, 2006, pp. 10–11).

In this context, the role of local and regional governments deserves special attention. Arguably, the sub-central governments have a share that is two to three times larger in total public procurement than national governments in the EU (Nyiri et al., 2007). At this time, however, there is no coherent evidence available to indicate the extent to which public procurement for innovation potential is realized at local and regional levels.[1]

This study aims to fill this gap by using the examples of six Nordic-Baltic Sea cities. Specifically, the purpose of the study is to address two important and inter-related issues on urban-level public sector innovation and public procurement. First, what kind of impact does urban-level public procurement have on providers' innovation? Secondly, what are the factors that determine the success of public procurement for innovation at the urban level?

In order to answer these questions, the study is organized into three sections. First, a conceptual framework of the link between public procurement and innovation policy is provided. Here, the potential of public procurement for innovation is explained. Secondly, an empirical analysis is presented of some of the main factors influencing public procurement for innovation at the urban level. Thirdly, based on the conceptual framework developed for the empirical study, some recommendations for future policy-making and administration are offered.

It is argued here that public procurement for innovation is an excellent case for understanding public sector innovation. While public sector innovation is one of the buzzwords in contemporary governance and public administration theory and practice, Pollitt (2009) rightly

argues that 'the sad truth is that many of today's management seminars on innovation are filled with a promiscuous litter of buzzwords
and woolly concepts whilst being almost entirely bereft of any specific,
empirically grounded propositions' (see also Moore and Hartley, 2008).
Indeed, existing literatures fail in their ability to differentiate public sector innovation from public sector change, modernization or reform – be
it in the form of new or improved policies, services or organizational
changes. In these literatures, innovation is regarded as just another
term for 'change' or 'modernization'. Most often, the term innovation is simply transferred over from the private sector literature without
any significant modification (see e.g. Albury, 2005; Walker, 2006). This
view, however, is bound to cause a considerable Humpty Dumpty effect:
that is to say, innovation in the public sector is whatever a particular user of the term wants it to mean. This study shows how public
sector activity (procurement of products and services) can be directly
linked with innovation in the private sector (new products and services). In doing so, it provides a more pronounced and direct meaning
to the concept of public sector innovation (see also Moore and Hartley,
2008, p. 3).

Public procurement for innovation: Setting the scene

From innovation to innovation policy

It is generally accepted today that throughout the history of
humankind, the generation, exploitation and diffusion of knowledge
has been fundamental to the economic development and well-being
of nations or regions (for a detailed discussion, see Reinert, 2007).
In 1613, for example, Antonio Serra analysed why his natural resource-
rich hometown of Naples remained so poor, while natural resource-poor
Venice was at the very centre of the world economy. Serra (1613) concluded that the Venetians at that time had built up an industry that was
making great use of knowledge in various ways. He also concluded that
'... effective government, when it occurs to perfection in any kingdom,
will undoubtedly be the most powerful cause of all of making it abound
in gold and silver.' Serra's work was appreciated by Joseph Schumpeter
who, in turn, was the first to produce a detailed approach to innovation
and entrepreneurship. Schumpeter's main argument was that economic
development is driven through a dynamic process in which new technologies, skills and industries play a key role. Today, Schumpeter's (1934,
p. 66) definition of innovation has been echoed in mainstream discourse

and policy of international institutions such as the Organisation for Economic Co-operation and Development (OECD) and the EU:

> An innovation is the implementation of a new or significantly improved product (good or service), or process, a new marketing method, or a new organizational method in business practices, workplace organization or external relations.
>
> (OECD and Eurostat, 2005, p. 46)

According to the technology lifecycle model, both process and product innovations develop through three main phases: fluid, transformation and specific (Abernathy and Utterback, 1978). In the early days of a new technology – the fluid phase – the application potential is imagined, but the market risks and R&D costs for an entrepreneur are very high. Once the technology enters the transitional phase, the entrepreneur benefits from, among other things, economies of scale/scope, possible exports to other regions and countries, and increases in companies' employment levels and real wages. These effects all bring positive spillovers or external economies to the whole region (e.g. development of supplier networks). In the final or specific phase, the sales volume declines or stabilizes, and prices as well as profitability diminish.

Particularly with technology-driven products, the fluid phase is often characterized by competing technologies or platforms. Such technological competitions create what is called 'winner-takes-all' markets, where a winning technology often captures the entire (potential) market, thereby creating huge scale economies for producers (for a classic discussion on this, see Arthur, 1994).

In most instances, there has to be a (systemic) interplay of various actors in order for innovation to take place. An innovation system refers to:

> Elements and relationships which interact in the production, diffusion and use of new, and economically useful, knowledge and that a national system encompasses elements and relationships, either located within or rooted inside the borders of a nation state.
>
> (Lundvall, 1995, p. 2)

Recently, various approaches to regional development have increasingly started to emphasize different aspects of skills development, technological advancement and industrial competitiveness. In his analysis of the economic and regional development of the United States, Porter (1990) introduced the idea of 'industrial clusters'. Porter argues that geographic concentration stimulates growth because of local advantages such as the concentration of highly specialized skills and knowledge, organizations, rivals, related businesses and sophisticated consumers. In 1992, Cooke et al. coined the term 'regional innovation systems', based on the works of Freeman (1987) and Lundvall (1992) on national innovation systems. Both of these works of seminal research in the early 1990s have given rise to various approaches to 'regional clusters' (OECD, 2007).

Innovation policies today, both at the national and sub-national levels, are based on these concepts. A widely popular activity-based framework has been developed, with ten of the most important activities taking place within national innovation systems (see Edquist, 2005), and the most widespread approach to innovation policy seems to be derived from looking at how policies affect various activities within the innovation system.

As Edler and Georghiou (2007) argue, innovation support has mainly been provided to enterprises through highly differentiated *supply-side* innovation policy measures (e.g. tax reductions, public venture capital funds, grants). On the other hand, *demand-side* innovation policies (i.e. all public measures that encourage innovations and/or speed up their diffusion by increasing their demand, defining new functional requirements for products and services, or better articulating demand) have been less prominent (see also Rothwell (1984) who argued in the same vein that supply-oriented instruments only address some aspects of the problem).

Public procurement for innovation

Users and their needs are central to innovation processes, often causing changes to be made to the product. Empirical research confirms this, leading von Hippel (1976) to identify the end-user innovation as, by far, the most important and critical. Lundvall (1992) has also written seminal works on how users and producers of innovations are mutually interdependent in a complex way. Public procurement for innovation represents one possibility that can be used to affect the technology life-cycle, promote clusters and innovation systems, and thereby increase urban and regional competitiveness.

Procurement offers much more refined options for government intervention and market enhancement than simple protectionism and/or subsidies. In fact, within the procurement process, it is often possible to enhance competition between different suppliers and thus avoid the usual traps of protectionism (e.g. rent-seeking) (for an excellent discussion on Taiwan, see Wade, 1990; and on other international cases, see Ades and Di Tella, 1997).

Public sector procurement in the current context can be seen here as a special case of user–producer interaction:

> In capitalist economic systems, where markets are effective mechanisms for articulating and satisfying most economic needs or demands, the point of departure in the application of public technology procurement must be the satisfaction of genuine social needs – in other words, specific societal needs unlikely to be met by the market.
>
> (Edquist and Hommen, 2000, p. 5)

In addition, the role of the central and local governments could be seen as facilitators of innovation processes in the fluid phase because both social and economic benefits for the region and/or nation state might follow.

In more concrete terms, there are several ways that public agencies can support innovations through procurement, namely:

- the creation of new markets for products and systems that go beyond the state of the art
- the creation of demand 'pull' by expressing its needs to the industry in functional or performance terms
- the provision of a testing ground for innovative products (Rothwell, 1984, p. 166)
- the provision of the potential of using public procurement to encourage innovation by providing a 'lead market' for new technologies (ECWG, 2006).

The public sector can act as a technologically demanding first buyer by absorbing risks for socially/ecologically demanded products (where significant financial development risks prevail) as well as by promoting learning (where procurement introduces strong elements of learning and upgrading into public intervention processes). Edler et al. (2005) have distinguished three basic roles that public technology procurement can play: (1) market initiation, where developmental technology is procured by the public sector (technology comes into existence only because of public demand); (2) market escalation, where public procurement is employed to diffuse the existing new technology into the market; and (3) market consolidation, which happens via bundled demand that leads to the harmonization of fragmented markets. The government can be the demander, bear higher entry costs, create critical mass, signal the market and link innovation to production – instead of just increasing the internal capacities of producers (Geroski, 1990; Edler, 2006, p. 8).

Public procurement as part of demand-side innovation policy measures may take three different forms: direct, cooperative and catalytic procurement (Edquist and Hommen, 2000; Edler et al., 2005). In *direct public procurement*, the public organization is the (primary) end-user of the product or service that is purchased. In the case of *cooperative procurement*, the public authorities buy together with private organizations and both also use the products or services purchased. In *catalytic procurement*, the government initiates or is merely involved in the procurement process, but the products or services that are purchased are used by private end-users. One should also distinguish between the procurement of commercially available products and pre-commercial products (see e.g. ECWG, 2006). The main difference between these two types of products comes from the risk-sharing perspective. In the latter case, the procuring authority covers some of the costs of the R&D process without considering the final results, whereas in the former case only the ready-to-use product is financed.

There have been several studies that compare R&D subsidies and state procurement contracts without direct R&D procurement (e.g. Rothwell and Zegveld, 1981). They have concluded that over longer time periods, state procurement has triggered greater innovation impulses in more areas than R&D subsidies. Geroski (1990, p. 189) highlights the direct links between innovation and production, showing that – in contrast to supply-side measures such as R&D subsidies – public procurement for innovations leads not only to technological capacities but also to increased production capacities for innovations. In the context of procurement, it is important to note that governments can become important end-users via the procurement process. In addition to direct technological or product innovations, quality and other standards (e.g. ecological) set by public agencies play a key role.

The following subsections outline some of the main factors influencing the effective and efficient use of public procurement for innovation at the urban level.

Multi-governance factors

Regional-, urban- and local-level governments are often dependent on legal regulations and financing at the level of the nation state. Public procurement is a highly regulated area, both internationally (e.g. World Trade Organization Government Procurement Agreement [WTOGPA], the EU directives) and on a national level, thus making the local and regional authorities dependent on this multi-level governance system.

Until recently, the EU procurement policy, for instance, has not favoured the use of procurement as a tool for wider social and economic goals, including innovation. The EU has not imposed exceptions permitted by the WTOGPA on restricting open competition in public procurement in areas where the EU suppliers are world market leaders. These exceptions are, however, used by other countries such as India, China and Japan in various areas such as information and communication technology (ICT) (ECWG, 2006). The norm has been to emphasize transparency, competitiveness, non-discrimination and cost-efficiency (the lowest cost principle) and to minimize or even avoid any risk-taking. This may be regarded as one of the reasons why the EU countries have concentrated so heavily on supply-side innovation policy measures and not so much on demand-side tools.

In 2004, the EU adopted a new package of public procurement regulations that includes several new tools and principles in favour of procurement for innovation (e.g. competitive dialogue), which has not yet been adopted into all national legislations. Thus, it could be emphasized that although the EU public procurement policy has been clearly unfavourable towards public procurement for innovation, the existing cases analysed in the literature (e.g. Edquist et al., 2000; Edler et al., 2005) indicate that public authorities, including urban governments, actually had the opportunity to use procurement as a tool for innovation policy even before the new EU regulations came into existence.

Small markets

In comparison with nation states or the EU as a whole, cities lack large potential markets and have less purchasing power. Small size and limited purchasing power make the bundling of demands more challenging and may also diminish the demand 'pull' effect as well as limit the potential of creating lead markets. It is a widely accepted view that competition is the main mechanism that leads to successful procurement. Small potential markets may have a negative influence on companies' incentives to invest in innovation and therefore reduce competition. As Cabral et al. (2006) have argued, in highly competitive markets it is the technological leader (i.e. the one who is willing to invest the most in innovation) who has a larger market share. However, this connection is not straightforward. Tight competition reduces the innovators' prospective rents and, therefore, may reduce the incentives to invest in innovation. Thus, in small markets, where potential rents are relatively smaller, a high level of competition may not be desirable.

Cities and regions have other clear advantages in procurement for innovation. Size constraints also mean that cities and regions often have advantages in:

- building and creating competencies and networks (key system elements in innovation systems) essential to the successful procurement of innovation, where cooperation, networking and learning by doing are cornerstones of success; thus making cities more attractive as testing grounds
- concrete and usually short-term demand: for example, procurement for a new m-parking system is relatively easier to handle – in terms of management capacities, finance, accountability and transparency – than long-term R&D ventures.

Administrative issues

For public administrators, modern public procurement tends to have too many goals – cost savings, transparency, sectoral policies (e.g. environmental, energy, industrial policies) all of which often contradict one another (Cave and Frinking, 2007; Nyiri et al., 2007) – and a dilemma can emerge between the micro cost effectiveness of a contract and the higher costs of R&D-based products/services that boost innovation (Cabral et al., 2006). Procurement for innovation is a costly and time-consuming process that demands strong coordination among stakeholders and constant evaluation and learning, and always involves transaction costs that have to be taken into account in the implementation of the process. Cave and Frinking (2007) have noted that there is a potential for expensive coordination failure. When the payoff is unclear, the innovative solution can be perceived as being the more expensive solution (Brammer and Walker, 2007).

Nyiri et al. (2007) have found that a lack of innovation orientation, budget and skills are considered the main barriers for local governments to the implementation of procurement for innovation. The shortage of proper know-how among procurement professionals about suitable procurement methods for fulfilling wider social goals seems to be a global phenomenon (e.g. Brammer and Walker, 2007). This may lead to a 'smart-buyer' problem in which the goals often remain unmet because the government does not know what to buy, who to buy from, and how to evaluate what has been bought – a challenge observed in cases of many public services contracting out initiatives (Nyiri et al., 2007).

Hence, a lack of administrative and financial capacity to manage and implement large-scale and long-term procurement processes is one of the most serious obstacles that may hinder governments from procuring innovative solutions. Lower administrative capacity at the urban level might be especially sensitive in important procurement for innovation areas such as conducting proper market intelligence, developing public technology platforms and managing high-risk projects. It has been found that small states, especially regions and cities, are particularly exposed to heightened rent-seeking and other corruptive pressures, due to their smallness.

Public procurement in Nordic-Baltic Sea cities

Research methods

A selection of Nordic-Baltic Sea region cities was made. The region is composed of highly developed cities (Helsinki, Copenhagen), emerging cities (Riga), relatively large cities (Stockholm) and clearly smaller cities (Tallinn, Malmö). All these cities are placed within the common European legal framework, which makes the comparison particularly interesting – not all the cities, however, have implemented the EU's new procurement guidelines. While the region has an apparent Nordic bias, it should offer an interesting analytical mix for the current purposes of this study.

Incorporating a thorough literature analysis and in-depth empirical data-gathering, the study employed a two-step approach to gather the empirical data. First, a Web-based questionnaire was delivered to the selected cities. This was designed to gain overall knowledge about procurement for innovation in the participating cities. An equally important goal was to find key study cases. The contact persons from the partner cities were given a list of the procurement and innovation-related characteristics the cases should match and then the contact persons made the initial selection of possible cases, indicating the responsible persons to be contacted. Due to the focus of the study (i.e. the implementation of a new or significantly improved technology), not all the cases were suitable for further analysis because the innovation aspect was missing and the regular procurement was carried out.

The case studies analysed here include those related to market creation, market escalation or market consolidation, as well as examples of direct, cooperative and catalytic procurement.

As a second step, structured interviews were carried out with representatives of the cities, the provider organizations and field experts. The interviews were aimed at gaining specific information about procurement for innovation cases in the participating cities. Altogether, seven cases were identified, and 18 persons from six cities were interviewed. Empirical information was also derived from secondary sources such as published and unpublished reports and documents.

The questionnaire and interview structures were, with some modifications, based on the framework used in the Fraunhofer Institute report for the European Commission (Edler et al., 2005). The results of the empirical investigation were categorized to reflect the research questions outlined in the introductory section.

The effect of public procurement on innovation

The case studies identified and analysed include those related to market creation (radical innovations not available on the [local] market), market escalation (established market, but technologies required further development), or market consolidation (establishment of critical mass) and present examples of direct, cooperative and catalytic procurement (Table 5.1).

The small number of the cases relates to the fact that public procurement for innovation in the cities that were studied is not very common. At the same time, the cases cover a wide range of types of public procurement for innovation, although not all possible types. Here, of course, the small sample size limits the ability to draw any definitive conclusions. The cases that were analysed indicate that the purchasing power of the cities is influencing not only adaptive but also radical innovations. All the radical innovations are about initiating a new market rather than generating radical technologies as such.

In budgetary terms, most of the procurements were small-scale initiatives when compared to city budgets. The share of public procurement budgets is relatively important in the cities' overall budgets, ranging from 15 per cent in Malmö to 40 per cent in Helsinki. In absolute numbers, the public procurement budget ranges from €160 million in Malmö to €2 billion in Helsinki. Although there is no data on the share of innovative-friendly procurement in the procurement budget, the numbers outlined indicate the potential of using the procurement

Table 5.1 A typology of innovative public technology procurement

	Role in relation to market		
	Initiation (Development)	Escalation (Adaptation)	Consolidation (Standardization)
Direct procurement Based on needs *intrinsic* to the procuring organization	Journey planner for the public transportation system (Helsinki)	ID-ticket for the public transportation system (Tallinn) Mobile ticketing for public transport (Helsinki)	Education software (Copenhagen)
Cooperative procurement Based on shared needs, *congeneric* to public and private sector users	Ethanol-fuelled pick-up cars (Stockholm)		Photovoltaic system for municipally owned premises (Malmö)
Catalytic procurement Based on needs of other end-users, *extrinsic* to the procuring organization	Development of the environmental city district Hammarby Sjöstad (Stockholm)		

Source: Authors, based on interviews; methodology adapted from Edler et al. (2005).

instrument as a vehicle for promoting innovation. In some cities, however, no relevant statistics are available (Table 5.2).

The cities employed very different procurement methods, ranging from direct procurement to cooperative projects and catalytic procurement; on one occasion, a sophisticated pre-commercial procurement arrangement was also implemented. The bundling of demand was a key element in Stockholm's cooperative procurement case, which was also perhaps the most complicated technology development project and had the strongest demand 'pull' effect. This implies that if urban procurement initiatives for innovation are aimed at supporting the development of complex technologies on a large scale, the demand aggregation becomes inevitable.

The cases suggest that local governments can act as market creators (see also Table 5.2). Market creation can usually happen in one of two

Table 5.2 Summary of cases in Nordic-Baltic Sea cities

	Journey planner for the public transportation system, Helsinki	Ethanol-fuelled pick-up cars, Stockholm	Development of the environmental city district Hammarby Sjöstad, Stockholm	ID-ticket for the public transportation system, Tallinn
Year of procurement	2001	2007	1998–2012	2004
Type of procurement	Direct	Cooperative	Mixed (200 projects), incl. technology competitions, market creation	Direct
Nature of innovation	Radical	Radical	Mixed	Adaptive
Level of risk for procurer	Medium	Low	Low	Low
Trigger for procurement	More efficient and effective public transport	Environmental policy goals	Environmental policy goals	Simplify collection of payments, attract people to register as local residents
Initiator	Helsinki Metropolitan Area Council	City of Stockholm (identification of demand; specification of common necessities)	City district Hammarby Sjöstad, Stockholm	City of Tallinn (Transport Department)
Procurer	Helsinki Metropolitan Area Council	Mostly private sector (Stockholm City itself might be buying 5–10 cars)	City district Hammarby Sjöstad, Stockholm	City of Tallinn
Supplier	WM-data LogicaCMG	Volkswagen	Different	Consortia: Certification Center Ltd., Eesti Ühispank and EMT

Price of good or service	€160 000	SEK 150 000/van (Volkswagen Caddy) [≈ €22.3 million (no guarantee of volume; supply of 1500 vehicles)]	–	Initial costs €700 000 Aggregate over €2 million
Number of competing bids	10 acceptable bids. 6 were then selected for the first qualification, then 3 were chosen for demonstration implementation	1 (Volkswagen – bid just for the smallest category; other processes postponed)	–	6
Intellectual property rights owned by	Core product – the company Adoptions – the city	Volkswagen	–	Supplier
Innovation effect	Increased export and competitiveness of company; cost benefit of €5 million; 90,000/day users of the service	Creation of new market (new transport service market using ethanol-fuelled cars)	Some suppliers have scaled up production processes and implemented process innovations	Effective solution in place, popularized national ID cards, similar system also implemented in other cities

Table 5.2 (Continued)

	Mobile ticketing for public transport, Helsinki	Education software, Copenhagen	Photovoltaic (PV) system for municipal premises, Malmö
Year of procurement	2001	2007	2005
Type of procurement	Direct	Cooperative	Direct/cooperative
Nature of innovation	Radical (unique validation method) and adaptive (SMS)	Market consolidation	Market consolidation
Level of risk for procurer	Low	Low	Low
Trigger for procurement	Easier and more comfortable access to the service, resulting in increased use of public transport rather than individual cars	To motivate students through a new education system using IT	Environmental issue
Initiator	Plusdial Ltd.	The Municipality of Copenhagen's Children and Youth Administration	City of Malmö (civil servants within the city administration)
Procurer	HKL Enterprise	Municipality of Copenhagen	City of Malmö, Real Estate Department
Supplier	Plusdial Ltd. with Add2Phone Ltd.	Crossroads Copenhagen	
Price of good or service	–	< €65,000 project (Copenhagen entered with c. €15,000)	The price for the PV part was €8 million. Fixed price: 30% was paid by Malmö and 70% by Sweden

Number of competing bids	–	Not applicable – negotiated procedure, not open due to the size	4 bids for the PV installation, and 1 bid for the steel construction; open procurement procedure; no search for local suppliers
IPR to	Provider	Alinea has the IPR, public schools of Copenhagen have free access	
Innovation effect	Creation of new market, fostering m-commerce; increased customer satisfaction; improved image of Helsinki City Transport and public transportation; increases in efficiency and effectiveness for the operator	A successful process, it attended to the necessities: children were motivated and teachers were satisfied	Energy being produced; inspiration for other cities; positive economical externalities; greater social welfare; marketing for the city

Source: Authors, based on interviews; methodology adapted from Edler et al. (2005).

ways. First, market creation can be a 'by-product' of a procurement process, where the main goal was to satisfy some sort of social need. Tallinn's ID-card case demonstrates that incremental procurement for innovation may lead to new solutions not foreseen by the stakeholders before the start of the process. Secondly, market creation is the main purpose of a purchasing activity. As demonstrated in the Stockholm case, market creation through the use of cooperative procurement can successfully be the goal of a local authority. The cases also demonstrate that procurements for innovative solutions do fail. The successful examples of Stockholm's ethanol-fuelled cars, Helsinki's journey planner and Tallinn's electronic ticket system have a common denominator: all the initial attempts to purchase the new solutions had failed; however, the experience gained was later turned into successful results.

Success factors

The main triggers for procurement for innovation have been specific public needs or policies, such as environmental policy. For example, Tallinn faced the challenge of introducing a universal ticket system for public transportation, which eventually led to the creation of electronic ID-card tickets. Copenhagen's case was initiated because of an emerging need in educational policy. Malmö's photovoltaic energy supply purchase was a direct result of its environmental policy, but it was also exploited as a marketing tool for the city. In Stockholm, public procurement for innovation is strongly driven by environmental goals as well.[2] The initiatives in Helsinki were launched to meet emerging problems in the city's public transportation sector. That said, it can be concluded that Nordic-Baltic Sea cities have not used procurement as a genuine innovation policy measure (e.g. to facilitate innovation processes in fluid phases) but rather as an additional key tool in achieving other social and environmental policy aims.

In the cases identified, the intellectual property rights were left with the providers. This should positively affect the future development phases of the procured products and therefore result in additional positive spillovers. There appears to be no correlation between the number of competitors and the success of procurement initiatives, thus supporting the theoretical claims.

The roles of regional and central governments stand out as being important in the cities' innovation systems. This becomes clear, for instance, from Tallinn's ID-card ticket, as this innovative service could not be introduced without the central government that initiated the development of the electronic ID-card in the first place. In Sweden, the central government assisted the City of Stockholm in creating a market for ethanol-fuelled cars by demanding that gas stations also sell alternative fuels and by introducing zero tax for alternative fuels. The city of Malmö was able to use the subsidies allocated from the central government in the framework of energy-efficient technology solutions to procure new energy systems. The cities themselves are also introducing supportive measures to promote the diffusion of innovative solutions, as procurement itself may not be sufficient. For example, when entering the City of Stockholm, a driver must pay the congestion charge but not in case of an environmentally friendly car, which can park for free. In Tallinn, an ID-ticket costs less than a regular ticket.

In most of the cases, procurement for innovation enjoyed direct support at the highest political level. In one particular case, a project leader of procurement for innovation was fired because of the unsatisfactory results in the procurement process. Procurement officials from Helsinki have admitted that because they are still struggling to get used to the new legal requirements, the question of the links between innovation and procurement is something 'for tomorrow'. Other representatives of the cities seem to be in the same position, saying that the whole issue is rather new to them.

The case studies reveal the inevitability of involving external consultants and experts in the complex process of procurement for innovation. Using external know-how, however, increases the transaction costs of public procurement for innovation projects. The cities thus face the challenge of measuring the potential positive spillovers that result from the procurement against the need to keep the transaction costs under control. This is something that cities still have to be introduced to.

Limiting factors

As has been argued above, public procurement for innovation is not very common in the cities that were studied. It can be claimed that the barriers to procurement for innovation identified earlier also hold in the cases of Nordic-Baltic Sea cities. There seems to be an overall lack of instruments in the cities regarding demand-side measures. There are no signs of allocating special local funds for procurement for innovation. The officials are not well aware of the possibilities offered by public procurement regulation for supporting innovation. In addition, the market and technology knowledge is small. A representative of the city of Copenhagen explained that:

> It is a challenge to motivate employees to spend the necessary time on projects that are not their primary task.

Innovation does not play any role in the current public procurement guidelines in the cities that were studied. The case of Malmö has shown that while some departments emphasize innovation in their everyday practices, others put more emphasis on off-the-shelf products to reduce risks. Copenhagen has participated in innovative development projects but not as part of public procurement. When it comes to the strategic level of public procurement and innovation, only Helsinki and Stockholm have developed a policy vision that links procurement and innovation in their region. For Helsinki, this is a relatively new issue, and no major actions have been carried out so far, but according to an official responsible for public procurement issues:

> It's recognized that we should be able to change our practices and views according to possible changes and needs of the market. We also have a new strategy for economic development, in which procurement is mentioned as one of the co-operation fields.

Stockholm can be regarded as a rather experienced city on the issue.[3] In addition to a long history of this kind of project (see the ethanol-fuelled lorries' case below), the city has also developed a framework for handling unsolicited innovative proposals. According to an interviewee, Stockholm's goal is to:

> Promote economic development, both in Stockholm and in the region, through procurement and competition, where a larger number of small companies are welcome as partners.

Stockholm's activity can be explained by the fact that Sweden is one of the few countries in Europe to have dealt with the issue since the 1990s (Edquist et al., 2000).

There is lack of awareness among city officials about the connection between procurement and innovation. The cities have so far not initiated public procurement that is aimed at supporting economic development.[4] There is no clear understanding regarding the transfer of intellectual property rights (IPR) in the cities. Most of the cases reviewed indicate that IPR are transferred to the providers, but the interviews reveal that this is not yet a common practice in the region and that cities are resistant to leaving IPR with the providers. As the CEO of a prominent ICT company in the region stated:

> The issue of IPR transfer is the single most eminent shortcoming of the current public procurement practice for innovation. It is vital for overall economic development that the IPR stays with the providers so that the results of procurement (i.e. innovative solutions) can be diffused into the market.

The public sector thus actually prevents the diffusion of new technologies into the market. When asked about the possible challenges and problems of public procurement for innovation, a respondent acknowledged the main obstacle to be:

> The national public procurement act does not define separately the purchase of innovative products or services.

The new EU public procurement regulation actually has many different tools specifically designed to promote innovation through procurement (for an overview, see ECEG, 2005). The existence of these avenues has simply not been realized or not yet been incorporated into national and local legislations. Civil servants in some cities seem to be better informed about the opportunities offered by public procurement for innovation and have first-hand experience (gained under the 'old' EU rules), both with and without success. However, this experience is neither disseminated nor discussed widely. The same applies to companies. Those that have had positive experiences consider it an important tool that should be applied more widely. At the same time, the cities have a different approach to training in procurement. There are examples of voluntary as well as strategy-based training, but no systematic training programmes or courses could be identified that targeted procurement and innovation.

The majority of the cities do not have procedures in place for carrying out a continuous market watch on what kind of new solutions private companies or universities can offer for meeting public needs. Stockholm stands out here as an exception. As stated by an official, Stockholm has:

> A constant dialogue carried out with different branches from the Executive Office and other departments. There is also a possibility

for companies or organizations from outside to (so-called) challenge existing activities throughout the city, where the responsible committee has to test the challenge.

The cities only infrequently procure and therefore influence the innovation of pre-commercial technologies. This also goes for the radical innovation examples included in the study. An outstanding exception is the City of Helsinki: in the journey planner procurement case (Table 5.2), the city reduced some of the financial risks of the bidders by awarding the three finalists monetary prizes. This is not to say that the procurement examples reviewed did not embrace any risks. Indeed, for instance Stockholm's ethanol-fuelled cars procurement did not actually produce the expected results after initial attempts. However, in terms of policy, the cities are not aware of taking any further steps to reduce the risks of providers associated with investments for R&D, production or field-testing.

Conclusions and implications for public administration

By exploring current public procurement for innovation practices in the cases of six Nordic-Baltic Sea cities, this study shows that public procurement can affect providers' innovativeness.

The mobile ticket case from Helsinki demonstrates the positive influence a public sector can have on markets through innovation-friendly procurement. The solution for a journey planner in Helsinki was exported to the United States and elsewhere; the company itself has been sold six times. The company that developed Tallinn's ID-ticket relies on knowledge and technologies developed for offering new products and services to other regions. Hence, the positive impact of public procurement on companies is evidenced by the increased exports and, most importantly, changes in companies' routines regarding how innovation is approached. The latter (immediate behavioural change) is considered the most important impact so far because some economic implications (exports, increases in value-addedness) may only be revealed in the future (OECD, 2006). It can be argued that most of the purchased solutions analysed here would not have come into existence if the cities were not playing the lead-user role. The cities have managed to positively influence the providers to overcome the fluid phase of the technologies under review.

Existing public procurement for innovation cases are mainly triggered by specific public needs or policies, such as environmental policy, which can be regarded as a good platform for future activities. However, the study also reveals that the public procurement for innovation potential is under-utilized and it is not seen as an inherent part of urban innovation policy: city officials are not aware of the connection between procurement and innovation.

There seems to be a contradiction here in the way in which public procurement for innovation is viewed. On the one hand, the phenomenon is understandable as shown in the enduring EU official policy that procurement is not to be used for wider social goals. On the other hand, in the context of urban competitiveness, the phenomenon is surprising because procurement for innovation has been, at least theoretically, regarded as a powerful demand-side tool that public authorities have for promoting innovation.

A number of important lessons can be learnt from this study's conceptual framework and empirical findings that have implications for policy and public administration activities in the cities.

First, there is a clear need for a strategy and guidelines for public procurement for innovation in the cities to address both the 'usual' commercially ready innovation and early stage pre-commercial innovation.[5] The strategy should bind together innovation policies (both demand-side and supply-side), R&D policies (where applicable), public procurement policies and field policies (e.g. environmental policy). This strategy for policy coordination, in effect, should form the basis for the introduction of the demand for innovation in the legislation of the regulation of a certain field of policy. The strategy formation could serve as an agent for overcoming the awareness problem and to change the current public procurement culture largely inherited from past policies of the EU.

Secondly, the cities should systematically deal with barriers and administrative issues related to the implementation of procurement for innovation in order to avoid the trap of the 'smart buyer' problem. Cities should build up their capacity to routinely collect information from the market on emerging (technological) solutions for social needs;[6] take full advantage of the new public procurement methods that are favourable to innovation;[7] and introduce appropriate evaluation mechanisms into everyday practices. Allocating specific grants to conduct pilot projects of procurement for innovation may signal to the public procurers that risk-taking is permitted by the political leadership. Cities should also advance their risk-management methods and techniques. Introducing innovation-related training schemes for procurement officials should be among the first steps to be taken.

Thirdly, cities should address the question of a limited market and resources by emphasizing the bundling of demand to increase the demand 'pull' effect. In addition to direct procurement – arguably the most dominant mode of public procurement today – more attention should be paid to cooperative and catalytic procurement involving other private as well as public organizations. Further, cities have to send out strong signals to the market that innovative solutions are sourced for and that innovative providers are welcome to approach cities.

Acknowledgements

Research for this study was partially supported by the Estonian Ministry of Education and Research (targeted financing grant no. SF0140094s08), the Estonian Science Foundation (grants no. 7577, 7441 and 8097) and the BaltMet Inno Project. The authors are also grateful for the research assistance of Caetano Penna and Margit Suurna and to all the people interviewed for this article.

Notes

1. There are only a few local and regional public procurement for innovation case studies available in the literature: e.g. Edler et al. (2005); Pohl and Sandberg (2005); Binks (2006).
2. In transportation, for example, waste collection contractors, public transportation providers and taxi companies must use clean vehicles in Stockholm. Contracts are made with, and licences are given only to, providers that guarantee use of a certain number of clean vehicles.
3. This is not to say that the other cities do not engage in procuring innovative solutions at all. On the contrary, the case studies reveal that it has been done only as single efforts and not as a coordinated activity.
4. When the representatives of the cities were approached in order to sort out possible candidates for procurement for innovation cases, the majority of cities stated that they had never had such cases. As the study demonstrates, all the cities actually do influence innovation through their procurement. Although in most cases, it is done indirectly or without this particular goal in mind.
5. Examples of existing policies on national level can be found, for instance, in the UK and the Netherlands (see ECEG, 2005).
6. This could include 'industry days', technical dialogues, handling unsolicited proposals and consultations with technology transfer agents.
7. Examples include most economically advantageous tender (MEAT) criteria, competitive dialogue, performance-based specification, references to standards and framework agreements.

Part III
Networks and Innovation

6
Innovation Inside Government: The Importance of Networks

Jenny M. Lewis, Mark Considine and Damon Alexander

Introduction

This chapter delves into networks and their relationship to innovation inside government. The concept of 'networks' is investigated, and an analytical framework is established through which the role of networks in the innovation process can be explored. It is argued that there is value in adopting a network approach for the study of innovation inside government, since networks offer a novel approach to understanding issues of power as well as issues of innovation.

Using results from a large survey of bureaucrats and politicians drawn from 11 local governments in the state of Victoria, Australia, different normative positions on innovation and different procedural orientations are first identified. This chapter then explores how these innovation norms and procedural types differ across governments, and according to the different political and administrative roles played by actors. In keeping with the age-old adage, it seems that where you sit very much determines where you stand, in terms of views on innovation and governance. The focus then becomes social network concepts and methods, and a detailed examination of the structure of advice and strategic information networks mapped for politicians and bureaucrats in the 11 governments is then provided. The overall structure of these networks is explored, and then the focus is on how network configurations around particular actors differ between politicians, the senior executive and middle managers, as well as across different municipalities. Politicians are important 'go to' people in some governments, while the senior executive or middle managers are more important in others. Different levels of connectedness between the political and bureaucratic sides can also be discerned across municipalities.

Finally, the chapter examines in detail who the innovators are, and what sets them apart from their colleagues, with a particular focus on network characteristics. It explores and attempts to disentangle the dual effects of formal (hierarchical) and informal (network) structures, concluding on the basis of both social network analysis and traditional quantitative statistical methods that the innovators are distinguished by specific networking patterns, beyond those attributable to hierarchy alone.

Innovation inside government: The importance of networks

The topic of innovation has often been approached using the much-discussed concepts of revolutionary ideas, breakthrough technologies and rule-breaking, and charismatic individuals. Much of this work deals with private corporations at the cutting edge, with high levels of flexibility and the freedom to pursue big ideas without the layers of oversight that accompany government and publicly funded services. If government is discussed, it is in terms of how government stifles innovation, or what governments should do to encourage others to innovate. The literature is largely silent on the topic of innovation inside government. This chapter turns this focus around to an exploration of innovation inside government.

A central task in examining innovation in a more public and political context is to disentangle expectations and claims about the various constraints on, and opportunities for, innovation inside government. How does it occur? What factors lead to its occurrence? What kinds of actors are involved? Are politicians, the professional representatives of the democratic process, important players in this game? In order to come to grips with this large topic, the study focused on several promising lines of inquiry generated by an examination of the literature (see Considine et al., 2009), which is briefly summarized here.

The first line of inquiry is one of normative frames, related to how those inside government understand the notion of innovation. The second is about the perceived impacts that the procedures of government have on innovation. These two rest on the (small) literature that tries to identify what innovation means in a governmental context (e.g. Dodgson and Bessant, 1996; Borins, 2000; Mulgan and Albury, 2003), and the larger management school literature on the effect of organizational processes on innovation (e.g. Drucker, 1985; Kanter, 1985; Damanpour, 1991; Jones and Beckinsale, 1999). The third is the familiar notion of hierarchy in organizations, and the fourth is the concept of 'networks', which is explored as a counterpoint to the formal structural relationships between individuals. Hierarchy needs no explanation as being important in shaping an individual's ability to achieve things in organizations, through their position. Networks are seen as a way forward in examining power relations among groups and individuals, by focusing on informal patterns of interaction rather than on formal positional power. Networks provide access to embedded resources (Lin, 2001), and the ways in which different groups and different types of network ties matter are important to innovation adoption (e.g. Coleman et al., 1966; Rogers and Kincaid, 1981; Valente, 1998). However, networks have, to date, contributed little to understanding innovation inside government.

The aim of this chapter is to examine the importance of networks to innovation inside government, compared with three other dimensions: innovation norms, innovation procedures and formal hierarchical positions.

Networks, innovation and public policy

Innovation is considered here as a characteristic form of policy development and governance. As already indicated, four important dimensions of the policy and administration process were analysed in this study. The first dimension is the normative or perceptual frame through which the key players in any system define innovation and orient themselves to a particular approach to innovative work. This provides contributors with a type of mental map to navigate their work. Also part of this map is the second dimension: the way in which participants understand and evaluate the main governmental institutions that might be used to create innovations within their environment. Is the planning and budget process helpful to innovation or a source of blockage? Are the committee systems and consultative institutions important to their innovation practices? By researching actor evaluations of their experiences with these procedures, this study expects to generate an account of innovation against specific expectations about the action channels, veto points and lock-ins that are characteristic of government.

While the first and second dimensions are normative and perceptual, the third is the more straightforward one of roles and positions. It seems likely that how one thinks about innovation and works to enact it will be shaped by where one sits within an organizational structure. Those in more senior positions have a higher organizational status, wield more formal power and have access to more resources. Important differences are also likely to be found between politicians and bureaucrats, since their roles reflect, respectively, the political and administrative arms of government. So, while innovation is viewed as an outcome of interactions among actors, shaped by the institutional structures they inhabit, role and rank are also expected to play a part in structuring those interactions and hence, innovation.

There is a logical connection from this formal structure to the final dimension, which is the informal pattern of communication or networking among actors within these governmental systems. We know who sits on committees and shares portfolio responsibilities, but who actually interacts with whom? Actors are connected by relationships through networks, which significantly shape political power (Knoke, 1990) and policy choices (Laumann and Knoke, 1987). Networks of influential actors have a set of embedded resources that can be used to wield informal power within a policy sector (Lewis, 2006) and to significantly shape the policy agenda (Lewis, 2005). In the (admittedly small) research literature on innovation inside government, there are accounts that stress 'the use of a systems approach', 'process improvement' (Borins, 2001, p. 6) and 'system values' (Swift, 1993, p. 18). Repeated and successful acts of innovation are seen to occur when a whole system is geared towards innovative outcomes. Lundvall's (1992) book on national systems of innovation points to such properties and to the very different histories driving them in different national systems.

On the other hand, there are many arguments that deny these explanations. First are those who say that innovation runs counter to existing structures and find that 'frustration with the status quo' is a major source of innovation. Second are the many observers who find innovation to be an individual rather than a collective property, or simply observe on the basis of the case study literature that 'innovative ideas spring up from all over the place' (Walters, 2001, pp. 9–11). Most relevant to our concerns here are the few attempts to integrate studies of policy diffusion processes with considerations of policy networks. Mintrom and Vergari (1998) have demonstrated the importance of different types of networks for different phases of innovation, with 'entrepreneurs' (akin to the innovators in this chapter) using external and internal networks for getting new items onto the policy agenda (external for generating new ideas from elsewhere, internal for shaping proposals so that they gain attention) and internal networks to obtain the required approval for the innovation.

Much can be gained by considering structures as something more than institutional roles and positions. If we allow for a model of structures that includes patterns of relationships or networks, we can examine innovation and what it means to be an innovator as some combination of individual and structural attributes. Mapping who talks to whom, where information is obtained and traded, and who seeks advice from whom, opens up the possibility of explaining the impact of both traditional forms of hierarchical interaction and the more lateral and informal links that could underpin innovation. Freeman (1991, p. 501) makes this case for firms, arguing that 'both empirical and theoretical research has long since demonstrated the importance for successful innovation of both external and internal networks of information and collaboration.' Given the small amount of research on innovation and networks in the public sector, it is postulated that networks might be equally important in this context, and this is a central empirical question that this research study addresses.

Another set of issues that should be canvassed relate to the character of the innovation itself, including who becomes an innovator. The research literature points us towards an enormous variety. The different kinds of innovations include those that transform techniques or processes, those that produce new products and those that alter the methodologies for drawing these different contributions into a system of value creation (Van de Ven and Rogers, 1988). Within this field, there is also great debate about what qualifies as an innovation, with some authors wishing to reserve the term 'invention' for substantially new products driven by research and development (R&D), leaving innovation to encompass any form of adoption of a 'device, system, policy, program, process, product or service that is new to the adopting organization' (Damanpour, 1991, p. 556). There is a substantial space between the demanding test required by new inventions and the permissive quality of adoption.

The modest range of studies dealing explicitly with public sector innovation was noted at the beginning of this chapter. If the definition of innovation is expanded to include all forms of policy change and organizational development, including such things as New Public Management (NPM), then there is an abundant literature of cases and country comparisons (Barzeley and Gallego, 2006). However, most of these studies focus on either policy or management, not the systemic attributes of innovation, or if they do they only describe systemic attributes in selected cases. The most prevalent source of accounts of more systemic forms of innovation is the public management field, where innovation is frequently defined as a desirable trait in the modern public manager. As a result, the model of innovation that emerges is often concerned with the role of entrepreneurial leadership. Sanders (1998), for example, makes this claim in relation to the US reinvention agenda.

Survey of 11 municipal governments

A research agenda that is capable of addressing the importance of networks to innovation inside government requires a large empirical study. In this case, local governments in the state of Victoria, Australia, were chosen. Limiting participation to municipalities within a single state means that they are all operating under the same statutory and regulatory framework. A call for expressions of interest to participate in this research went out through the regular newsletter of the Victorian Local Governance Association (VLGA), an umbrella industry association for local governments, community groups and individual citizens. This association has 46 of the total 79 municipalities in the state as members. In response to our call, 11 municipalities volunteered to participate and they were all accepted.[1]

On average, each municipality in Victoria has around nine politicians who are elected to a three-year term and then elect their mayor for a one-year term which may be renewed. State legislation provides for a strong managerial mandate for chief executive officers (CEOs) who are appointed to a three-year renewable term by a committee of elected politicians. The average size of municipalities in Victoria is approximately 60,000 residents. Municipal governments raise their own taxes through property rates and charges, but receive up to half of their total revenue from state or federal funds for the running of various devolved activities. The municipalities vary widely in terms of population and geographical size, and this diversity is reflected in the 11 governments in this study, some characteristics of which are shown in Table 6.1.

The top four levels of bureaucrats (the CEO, directors, managers and team leaders/coordinators) and all the politicians at each of the 11 participating local governments were surveyed using a self-completed questionnaire. This was distributed either at meetings of staff, through the internal mail system, or in person by the research team.[2] The questionnaire collected information on respondents' social networks and asked a range of questions concerning how they framed innovation as a concept, and how different institutional, structural and personal traits influenced innovation in their municipality. Overall, 765

Table 6.1   Characteristics of the 11 municipalities in the study

Municipality	Total persons[a]	Median weekly household income[a]	Area (sq. km)[a]	Urban-rural[b]	% Male politicians[c]
Bankview	114,222	$800–$999	62	Suburban	71.4
Bilstown	24,075	$400–$499	864	Rural	57.1
Kilbourne	141,912	$800–$999	114	Suburban	55.6
Lassiter	35,667	$800–$999	1747	Rural	66.7
Melville	107,920	$1000–$1199	114	Suburban	62.5
Millside	59,770	$600–$699	31	Inner city	42.9
Netherton	67,784	$800–$999	36	Inner city	44.4
Oberon	131,359	$700–$799	51	Inner city	80.0
Parkside	80,157	$800–$999	21	Inner city	71.4
Wallerstrum	114,082	$800–$999	490	Urban fringe	100.0
Yarwood	137,539	$800–$999	2470	Urban fringe	66.7

Source: ABS Census (2001).
Notes:
[a] These data are taken from: ABS Census (2001): Basic Community Profile and Snapshot
[b] Based on the following distinctions:

- Inner city – 10 km or less from Melbourne centre
- Suburban – more than 10 km and less than 30 km from Melbourne centre
- Urban fringe – 30 km or more from Melbourne centre
- Rural – outside Melbourne metropolitan area

[c] Based on incumbent politicians at the time of the survey (2008)

responses were received (an 80.8 per cent response rate). Table 6.2 contains detailed information on response rates for individual governments. Pseudonyms have been used to identify the governments throughout this chapter.

Innovation norms

The first part of the puzzle was to identify different normative positions on innovation and different procedural orientations. As the authors have argued elsewhere (Considine et al., 2009), innovation is an elastic term that needs to be understood as a practice of real actors with their own dispositions and preferences. In this study, the authors were particularly interested in how these dispositions and preferences varied according to innovator status. That is, did the innovators in the sample have different ways of framing innovation as a concept? Did they hold alternative perceptions of the role and influence played by different organizational and institutional procedures?

Table 6.2   Response rates for the municipalities in the study

Government	Staff identified in sample*	Returns	Response rate (%)	Politicians	Returns	Response rate (%)
Bankview	77	63	81.8	7	3	43
Bilstown	48	41	85.4	7	6	86
Kilbourne	88	78	88.6	9	7	78
Lassiter	66	51	77.3	9	4	44
Melville	54	45	83.3	8	7	88
Millside	65	57	87.7	7	2	29
Netherton	233	162	69.5	9	7	78
Oberon	93	74	79.6	10	8	80
Parkside	102	89	87.3	7	5	71
Wallerstrum	52	46	88.5	5	3	60
Yarwood	69	59	85.5	9	7	78
Overall	947	765	80.8	87	59	68

*This is the number of staff identified from organizational charts and other information provided by the councils as being at the top four levels – chief executive officer, director, manager and team leader/coordinator.

Politicians and bureaucrats were asked to locate their own norma-tive accounts of innovation by responding to a series of statements concerning the nature of innovation. The 16 statements used in the questionnaire included items such as 'innovation means making small, continuous improvements'; 'innovation means making major changes'; 'accountability requirements limit innovation'; and 'my organization values innovative individuals'.[3] Each respondent was asked to indicate their level of agreement with these statements on a five-point Likert scale, ranging from strongly disagree to strongly agree. The 16 items were then factor analysed using principal components analysis in order to determine underlying or latent structures in the ways in which inno-vation was understood across this population. Details of this analysis can be found in Considine and Lewis (2005).

The five factors that emerged have been called *institutional, structural, sceptical, incremental* and *adaptive* accounts of innovation. The institu-tional factor describes innovation as the work of internal structures and certain standard organizational factors. The structural type refers to innovation as radical, externally focused and sometimes based on conflict. The sceptical outlook defines innovation as being of limited applicability to the public sector, while the incremental factor refers to the role of small and planned efforts. The notion that innovation is largely about adaptation refers to sourcing ideas from elsewhere, while also seeing governmental innovation as being quite different from other types. Box 6.1 contains a summary of what is captured by each of these.

Box 6.1   The five normative positions on innovation

Institutional	'Innovation relies on organizational factors'
Structural	'Innovation is about large external changes'
Sceptical	'Uncertain if government has a role in innovation'
Incremental	'Innovation is about small, planned improvements'
Adaptive	'Innovation means adapting things from elsewhere'

Tables 6.3–6.5 present the mean factor scores for each government, role and position, wherever the one-way analysis of variance (ANOVA) showed statistically significant differences (at $p < 0.05$) across these categories. In keeping with the age-old adage, it seems that where

Table 6.3   Institutional innovation norms (mean factor scores)

Government		
	Bankview	0.614
	Bilstown	−0.080
	Kilbourne	−0.132
	Lassiter	0.142
	Melville	0.314
	Millside	−0.027
	Netherton	−0.368
	Oberon	−0.197
	Parkside	0.171
	Wallerstrum	0.349
	Yarwood	−0.087
Position	Mayor	0.280
	Politician	0.083
	CEO	0.644
	Director	0.422
	Manager	0.033
	Coordinator/team leader	−0.075
	Other	−0.087

Table 6.4 Structural innovation norms (mean factor scores)

Group	Mean factor scores
Bankview	0.190
Bilstown	−0.255
Kilbourne	−0.181
Lassiter	−0.120
Melville	−0.238
Millside	0.058
Netherton	−0.014
Oberon	0.016
Parkside	0.265
Wallerstrum	−0.260
Yarwood	0.260

Table 6.5 Sceptical innovation norms (mean factor scores)

Group	Mean factor scores
Mayor	0.119
Politician	−0.170
CEO	−0.999
Director	−0.192
Manager	−0.046
Coordinator/team leader	0.040
Other	0.143

you sit very much determines where you stand, in terms of views on innovation. Significant differences were found for the institutional type across governments, and across positions, but not between politicians and bureaucrats. This suggests a different normative frame for innovation in each government. Bankview is the government most in agreement with the institutional view, while Netherron is the least in agreement. CEOs identified most with the institutional model of innovation, followed by directors and then mayors, then politicians and managers, while team leaders/coordinators identified least with this view (see Table 6.3). The structural view was also significantly different across governments, with Parkside and Yarwood strongly supporting this view (see Table 6.4). This difference was close to significant for politicians versus bureaucrats ($p = 0.08$), with politicians being more likely than bureaucrats to view innovation as something involving large changes out in the community, sometimes involving conflict.

The adoption of a sceptical view of innovation (seeing it as having little to do with government) varied significantly across organizational positions (see Table 6.5). Mayors and others (generally people at the fifth level down in organizational terms) were the most sceptical about whether government could contribute much to innovation, followed by team leaders /coordinators, then managers. Politicians and directors were less sceptical and CEOs were the least sceptical about innovation inside government.

The incremental view did not vary significantly either between governments, when comparing politicians and bureaucrats, or in relation to position in the hierarchy. The idea that innovation could best be expressed as a process of adaptation did not differ significantly across governments, politicians versus bureaucrats, or positions either. That is, although these two norms describe coherent positions, they do not differ significantly across governments, roles or ranks. It is concluded from these five normative frames that people construct their own cognitive understandings of innovation, and these reflect, in part, their role, their rank and the normative climate (or 'culture') of their particular government.

Innovation procedures

Using the same approach, respondents were also asked to assess, using a five-point Likert scale, the extent to which 13 key institutions and instruments used in local government helped or hindered innovation. These items included such things as statutory meetings, the budget, corporate plans, election campaigns and their organization's pay and promotion system.

Three coherent positions expressing different views of the procedures most likely to help and hinder innovation emerged from the analysis. The position that has been called *political* covers assessments of all the formal legislative procedures of local government such as municipal meetings and committees. The annual budget process and the corporate plan load on both this factor and the *managerial* factor, reflecting the fact that these items are seen as being part of both political and internal management procedures. *Managerial* also includes the internal management procedures associated with the organizational machinery of each municipality and its staff (e.g. pay and performance, quality procedures), but not politicians. The items making up the *electoral* factor centre on the role played by elections, state government regulation and the culture, values and other characteristics of local politicians, so far as innovation is concerned. Details of this analysis can be found in Considine and Lewis (2005), and a summary of the types is provided in Box 6.2.

Box 6.2   The three types of innovation procedures

Political	Budget, committee meetings and municipal meetings
Managerial	Corporate plan, structure, systems and officials
Electoral	Elections, state government and municipal politicians

---

Analyses of these three types of innovation procedures across governments, roles and positions are presented in Tables 6.6–6.8 where there are statistically significant differences. The view of whether political procedures help or hinder innovation varies significantly between bureaucrats and politicians, with politicians being far more positive about what this set of procedures delivers than bureaucrats, and CEOs being the most negative (see Table 6.6). These are the parts of government over which politicians have the most control. Bureaucrats at all levels see them as hindering innovation. The view of the impact of managerial procedures on innovation also differs significantly between governments and across positions (see Table 6.7). CEOs were (not surprisingly) the most positive about the impact of plans and structures in helping innovation, followed by directors then mayors. Mayors are the only full-time politicians in these governments and, as such, spend

Table 6.6   Political procedures (mean factor scores)

	Group	Mean factor score
Politician vs bureaucrat	Politician	0.477
	Bureaucrat	−0.035
Position	Mayor	0.319
	Politician	0.515
	CEO	−0.107
	Director	−0.076
	Manager	−0.016
	Coordinator/team leader	−0.073
	Other	0.040

Table 6.7 Managerial procedures (mean factor scores)

Government		
	Bankview	0.465
	Bilstown	−0.183
	Kilbourne	0.130
	Lassiter	−0.043
	Melville	0.069
	Millside	0.097
	Netherton	−0.266
	Oberon	−0.260
	Parkside	0.013
	Wallerstrum	0.501
	Yarwood	0.013
Position		
	Mayor	0.343
	Politician	0.104
	CEO	1.035
	Director	0.420
	Manager	0.140
	Coordinator/team leader	−0.157
	Other	−0.158

Table 6.8 Electoral procedures (mean factor scores)

Bankview	−0.272
Bilstown	−0.135
Kilbourne	−0.777
Lassiter	−0.047
Melville	0.100
Millside	0.128
Netherton	0.074
Oberon	−0.063
Parkside	0.584
Wallerstrum	0.224
Yarwood	0.000

more time in the town hall than their colleagues. Electoral governance was seen as having a different impact on innovation in different governments, with five of them regarding it as helping while the remainder seeing it as a hindrance (see Table 6.8). There were no significant differences across positions in relation to electoral governance helping or hindering innovation.

These normative parts of the innovation story show that there are more or less coherent normative positions among these actors with respect to two different dimensions: the way innovation gets defined,

Table 6.9   Correlations* between innovation norms and procedures ($n = 715$)

	Political	Managerial	Electoral
Institutional	0.17	0.47	0.13
Structural	–	–	–
Sceptical	–	–	–
Incremental	0.17	–	–
Adaptation	–	–	–

* Spearman's rank correlation coefficients (ρ), significant at $p < 0.01$ shown. Note that because orthogonal rotation of the factors was used, there are no significant correlations amongst the five innovation norms, or amongst the three innovation process factors.

and the role they believe governance plays. Table 6.9 shows that there are also important relationships between the normative views about innovation and the assessments that actors make of the procedures. The institutional norm is significantly associated with each of the three procedures, but is most strongly correlated with managerial. That is, people who view innovation as being about internal structures and organization also see things like pay and performance systems as helpful. Not surprisingly, the structural view is not related to these internal processes, since in this view, innovation is primarily about changes occurring externally. Neither the sceptical nor the adaptation norms of innovation are correlated with internal processes, indicating that if the view of innovation is limited and uncertain, or simply adaptation from elsewhere, then institutional processes are not likely to be seen as being all that important.

In brief, politicians are most positive about the role of political procedures, while CEOs and top officials are negative about this aspect in relation to innovation. Whether you favour managerial and electoral procedures is likely to depend on what government you work in. However, regardless of this, you will favour managerial procedures if you are a CEO, a mayor or a senior bureaucrat. If you are a lower-level official, you are likely to regard these organizational procedures as an impediment to innovation. Views of electoral procedures vary between governments, but not across positions.

Little needs to be said about formal position, beyond the already demonstrated impact that location in the hierarchy has on innovation norms, and the expected relationship between position and innovator status, which is returned to later. The focus now moves to informal networks. The study aimed to trace networks and networking of different types, and so looked at levels of external contact with other organizations, levels of conference attendance and membership in associations. Social network concepts and methods were also used to provide a detailed examination of the structure of advice and strategic information networks for politicians and bureaucrats in the 11 governments. These different types of networks are examined next, before their relative contribution to the innovation story is assessed.

Networks – external contacts

Networks are a prime means to facilitate information exchange within organizations and governments. Being linked to other organizations provides opportunities to learn new ways of doing things (Borins, 2000; Martin, 2000), and in this context, the innovative capacity of local governments has been linked to the presence of strong internal and external networks (Newman et al., 2001). In this study, a number of approaches were taken to explore such networks and their link to the innovative capacity of individuals.

The first involves an examination of the level and scope of specific *external contact* that politicians and bureaucrats have with other governments and organizations that are relevant to their work. In the case of local government in Australia, the important external agents are other municipal governments, the two municipal government associations, state and federal government departments, local business associations, private for-profit and not-for-profit organizations, residents' groups, trade unions and community sector peak organizations. Bureaucrats and politicians who answered the survey were asked to indicate how frequently they had some form of direct contact with people in each of these different organizations, in regard to some aspect of their work role.[4]

Data were also collected from survey respondents on two other proxy measures of external interaction – how frequently they attended conferences in the previous 12 months and how many professional associations they were currently members of. Prior research suggests that both activities are important sources of new information and ideas, and are closely linked to innovation performance. Teske and Schneider, for example, found that two-thirds of the city managers identified as 'entrepreneurial' were active in professional organizations, with the latter identified as the source of new ideas and policies in 75 per cent of cases (1994, p. 336). Other studies (Martin, 2000; Borins, 2001; Newman et al., 2001; Walker and Enticott, 2004) have similarly pointed to the importance of participation in professional networks, conferences and seminars as important catalysts for organizational learning and innovation in the public sector. Further details of each of these forms of networking can be found in Considine et al. (2008). These are returned to in the analysis of what predicts innovator status.

Networks – internal connections

The third and final network dimension involves the use of social network analysis to examine how extensively individuals are connected to other actors through networks of embedded resources. Network information was collected during the survey using a 'name generator', with respondents asked to nominate up to five people they went to most, firstly when they wanted to get advice on a work-related issue; and secondly, when they wanted to get strategic information about something in their government. The advice question was unbounded – that is, respondents could nominate any five individuals they chose. For the strategic information question, however, nominations were limited to five people from within their own organization. Having collected this data for both networks in each government, the network structures were mapped to provide a visualization of the global and local patterns of communication in different governments. These network maps are shown in Figures 6.1–6.3. The mapping option used here places those with the most network ties in the middle, while those with fewer ties are placed around the periphery.[5]

Figure 6.1 is the strategic information network for Melville, showing the overall structure of the interpersonal network within this government. The nodes (each of which is an individual) have different shapes and shades which refer to the individual's position in the organization. Quite a distinct configuration of nodes and ties can be seen within the network. The CEO (black circle), with a large number of ties, is placed in the centre of the network, and is quite clearly surrounded by a ring of directors (dark grey circles) from each of the directorates within this government. The mayor (black hourglass) and a number of other politicians (black squares) are also quite centrally placed, and appear to be closely integrated with these senior members of the executive. Surrounding this inner group of senior bureaucrats and politicians, there is a ring of middle managers (light grey), with coordinators/team leaders and others (people in other positions within the government) generally placed on the periphery. This reveals a pattern of strategic information-seeking which shadows the traditional hierarchical bureaucracy. This pattern

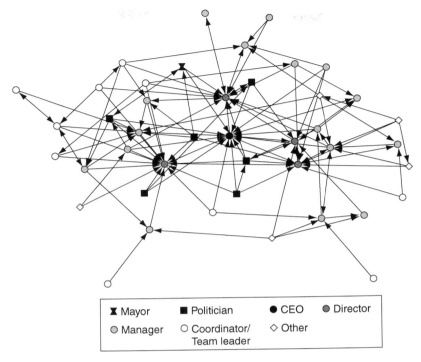

Figure 6.1 Strategic information network by position for Melville

is quite common among the 11 municipal governments, although its strength varies from place to place.

Figures 6.2 and 6.3 shift the focus from global network structures and characteristics to the local network ties (both inwards and outwards) surrounding the mayors and CEOs. They are strategic information ego networks of mayors and CEOs; that is, their immediate network surroundings comprise all actors with a direct tie (either in or out or reciprocal) to each of these actors.

The combined CEO and mayor ego network at Parkside (see Figure 6.2) is the most elaborate of the 11 governments. Indeed, the Parkside CEO and mayor each individually have the largest ego networks of all their bureaucratic and political colleagues respectively. In total, there are 27 actors in the CEO's network including the mayor and three other politicians, four of the five directors, eight managers, eight coordinators/team leaders and three others. The mayor's network is smaller, with 15 actors – this includes the CEO and all five directors,

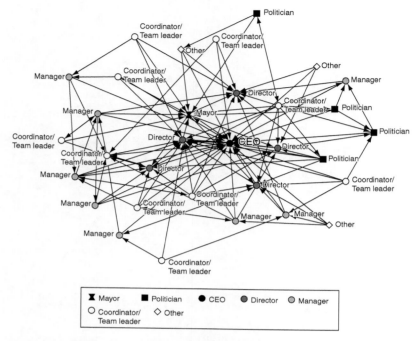

Figure 6.2   Parkside strategic information network around the CEO and mayor

two other politicians, a manager, five coordinators/team leaders and one other.

There is a reciprocal tie linking the mayor and the CEO, as well as a large number of ties linking the senior members of the bureaucracy to the elected members. Overall there are 17 ties linking the politicians and senior bureaucrats (CEO and directors), with the majority of these (14) being politicians seeking strategic information from bureaucrats. In terms of overlap between the two configurations, one politician, four directors, a manager, two coordinators and one other actor appear in both the CEO's and the mayor's ego networks. This again suggests quite a closely integrated relationship between the political and bureaucratic branches of government at Parkside.

In contrast, Figure 6.3 shows the smallest combined CEO and mayor strategic information ego network that was found – Wallerstrum, with 16 actors. Here, the CEO's network contains just 12 actors, including the mayor, one other politician, six directors, two managers and two coordinators/team leaders. The mayor's network contains eight actors – the

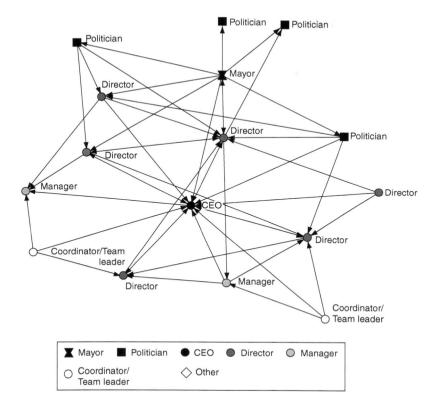

Figure 6.3 Wallerstrum strategic information network around the CEO and mayor

CEO, three directors and all four of the other politicians. There is a small degree of overlap between the two networks, with one politician and three directors appearing in both. Interestingly, and in marked contrast to Parkside, there are no mid-level bureaucrats in the mayor's ego network at Wallerstrum, and just four in the CEO's network, a configuration that suggests that the strategic information network is heavily influenced by hierarchy in this government. It is also much easier to see a clear distinction between the political and bureaucratic sides of government at Wallerstrum, with the politicians concentrated around the mayor at the top of Figure 6.3.

Mapping a network structure provides a visualization of interpersonal connections, which can prove to be difficult to decipher. Network measures give more precision, so normalized in-degree centrality scores

Table 6.10   Strategic information network centrality across position (mean in-degree centrality)

	Mayor	Politician	CEO	Director	Manager	Coordinator/ team leader	Other
Bankview	n/a	0.85	20.34	25.42	9.18	2.05	3.00
Bilstown	5.13	0.51	n/a	30.13	7.89	0.99	0.64
Kilbourne	5.26	2.41	11.84	20.26	9.95	0.93	0.94
Lassiter	10.00	0.67	32.00	34.67	10.77	1.09	2.00
Melville	4.76	2.38	38.10	32.14	6.85	1.43	0.95
Millside	10.91	3.64	58.18	42.91	12.55	2.99	4.96
Netherton	3.27	1.20	1.31	0.65	1.33	1.17	1.36
Oberon	1.43	1.90	20.00	19.43	5.06	1.11	1.19
Parkside	12.79	2.03	31.40	19.53	5.55	1.31	1.03
Wallerstrum	2.22	2.22	24.44	21.11	6.52	1.98	5.93
Yarwood	3.70	1.85	29.63	21.48	9.39	1.99	0.93
Total	5.95	1.72	26.72	24.01	7.27	1.48	1.84

were calculated for each actor. In-degree centrality provides an indicator of the 'prominence or importance' of actors in a social network (Wasserman and Faust, 1994, p. 170).[6] This does not necessarily translate into power *per se*, but simply measures the number of connections to other actors – indicating potential power through ties. It is postulated that networks yield important resources for innovators, so it is expected to be found that innovator status is positively associated with in-degree centrality. This is indeed the case.

Table 6.10 presents the in-degree centrality measures for each government for strategic information.[7] It shows that CEOs and directors are the most central, followed by managers. However, politicians and especially mayors are more central than lower ranked bureaucrats. In one government (Netherton), the mayor is the most central actor overall.

Who are the innovators?

Following the first survey-based stage of this study, four of these 11 governments, representing a diverse range in terms of socio-economic climate, political orientation and geographic location, were then selected to participate in a more detailed second stage of the research. The most important priority was to ensure that there was substantial variation between them in terms of socio-economic status of the citizens, political orientation of the governments, whether they were close to the city centre or further out, their dominant innovation norms and procedures,

Table 6.11 Key characteristics of four municipalities

		Kilbourne	Melville	Millside	Parkside
Geography	Location	Fringe metro	Middle metro/fringe metro	Inner metro (industrial)	Inner metro (bayside)
Socio-economics	'Class'	Lower middle/ middle	Middle/ upper middle	Old working class/ gentrifying	Gentrified with pockets of disadvantage
	Access to resources	Middle	High	Low	High
Politics	Party orientation	Divided	Conservative	Old Labour	New Labour
	Stability	Unstable	Very stable	Traditionally stable but shifting	Very stable
Innovation norms (placement)	Institutional	Lowest	Highest	Middle	Middle
	Structural	Middle	Lowest	Middle	Highest
	Sceptical	Middle	Middle	Lowest	Highest
	Incremental	Middle	Lowest	Middle	Highest
	Adaptive	Middle	Lowest	Highest	Middle
Innovation procedures (placement)	Political	Middle	Highest	Lowest	Middle
	Managerial	Highest	Middle	Middle	Lowest
	Electoral	Lowest	Middle	Middle	Highest
Freeman Network Centralization (in-degree)	Advice network (internal and external)	15.7	23.9	18.0	16.1
	Strategic information network (internal only)	23.6	36.9	47.5	28.2

and different network structures. The main characteristics of the four governments are summarized in Table 6.11.

Follow-up interviews were conducted with 104 respondents from across these four governments in order to gain a more detailed understanding of the nature of innovation at each location. In total, 26 interviews were conducted at Kilbourne, 27 at Melville, 26 at Millside and 25 at Parkside, with 41 per cent of interview respondents being managers, 26 per cent politicians, 19 per cent senior executives (CEOs and directors) and 14 per cent coordinators/team leaders or other ranks. Respondents were asked to identify important innovations in their municipality, to detail who was involved in each case, and to nominate the key innovators in their municipality.[8]

In order to allow for identification of the innovators in each municipality and to test their innovator status against a range of variables, a 'key innovator' score was developed to use as the dependent variable. In identifying key innovators in the interviews, no limitations were placed on the number of 'key innovator' nominations that could be made, and these could include politicians, bureaucrats or people outside the government.[9] Using these nominations, politicians and bureaucrats in each municipality who had completed the initial survey were assigned a score that is the percentage of total 'key innovator' nominations they received from the respondents in their municipality. Those who were not nominated at all were assigned a score of zero. As the results in Table 6.12 indicate, scores on this scale ranged from 0 to a high of 16.8 per cent at Kilbourne, 13.4 at Millside, 12.4 at Parkside and 10.3 at Melville. The standard deviation figures indicate variation was highest at Millside (3.5) and lowest at Parkside (2.2).

This investigation of who is regarded as an innovator gives us a measure of who the innovators are, and allows us to answer the central question about the importance of networks to innovation. A multivariate approach was used to explore the relative effects of norms and procedures, and formal (hierarchical) and informal (network) structures on innovator status. Ordinary Least Squares multiple regression was employed, using the key innovator score as the dependent variable. Given the large number of potential independent variables available for inclusion in the models, a series of exploratory bi-variate analyses and step-wise regressions were first used to separately identify the most important variables.

Table 6.12   'Key innovator' score (percentage)

	Kilbourne	Melville	Millside	Parkside	Total
N	78	44	57	89	268
Mean	1.3	2.3	1.8	1.1	1.5
Std. deviation	2.9	3.0	3.5	2.2	2.8
Minimum	0	0	0	0	0
Maximum	16.8	10.3	13.4	12.4	16.8

The authors have already pointed to the important relationship between structural position and innovator status, noting how successful innovators tend to reside further up the hierarchy where they are able to profit from the strategic benefits that seniority confers. To measure the relative impact of structural position on innovator status, a set of dichotomous variables was included for position in the regressions. The largest group of respondents in the survey cohort (44 per cent) was made up of coordinators/team leaders. Using this group as the reference category allows for the measurement of the relative effect of being positioned at the level of mayor, politician, CEO, director, manager or other (those holding other positions within these governments) on innovator status.

Based on the initial exploratory analyses, 10 independent variables were selected for inclusion in the final model – managerial procedures, external contact with a politician from another government and with a community sector peak organization, normalized in-degree centrality (strategic information network), and the full set of variables representing structural position. Having selected the independent variables, a series of regressions was run using the enter method, for each of the four governments individually and for the four combined ($n = 210$). The results are shown in Table 6.13 with standardized regression (Beta) coefficients statistically significant at $p < 0.05$ or 0.01 marked with an asterisk and those close to significant (between 0.05 and 0.10) in italics. As the Adjusted R^2 statistics show, the models account for just over 41 per cent of the variance in key innovator status for the survey cohort overall, and for between 33 per cent (Kilbourne) and 74 per cent (Parkside) for the four governments individually.

Both position and networks were important predictors of innovator status. Managerial procedures returned a marginal coefficient just outside standard measures of statistical significance.[10] All three of the network variables (contact with a politician from another government, contact with a community sector peak organization, strategic information centrality) returned statistically significant coefficients in at least one government. Normalized in-degree centrality scores for the strategic information network were by far the most important predictor of innovator status overall, and were also significant in Kilbourne and Melville, and almost significant in Parkside. Innovators overall, and those from Parkside in particular, were more likely to be in contact with community sector peak organizations, while those from Parkside were also likely to be in contact with politicians from another government. Interestingly (although just beyond the 0.05 significance level)

Table 6.13   Regression results for key innovator status

	Kilbourne	Melville	Millside	Parkside	Total
N	60	35	44	71	210
Adjusted R^2	0.332	0.379	0.574	0.741	0.414
Std. error	2.349	2.541	2.199	1.042	2.173
Beta coefficients					
Managerial				0.115	
Politician from another government	−0.259		0.285	0.221**	
Community sector peak organization				0.172**	0.159***
Normalized in-degree centrality (Strategic information)	0.644***	0.811**		0.305	0.368***
Mayor					
Politician			0.459***		0.163***
CEO			0.264	0.472***	0.184***
Director			0.427**		0.157
Manager					0.114
Other					

** – $p < 0.05$
*** – $p < 0.01$

the latter variable was negatively correlated with innovator status at Kilbourne.

The evidence linking structural position to innovator status was slightly more mixed. For the four governments overall, two of the five position-based variables were statistically significant and a further two (being a director and manager) were close to significant. Compared with the reference group of coordinator/team leader, the coefficients rose in an almost linear fashion up the bureaucratic hierarchy. That is, recognition as an innovator increased with positional seniority. Being a politician was also a significant predictor of innovator status overall, particularly in Millside. The importance of structural position as a predictor was quite mixed across the governments. While bureaucratic seniority and political function appeared to be important in Millside, neither were influential in Kilbourne and Melville, and only bureaucratic seniority was important in Parkside, where the CEO stood out.

Conclusion

This research aimed to examine how informal networks contribute to an explanation of innovation inside government. The results clearly show that how you conceive of innovation, what position you hold and who you communicate with are all significant in shaping whether you are regarded as an innovator. However, network relationships are the most important predictors of innovator status. Although network centrality is related to hierarchical seniority, and it is not possible to assess the separate contribution of these two variables, these findings fit with the view that innovators are those who are adept at working through relationships outside formal structures, in order to get things done. Innovators are central in networks, and this is their most important attribute out of those examined in this study.

Networks are important, and explain more than can be found by a focus on position alone. This finding resonates with network-based studies of politics and policy (Lauman and Knoke, 1987; Knoke, 1990; Mintrom and Vergari, 1998; Lewis, 2006). In addition, as the authors have reported elsewhere (Considine and Lewis, 2007), strategic information networks are more crucial than advice networks in signalling innovator status. It is postulated that strategic information centrality is important for innovator recognition because these actors are doing the visible, internal work of getting innovations approved and in place. Seeking advice through networks might well lead to the initiation of innovation, but this is more intangible and diffuse. The most important finding is that innovation and innovators inhabit a specific kind of institutional space, defined in part by structural position but more by their place in informal, actor networks.

This last point indicates that this research has settled some questions about the link between formal and informal structures, and the importance of local cultures. The importance of government itself as a variable has been demonstrated. Each of our governments has a set of characteristics which, woven together with network structure, explains what in common parlance might be called a local culture of innovation. This is what is meant by the claim that innovation occupies a particular institutional space. This study has captured important characteristics of these governments, and shown that, net of all other factors, networks explain more about innovation than anything else in the study.

Important steps have also been made in exploring innovation in the public sector. Networks obviously provide a viable and robust way to describe and understand the links between structural and individual elements in the innovation story. The application of social network concepts and methods to this puzzle has been rewarding, allowing us to make robust claims about the importance of networks. It has been shown how different the networks of politicians are compared to those of senior bureaucrats in these systems. The study reinforces the idea that politicians' structural positions are fundamentally different, and nowhere is this more evident than in regard to the normative frames that shape their approach to innovation and guide their evaluations of governmental procedures. The theoretical gains from this approach are worth emphasizing. Substantial progress has been made on better ways to study structure and action together, by focusing on the interaction between them.

It is concluded that this research opens up three exciting research opportunities. First, the networks approach can profitably be applied to other levels of government now that some key methodological issues have been resolved. Secondly, the analysis can be extended beyond advice and strategic information to a greater range of networks, such as political support and know-how trading. Thirdly, the social network analytical techniques used here represent substantial methodological advances that can be usefully applied in further studies of innovation inside government.

Notes

1. Taking volunteers in this fashion obviously skews the sample towards those more interested in this topic. Since our purpose is to understand how innovation works, this slight bias represents no threat to our aims, although it limits how far our findings can be generalized to governments with little interest in innovation.
2. The sample group was identified by an internal liaison officer at each council based on internal staff lists. Response rates were maximized by a minimum of two follow-up calls to all potential respondents within the sample.
3. The list of items was tested extensively during a pilot study.
4. Respondents were asked to include communication by phone, email or in person, but to exclude bulk email circulars. People were asked to score the frequency of contact on a five-point scale ranging from 'never' (zero) to 'daily' (four).
5. Maps were created for both advice and strategic information networks, but only examples of the strategic information networks are provided here as these are more important in determining innovator status (see Considine and Lewis, 2007).
6. Normalization makes the in-degree centrality scores comparable across networks of different sizes (Scott, 2000). This is important given the large variation in network size across the governments.

7. Only the strategic information network is included here as it has greater explanatory power in predicting innovator status (see Considine and Lewis, 2007).
8. While nomination-based methods for locating key actors have attracted criticism for being highly subjective, when dealing with small- and medium-sized groups who work in close proximity with one another, it is reasonable to expect that they will be well informed about one another's reputation for work-related performance. This is supported by the close correlation between 'key innovator' nominations and the prominence of those identified as important actors in the 16 innovation case studies that were examined as part of the larger study.
9. In total, 464 nominations were received across the four local governments. Only politicians and bureaucrats were nominated, with not a single nomination directed to actors outside.
10. More extensive modelling using alternative normative variables confirmed that this dimension had no significant bearing on innovator status.

7
Competing Values in the Management of Innovative Projects: The Case of the RandstadRail Project

Haiko van der Voort, Joop Koppenjan, Ernst Ten Heuvelhof, Martijn Leijten and Wijnand Veeneman

Introduction: A problem of 'innovative projects'

Large engineering projects without late delivery, cost overruns or technical problems seem to be rare (Flyvbjerg et al., 2003). Illustrations of this statement are abundant worldwide (e.g. the French Superphenix project, the German Transrapid project, the Channel Tunnel, Denver International Airport, Boston's Central Artery Tunnel (Dempsey et al., 1997; Bell, 1998; Altshuler and Luberoff, 2003; Flyvbjerg et al., 2003). The political and societal environments of these projects all ask for safe delivery on time and within a budget. A variety of project management tools have been developed to meet such expectations. However, these projects also have innovative elements, providing situations that implementers (e.g. managers, engineers, operators) of the projects have not met before. These elements require room for improvisation and interaction between implementers, which most project management tools typically do not provide. They are 'innovative projects': projects with clear ends (time, budget), but without straightforward solutions. Managers of such projects continuously face a tension between the project character and its innovative character. How can project managers respect the competing values between being innovative and meeting the clear ends?

This central question is relevant to analysts who have to evaluate innovative projects in hindsight. This contribution aims to provide steps for producing a framework for valuing the management of these 'innovative projects'. This will be done by exploring the tensions between innovation and project management of an 'innovative project' in the Netherlands: the RandstadRail project. The aim of the RandstadRail project was to realize an innovative regional public transport system in the southern wing of the Randstad area in the Netherlands. This was done by linking two old 'heavy rail' connections between Zoetermeer and The Hague and Rotterdam and The Hague respectively, The Hague's tram network and Rotterdam's metro network. The intention was to create a new high-quality light-rail system, able to compete with car traffic through high frequency and a high level of comfort, as well as with connections penetrating into the hearts of the cities.

After introducing the project and determining its innovative aspects, this chapter conceptualizes the tension further and presents an analytical framework for assessing innovative projects. The RandstadRail case serves as an illustration for the use of this framework for analysts. The framework is used to analyse the efforts of project managers to run this innovative project. A 'project manager' refers to any actor who has the formal or informal ability to shape the management of – in this case – an innovative project. This means that a specific predefined actor is not referred to.

RandstadRail as an 'innovative project'

The RandstadRail project comprises the construction and conversion of infrastructure, the management and maintenance of infrastructure and the operation of transport services. In Figure 7.1, the planning of the line is being sketched, while in Figure 7.2 the organization of the project is being sketched.

In fact, the project consists of two distinct parts, separated geographically by administrative borders. The Rotterdam part is the responsibility of the Rotterdam urban region – a cooperative body of municipalities in the region. Rotterdam metro trains run on this part. The Hague part consists of the tramlines linking Zoetermeer with The Hague and the tramlines in The Hague, for which the Haaglanden urban district is responsible. There is a short 'concurrent section' where metros and trams use the same rails. The Haaglanden urban district is responsible for the interconnecting 'Hofplein line' from the border of the region to The Hague Central railway station, while the Rotterdam urban region is responsible for the other part (from the border to the City of Rotterdam).

This chapter focuses only on RandstadRail on the side of The Hague. The Haaglanden urban district contracted out the construction of the

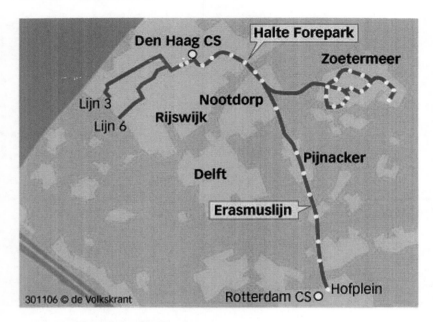

Figure 7.1 The RandstadRail tracks

Note: The 'Hofplein-line' (also called the Erasmusline) is the line between the south of Rotterdam and the cental railway station of The Hague ('Den Haag' on this map); the 'Zoetermeer-line' are line 3 and 4/6 connecting Zoetermeer to The Hague.
Source: De Volkskrant, 2006.

infrastructure on The Hague side of the project to the municipality of The Hague as a 'turnkey' project – The Hague would realize the project for a fixed price within functional constraints from Haaglanden and without additional interference. Within the municipality, the RandstadRail Project Organization was responsible for the construction of the infrastructure. In addition, the municipalities of Zoetermeer, Leidschendam-Voorburg and Pijnacker-Nootdorp, which were dependent on RandstadRail for transport, were closely involved in the project as members of the RandstadRail Administrative Consultative Body (RACB). The portfolio holder at Haaglanden, the chair of the RACB and the relevant Hague alderman were one and the same person. The operation and management of the Zoetermeer and Hofplein lines (in Haaglanden territory) were made the responsibility of The Hague and Rotterdam city carriers HTM and RET, respectively.

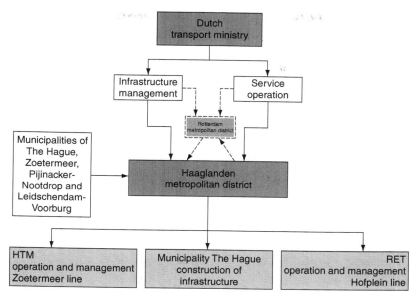

Figure 7.2 The organization of the RandstadRail project (simplified)

The multi-layered innovative character of the RandstadRail project

Despite the fact that RandstadRail was a combination of existing systems, the project was innovative in numerous respects.

- From a technical point of view, the tram, metro and heavy rail were well-known systems. Still, the couplings between them were new and had many implications that were not covered by existing expertise. Two types of vehicles had to run on a system that consisted partly of new infrastructure, partly former 'heavy rail' infrastructure and partly tram infrastructure. In addition, the safety management systems differed along the railway tracks: parts of it were managed by traffic lights, while other parts were dependent on each individual driver's sight.
- At the institutional level, the division of roles between the parties was new. The central government gave the project autonomy. The Haaglanden urban district had limited experience as a principal. The central government funded the construction of the infrastructure through a lump sum (413 million euros for the construction of The Hague portion), an arrangement not often used in this context. This

sum of money was channelled to the municipality, which carried out the project on its own account and risk. Also new was the fact that the municipality of The Hague had to build infrastructure outside its municipal borders. Tenders were invited for transport concessions for the first time; this was new for both the principal (Haaglanden) and the carriers.

- The legal context of the project was new. Safety regulations for railways were applied to heavy rail, tram rail and metro rail, but not to light rail, which falls somewhere between tram rail and heavy rail. The extent to which existing regulations for tram, metro and heavy rail applied to RandstadRail was unclear. The Dutch Ministry of Transportation delegated the responsibility for regulation to the principal of the project, Haaglanden. The ministry issued a Standards Document (as policy guidelines, not as formal law), which contained procedures and roles to support safety management. RandstadRail was the first project where safety was managed according to these standards.

Project results

As is the case with many large technically complex public projects, the aim of this project was to realize a new transport system that would immediately result in a fully fledged, 'normal' service. However, this did not occur without hitches. The realization of the RandstadRail project began in 2001, when the central government pledged approximately 1 billion euros to the project. Converting the existing lines would take place quickly, in 13 weeks during the 2006 summer holidays. The idea was to keep the disruption to passengers at a minimum, at the urgent request particularly of administrators from the municipalities involved. However, this time period proved to be too short and the system was delivered only after a few months' delay. Subsequently, it was plagued by many interruptions. Even worse, a number of derailments occurred shortly after each interruption. Seventeen people were injured in a derailment at Forepark station on 29 November, after which the Traffic Inspectorate closed down the line. The entire system did not become operational until October 2007, although the promised frequencies were not achieved at that time. In the interim period, passengers had to use other modes of transport. On 7 February 2007, the relevant Hague alderman resigned because of the problems with the RandstadRail project. However, the project was delivered within the budget, although the delay led to claims by aggrieved parties, which have been kept outside the budget.[1]

Towards an analytical framework for innovative projects

Over the course of the last few decades, project management has taken off as a tool for the realization of technological systems. More and more, temporary organizations are given a temporary assignment: to realize a technological system (which is the focus here). A growing set of tools supports the use of project management. These tools are aimed at predicting: the design through system engineering; the tasks through a work breakdown structure; the time to spend through network-planning tools; and the budget through various cost-estimation techniques (see e.g. Winch, 2002). Project management uses instruments to ensure that the predicted outcome is actually the real outcome of the project. Change management, risk management and progress management are tools used to ensure that the prediction is realistic and realized. The dominant values are controllability and meeting preset goals (Pinto, 1986; Shenhar et al., 2001). This predict-and-control approach to project management is referred to as the Type I approach in this chapter.

It is, however, increasingly being recognized that traditional project management tools do not get along very well with innovation (Baccarini, 1996; Keegan and Turner, 2002). The more innovative a project, the more uncertainties managers have to cope with (Kline and Rosenberg, 1986). Standard technologies and operating procedures are often absent in innovation, leaving project managers with the need to invent unique new solutions by combining technologies, knowledge and expertise – dispersed across various actors (Von Stamm, 2003). These solutions emerge on the run, during the projects. However, this poses serious challenges if a project is deemed to be 'complex'. This complexity refers to the existence of many varied and inter-related parts (Baccarini, 1996; Perrow, 1999, pp. 85–86; Williams, 1999), on a technical level (vehicle, infrastructure, safety systems), an institutional level (principals, politicians, carriers, operators) or a legal level (different regulations and legal standards).

The emergence of new solutions and ideas during the project requires flexibility, that is the ability to adapt to new conditions (Floricel and Miller, 2001). If parts are varied and inter-related, flexibility implies a lot of horizontal and vertical coordination, cooperation, learning and trust as alternatives to predefined functional relations and planning that characterize traditional project management tools (Barlow, 2000; Keegan and Turner, 2002; Pich et al., 2002). In other words, the ability to predict is compromised severely by uncertainty and complexity that characterize many innovative projects. As such, the predictions of project management are less accurate, and control focused on realizing that prediction is less apt.

Thus, in more innovative projects, the Type I approach becomes vulnerable. Miller and Floricel (2000) underline the need for 'bonding for internal cohesion' and flexibility to respond to surprises that occur in complex projects, for example because of changing customer demands (Turner and Keegan, 1999; Dvir and Lechler, 2004). In these situations, the project manager does not need team members, partners and contractors with neatly and narrowly described tasks but rather, broad-thinking and committed collaborators with room to manoeuvre. Where traditional project management would focus on predict-and-control, this approach would focus on prepare-and-adapt. This alternative, which is called a Type II approach here, implies a shift towards forms of management, contracts and cooperation that focus more on flexibility, learning and trust (comparable with the 'bonding' concept derived from Miller and Floricel). From bodies of knowledge outside the world of traditional project management (e.g. literature on innovation and networks), several approaches are suggested, all of which stress horizontal coordination rather than a vertical hierarchy and stimulated learning. Examples of these suggestions are adaptive planning, concurrent engineering and process management (Dempsey et al., 1997; De Bruijn et al., 2002; Koppenjan and Klijn, 2004; Loureiro and Curran, 2007).

The project team in a typical Type II approach needs to prepare for surprises by committing everyone involved to dealing with and adapting to these surprises. Part of this preparation can be to stick to a functional description of the terms of reference (ToR) (see Morris and Hough, 1987, p. 218). During the process of design and even construction, lessons will be learnt by the client about what it wants and by contractors and engineers about what is possible and efficient. Learning requires room in terms of resources, time and budget, allowing for experimentation, the making, detecting and correcting of mistakes, and the exchange of experiences. Working in a learning and flexible environment demands the use of suitable contracts that focus the contractors on the realization of a prescribed function rather than on a prescribed system. Furthermore, the project management is in need of a negotiated environment; with administrators, politicians and stakeholders allowing it discretionary freedom. Table 7.1 sums up the differences between the two approaches.

In order to allow for proper control, the Type I (predict-and-control) approach needs a detailed ToR and a narrow task definition for the contractors. The Type II approach needs a more functional ToR and broader task descriptions.

Table 7.1 Two competing approaches to managing innovative projects

	(Type I) Predict-and-control	(Type II) Prepare-and-adapt
Dominant values	Controllability, meeting preset goals	Flexibility, learning, trust
Terms of reference	Blueprint	Functional
Task definition	Narrow for best control	Broad for best cooperation
Contract	Task execution	Functional realization
Change	Limit as much as possible	Facilitate as much as needed
Steer	Vertical (hierarchical)	Horizontal
Information exchange	Limited	Open
Interface management	Project management task	Shared task
Standards	Strict and predefined	Broad and emergent

The broad task description in the Type II approach does not put a focus on the contractor. In order to add focus, it needs strong system- and output-related incentives. The contractors are paid to realize the functionality of the overall system, rather than for carrying out their own limited task. This is reflected in the way in which the contract describes what is needed from the contractor: task execution (Type I) or realizing a system function (Type II).

Every change clouds the relationship between the original blueprint ToR and the reality of the realization, which hampers control. Thus, in the Type I approach, change is a liability and strict change control is required. In the Type II approach, change is a given and change facilitation is required. The same holds for standards, such as those for safety regulation. Safety standards in a Type I approach are, as are other requirements such as in the ToR, predefined based on rigid research and controls, whereas safety standards in a Type II approach are the result of an emerging learning process that could continue well into the runtime of the project.

In the Type I approach, the client has defined its needs in the ToR and will hierarchically steer in that direction, whereas in the Type II approach the client and contractors are on a shared journey, discovering together what is needed and what is possible, as in horizontal networks (Koppenjan and Klijn, 2004). This demands intensive and open information exchanges between the client and the contractors, as opposed to in the Type I approach, where limited progress reports are standard.

In the Type I approach, the ToR should standardize the interfaces between different subsystems, whereas in the Type II approach, contractors have to constantly evaluate the interfaces; the innovative and flexible character of system development hampers a priori standardization.

Both approaches are described here as extremes, which implies that they are hard to find in real-life engineering cases. An extreme Type I approach fits well with relatively simple, routine projects. An extreme Type II approach fits best with extremely turbulent environments, where coping with the turbulence and arriving at a solution are more important than meeting time and budget constraints (e.g. Burns and Stalker, 1996, pp. 96–98; Galbraith, 2004, p. 206). A real-life innovative project is often a combination of both approaches. Complexity, that is the variety of and inter-relations between parts, means that there are a huge number of potential combinations of these two approaches.

Mind the countervalue

It is concluded that a single approach is likely to fail as an analytical framework for innovative projects. In working to respect the efforts to manage innovative projects in the analytical framework, both approaches are needed in some ways. To summarize, four assumptions are formulated on which the normative point of departure for analysing RandstadRail are based:

1. Innovative projects are the subjects of competing values that can be derived from their project characteristics and their innovative characteristics. As described, possible competing values are controllability and flexibility.
2. These competing values call for distinct approaches to managing innovative projects, which are defined as Type I and Type II approaches. For example, controllability is best served by a Type I approach, while a Type II approach allows for more flexibility.
3. The reality of managing innovative projects is always finding a mix between the two approaches. Since innovative projects have both project characteristics that demand controllability and innovative characteristics that demand flexibility, somehow the management of innovative projects needs the best of both worlds.
4. As innovation presents itself throughout the project, project management choices are made continuously from design to operational realization. The project characteristics require predefinitions (such as project definitions and project design), while the innovative

characteristics require an openness to new ideas and solutions on the run. All these decisions can, in hindsight, appear to be of vital importance.

These assumptions imply that an adoption of a single approach bears the risks of undervaluing the other. Therefore, the concept of 'mind' is introduced as the normative point of departure for the analysis of RandstadRail. 'Mind' refers to being aware of the countervalue when crucial management decisions conform to one of the two extreme approaches. Using 'mind' as a norm reveals how decision-makers and project managers could tune the project as a reaction to a given approach, counteracting the weaknesses of that particular approach by introducing counter-arrangements based on the principles of the competing approach. Following this normative line of thought allows us to dig deep into the continuous processes of managing innovative projects and showing its dynamics from initiation to completion.

The innovative project management of RandstadRail

It has now been shown that the project management of innovative projects is best described as a hybrid of the two approaches. It has also been stated that decision-makers and project managers tune their project as a reaction to a 'given' approach. This section describes crucial decisions in the RandstadRail project in the course of its development along three broad themes: project definition, governance and safety regulation. The themes and characteristic choices are defined broadly, so a majority of issues are covered, which will help achieve the main goal – to explore the tensions between innovation and project management.

For each theme, the following is described:

- What characteristic choice in the project design determined the project management of RandstadRail during the runtime of the project
- What this choice implied and how it can be characterized from a project (Type I approach) or innovation (Type II approach) perspective
- To what extent and how the parties tried to compensate for the possible one-sidedness of this choice during the project
- To what extent they succeeded in doing so and what factors played a role in this.

1. Project definition: Starting with a broad ToR

The run-up to the RandstadRail project extended over a very long period of time. When the project eventually seemed to get off the ground, there was a strong sense of urgency among local administrators and carriers. There was momentum at the ministry, and, in order to exploit this, the project had to be formalized quickly. This required terms of reference (ToR).

In this context, broad and functional ToR were drawn up. This fitted in with the quick formalization of the project; the wishes could quickly be translated into functional requirements. This matched with a Type II approach. It was appropriate because the project contained many uncertainties as to what technical realization would function. The ToR created room for project workers, building contractors and suppliers to learn and to solve problems surrounding that uncertainty. Functional ToR offer this room while at the same time defining the customer's preconditions. In such a case, the customer and building contractor have to work out requirements and the technology needed together, after the contract has been awarded.

Minding the countervalue: System integration through stronger control of interfaces

However, ToR, particularly technical realization, are also an important means to realize system integration. Vehicles, rails, construction works, the safety system and operation need to be properly coordinated in order to be able to arrive at a well-functioning system. Broad ToR do not predefine interfaces narrowly. Some predefinitions are required, however, because the different subsystems do not automatically fit with one another. Definitions and control of interfaces, typically Type I values, should therefore be done later in the project. For instance, appointing a strongly integrating party that is responsible for interface management and has the ability to steer vertically could facilitate this during the realization phase. If system integration is not guaranteed at an earlier stage, the test and trial period could be strictly regulated. The latter would be a Type I correction in the final stage of the project.

Ensuring system integration at RandstadRail

RandstadRail stimulated system integration in the follow way:

1) A first form is setting up a strong system integrator, in line with the Type I approach of hierarchical interface management. This role was assigned to HTM (the carrier) for the inner-city area, with

the responsibility for vehicles, infrastructure, operation and maintenance. However, this situation only arose at a later stage (i.e. in 2005), because HTM was not certain of its position as a carrier until well into 2005 as a result of the tendering out of the transport on RandstadRail that year.

Outside the municipality of The Hague, there was less organizational integration. The RandstadRail Project Organization (RRPO) was responsible for the infrastructure and HTM for the vehicles, the operation and management. Initially, it was unclear who was responsible for the system integration. The initial idea was that the RRPO was responsible. However, Haaglanden was the manager of the ToR. This uncertainty about the division of responsibility hampered system integration. This led, for example, to the purchase of a type of switch in the convergence area which the carriers and managers did not want to use and in which they had no expertise either.

2) A second form is to allow the ToR to play this integrating role after the design phase. That was done by installing the 'configuration control board' (CCB), which managed the ToR, matching a Type I approach of change management (see Table 7.1). However, the CCB only got off the ground at a later stage, which consequently resulted in it being unable to gain sufficient authority within the project. This is why decisions made by the RRPO or the administrators were insufficiently tested for their consequences for other parts of the system.

3) The lack of powerful forces for system integration resulted in a very busy conversion, test and trial period (CTP). This is the final period where the control of interfaces can be enhanced. During this period, all construction activities converge and, for the first time, are integrally tested. The lagging system integration left lots to do in the CTP. The authorities, however, kept the time pressure high. This was probably the period in which construction workers damaged a switch, without it being detected. This was one of the causes of the derailment in which people were injured at Forepark. Under this immense time pressure, Haaglanden formulated relatively loose standards for the trial and test period in 2006. This time pressure also influenced the way in which the standards were dealt with. In accordance with the standard, trains ran below a stipulated interruption level for exactly three days. During the preceding and following days, the interruptions were above that level. Thus, formally, the standard was interpreted correctly, but in fact, the performance was problematic.

Consequently, provisions for system integration were made after the design phase, particularly at the operational level, as a counter-arrangement to the Type II approach that had been chosen, which involved working with broad ToR. However, these proved insufficient to compensate for the broad, dynamic ToR. It seemed to have been difficult for interface managers to gain enough authority in the project. This resulted in suboptimal solutions (e.g. a procurement of unfamiliar switch motors), misaligned standards between parts of the infrastructure (e.g. a problematic interface between the switch control systems and the traffic control systems) and between material and infrastructure (e.g. a mismatch between carriages and rails). Finally, a lack of system integration put too much pressure on the CTP, and there was insufficient time to try out innovative technical solutions, detect errors and remedy them.

2. Governance: Commercializing and unbundling of the relationships in the project

From 2001, the funding by the central government materialized and RandstadRail was designed as a project. Traditional principal–agent relationships evolved: the hierarchy of a Type I approach gained the upper hand to control the budget and time span of the project. The project was contracted out 'turnkey' to the municipality of The Hague, which took on the financial risks for the construction of the infrastructure in the municipality. This created strong incentives for quick progress and strict money-oriented steering. This incentive was strengthened by the setting up of lump-sum funding by the central government and the agreed financial phasing of the payments by the Ministry of Transport.

Minding the countervalue: Creating horizontal cooperation arrangements

The risk of such commercialization and unbundling is that the hard values of time and money are overvalued against the softer values of scope, quality and safety. This is particularly dangerous in the case of innovative projects, because devising, developing or trying out new solutions requires room with regard to both time and budget. Moreover, commercialization potentially hampers horizontal cooperation and shared involvement that is desirable for innovation. The question is then to what extent this involvement is institutionalized in the project and how it safeguards soft values.

Horizontal cooperation arrangements at RandstadRail

At RandstadRail, attempts were made to mitigate the focus on project management by supplementing the commercialized and unbundled relationships with a number of cooperation arrangements:

1) The most important of these was the RandstadRail Administrative Consultative Body (RACB). The RACB worked as a sounding board for Haaglanden's transport portfolio holder, who was also an alderman of the municipality of The Hague. In practice, administrative agreement was realized in the RACB, which provided the portfolio holder with support for his decisions.

2) The double role of the Haaglanden portfolio holder for transport (principal) and alderman of the municipality of The Hague (agent) was a horizontal arrangement in itself. This double role allowed for a commitment of two layers carried over by this one person.

3) The tripartite consultative body provided coordination at the civil service level between the municipality of The Hague, Haaglanden and carrier, HTM. In the project management team (PMT), The Hague and the Rotterdam project organizations mutually coordinated their activities. The PMT was busy coordinating the efforts of the carriers, HTM and RET. They became responsible for transport and the management of the infrastructure. Since HTM was uncertain about its role as a carrier until 2005, this company only contributed its expertise and wishes regarding the project at a later stage, which was suboptimal for a Type II approach.

The horizontal arrangements made it possible to make some far-reaching choices at a late stage during the realization of the project. These were the decisions to equip RandstadRail with a safety system (November 2003), not to adapt the switches in the city of The Hague but the switches in the outer area (June 2004), to change the overhead wire voltage (December 2004) and to replace all of the tracks on the Zoetermeer line (August 2005). From a project management perspective (Type I), such late changes would have been turned down. On the other hand, responding to changing insights and new circumstances fits in well with a Type II approach. In the RandstadRail project, it was decided that these interventions would be carried out. This was possible through consultations in the cooperation forums, which accumulated in the decision-making in the RACB, where these proposals were approved.

It would have been reasonable if The Hague had turned down these late change proposals, for which it would bear the financial risks. That it did not do so can be explained by the fact that The Hague alderman was also the portfolio holder and, therefore, always had to juggle two separate loyalties in his actions.

Yet, in the end, there was no balanced trade-off between project management and innovation with regard to the consequences of these decisions. It could be said that on an administrative level, the commercialization and unbundling of relationships have been overcompensated by Type II arrangements. Indeed, they seem to have lost touch with the lower management levels. They have facilitated changes, but the late changes in scope were drastic and greatly enhanced the complexity of the project. The lower levels of project management felt the consequences of these changes. At these levels the problems of system integration, as described earlier, surfaced. Without the help of sharply defined ToR (see above), they had a hard time applying these changes and integrating them into the system. Most of these drastic activities, again, had to be realized during the CTP, which was both busy and brief anyway. Despite warnings from the project organization, the RACB did not decide to extend the length of the CTP substantially. Illustrative of the administrators losing touch with the 'work floor', within the RACB there was little tolerance for extension. This was due to the fact that its members included aldermen of municipalities that had no rail transport during the RandstadRail conversion phase. This strongly contributed to the hectic atmosphere and unmanageability of the CTP.

3. Safety regulations: A process-based approach

Traditionally, ensuring safety in a large project takes on a typical Type I approach: the standards are drawn up and the system is checked to comply with these standards. Such an approach was hampered at RandstadRail by a lack of substantive standards. Although standards had been included in the ToR, many were not explicitly based on knowledge of light rail, but on expertise on the metro or tram. At the ministry's instigation, Haaglanden and the Traffic Inspectorate worked together to develop a new institutional regulatory framework. The ministry laid down this framework in the 'Standards Document on Safety in Lightrail Projects', which contains procedures and roles. It delegates responsibility for regulation: the principal itself (in this case, Haaglanden) formulates substantive standards and demonstrates that the standards are being met. In addition, the principal hires an independent safety assessor to inspect the 'evidence' and approve it if it is satisfactory. The regulator approves the standards and further provides broad regulation. The Standards Document also includes a procedure for the submission of safety documents. It does not contain substantive standards. This process-based approach leaves the parties involved with a great deal of room for the substantive realization of the safety regime and thus fits in very well with a Type II approach, in keeping with the project's innovative character (see Table 7.1).

Minding the countervalue: The codification and internalization of standards

The lack of substantive standards for light rail makes knowledge development important. Intensive knowledge exchange between experts from different parties within and outside the project is a condition for such knowledge creation. Gradually, this interaction should lead to codification and internalization: learning about safety leads to substantive standards, which are internalized by those involved in the project and which test both the processes and the system. This ensures safety and brings the Type II approach (interaction and learning) and the Type I approach (definition of standards – although late) together. A procedural working method as used at RandstadRail therefore only works if the processes of knowledge development, codification and internalization are properly facilitated.

Ensuring knowledge development, codification and internalization at RandstadRail

The codification and internalization of safety standards occurred as follows at RandstadRail:

1) 'Safety managers' – one in the Rotterdam part and three in the Haaglanden part – coordinated the standardization and evidence of safety. Conforming to the procedures of the Standards Document, they gathered information about standards and evidence. This information came from all those who supplied to the project: Haaglanden itself, the RRPO (project organization), HTM, RET, manufacturers of material and so on. This provided safety management with a visible horizontal coordination arrangement and a recognizable 'spider in the web' of safety issues.
2) RandstadRail's safety organization was particularly open to outside organizations in an authoritative knowledge position. Much of

the development of standards was contracted out, thus admitting technically substantive knowledge from outside the organization. In addition, the Transport Inspectorate (i.e. the regulator) and Lloyd's Register (the auditor) were consulted about standards and evidence regularly.

RandstadRail succeeded in developing a safety approach that also attained a position within the project organization. On the other hand, the interruptions and derailments that occurred shortly after bringing the system into use indicate that attempts to combine the Type II approach with a Type I approach were insufficient. The following observations reveal some problems with integrating the two approaches.

1) Because of the innovative character of light rail and the absence of appropriate safety standards, it was occasionally difficult, when important decisions had to be made, to classify them in advance as being relevant from a safety perspective and to lay down safety standards. This was a task for the Haaglanden safety management. It was dependent on the discipline of other parties to detect issues relevant to safety and report them to the safety management. This required the internalization of safety among these parties, but this proved to be a tricky point: the safety management appeared not to be aware of some crucial safety-relevant decisions that were made outside Haaglanden. For example, the project organization decided to use a special type of switch in the section used by both metros and trams. The switches fully complied with the broad standards in the ToR and the procedural standards of the Standards Document, because the documents were in order. Nevertheless, the problems in the interface between the switch and safety system later appeared to result in many interruptions in operations and to play a role in the derailment at Forepark. However, these switches were never regarded as a safety problem during the realization phase, and the CTP and the safety manager did not have the opportunity to analyse the safety risk and lay down extra safety standards.

2) The roles fulfilled by actors responsible for safety were new and no role models were yet available. Actors mainly interpreted their roles procedurally. The safety managers coordinated the safety documents, Lloyd's Register mainly imposed process-based requirements and the Transport Inspectorate, as a system regulator, failed to provide more detailed substantive standardization. This accumulation of procedural approaches caused the substantive vacuum of standards to persist.

This gave rise to ritualization: ensuring that safety was equated with compliance with procedures, and this became most evident during the test and trial period. Despite the fact that the CTP was assessed by everyone after the fact as having been too brief, it was approved of and proceeded largely according to plan. Besides, as stated above, the standards were interpreted by the letter during the test and trial operations (three interruption-free days), while the many interruptions outside this time period could have been a reason to discuss the safety of the system. In the absence of substantive standards, the safety management hardly had any arguments to oppose the brief conversion period and halt the quick bringing into use, on which the administrators in the RACB insisted.

As far as safety was concerned, a Type II approach dominated. The counter-arrangements, aimed at compensating the lack of a Type I approach, did not materialize sufficiently to prevent the accidents.

Discussion: Concluding on innovative projects

Once the well-known problems of delays, cost overruns or technical problems occur, it is easy for an analyst to formulate difficult conclusions about the management of innovative projects. An obvious one for the RandstadRail project is that the CTP was far too short as a result of the overvaluing of time and money. These kinds of conclusions, however, do not respect the continuous effort it takes to run an innovative project. The framework put forward in this chapter helped to unveil the story that had the short CTP period as an ending:

- Weak counter-arrangements for a broadly defined ToR, resulting in system integration problems until and during the CTP
- Relatively smooth cooperation among administrators who, however, have lost touch with the lower levels of project managers and their system integration problems. The innovations of administrators put extra pressure on the CTP, and the administrator's tolerance for lengthening the CTP period was low
- Problematic internalization of self-developed safety standards and, related to this, the perception of the desired length of the CTP period.

The concept of 'mind' directs the analyst to the countervalues of design choices and the dynamics of the projects. By using this framework and the 'mind' concept, an analyst can explore the tensions between project management and innovation in a real-life project such as RandstadRail. In the case of RandstadRail, four observations illustrate these tensions. These are discussed below.

Mixture of approaches, but little free will for project managers

The RandstadRail project did not use just one approach, but quite a refined mix. A conclusion that RandstadRail was run as a traditional project (Type I) cannot be justified by our analysis. In fact, one of the three guiding choices, the unbundling and commercialization of the relationships in the project, was Type I-inspired. The other two guiding choices were typically Type II-inspired. It was found that the choice of approach was determined heavily by the political conditions at the initiation of the project and not by some thought to respect one of the two competing values in innovative projects. The political momentum provided incentives to adopt functional ToR (Type II). The initiators could not afford the luxury of waiting for the specification of the ToR. For safety regulations, the lack of standards and the political will to decentralize responsibilities for safety 'forced' RandstadRail to adopt a Type II approach.

This suggests that project management already begins with formulating counter-arrangements for decisions that take place outside of its range of influence.

Hard to counter 'prepare-and-adapt' approach

There seems to be a pattern in the distribution of approaches over different project values (e.g. time, money, quality and safety). In particular, the dimensions of money and time were managed in a Type I manner. This resulted from the incentive structure, which arose out of a combination of the lump-sum funding with the turnkey contract for The Hague. Strictly money-based steering would, therefore, bring great rewards. The broadly supported wish to interrupt regional public transport by rail as little as possible also influenced the process. It was found that the (Type II) counter-arrangements for the unbundling and commercialization of relationships worked quite well. Horizontal cooperation arrangements, such as the RACB (the administrators), helped in making important innovative choices at a later stage of the project. The dimensions of quality, scope and safety were managed in a Type II manner. The two (Type I) counter-arrangements had their shortcomings. This means that they did not institutionalize the lessons learned so that these lessons had sufficient countervailing power to compete with the values of time and money. The requirements around time and money were clear; the requirements to do with quality and safety remained functional and process-based.

Based on this observation, it seems to be difficult to define integrated and authoritative standards during the runtime of a project once room for innovation has been provided.

Multiple levels meet at the conversion, test and trial period

The line of thought adopted might imply that there is some central actor that assesses project design decisions and consciously defines counter-arrangements. This is, of course, not the reality of project management. Most large engineering projects involve decisions made by politicians down to workmen, considering a wide variety of issues at different phases in time. The different levels come together at the end of the preparation phase. In the case of the RandstadRail project, this was the CTP. In this brief period, the lack of system integration and authoritative predefined standards, the results of an ill-countered Type II approach, appeared and had to be solved by managers on an operational level. At the same time, the political level (local administrators) became more involved because the long-awaited exploitation phase abounded in their perception. This expectation compromised their tolerance for more delays. More time is exactly what the operational managers and safety managers needed to integrate the different systems and standards properly.

Multiple layers of innovation, multiple effects on management approaches

It was assumed that a Type II approach fits in with innovation better than a Type I approach. However, not all innovations have resulted in a Type II approach. The innovation in the RandstadRail project was multi-layered. The project was legally, institutionally and technically innovative. The legal innovation and some institutional innovations implied the decentralization of project management, safety regulation and standard setting. These innovations had their origins outside the project – they were instigated by a national policy trend – and resulted by definition in a Type II approach. In addition, the technical innovation – new interfaces between a variation of new and old technical systems – were served by a Type II approach as well, although the decision to adopt this approach was not motivated by innovation considerations, but by political momentum. However, the financing of the project, including the combination of the lump-sum funding with the turnkey contract for The Hague, provided incentives to steer on time and money, which is typical for a Type I approach. Furthermore, the new tendering of carriers hampered horizontal cooperation (Type II), as the carrier HTM was unsure about its role as the future carrier at a time when the commitment of HTM was vital to the project. This suggests that not all types of innovation direct project managers to a Type II approach. Thus, if innovation comes from different layers, project managers might very well be confronted with conflicting demands on which approach to adopt.

The framework (Table 7.1) combined with the 'mind' concept was helpful in exploring the tensions between innovation and project management using a real-life innovative project. In actuality, there are predefined dominant values and principles behind both 'project management' and 'innovation', based on the literature. Meandering attempts of project managers in the case have then been searched out. Of course, as has been concluded, a real-life project manager has limited room to manoeuvre in conducting such an analysis, as has been done here in hindsight, and actually act upon it. In the multi-actor and multi-layered context described, it is difficult to believe that a single project manager has the ability to find and realize an ideal mix of project management and innovation. However, they can at least keep in mind and put their efforts into balancing out the competing values behind innovative projects.

Note

1. This prompted the urban district to have the course of events examined during the construction and the bringing into service of RandstadRail from 2001. This study was conducted by the authors, and the analysis in this chapter is based on this study. See Ten Heuvelhof et al. (2008).

8
Exploring the Innovative Capacity of Intergovernmental Network Managers: The Art of Boundary-Scanning and Boundary-Spanning

Joris Voets and Filip De Rynck

Introduction

This chapter explores how network management is innovative from an intergovernmental perspective. The following questions are dealt with: who are the actual network managers; what management roles can be identified and how do they help create innovative capacity for intergovernmental problem-solving? These questions are answered through the use of a semi-inductive approach. First, network management is mapped using the framework developed by Kickert, Klijn and Koppenjan, and some additional elements are suggested for inclusion. Secondly, a role typology is developed and it is shown how the mix of these roles creates new intergovernmental capacity. The empirical evidence is drawn from case study data on two Flemish intergovernmental networks.

All kinds of networks are based on resource dependencies between (semi-)autonomous actors, and are driven by trust (Scharpf, 1997). Intergovernmental networks are a specific type of network, because the actors involved are different governments. As such, their distinctive character is that they involve 'boundary spanning activities of distinctive units that possess territory, identity and ascribed powers' (Agranoff, 2008, p. 1).

Like all networks, intergovernmental networks need to be triggered (March and Simon, 1958) and managed actively (Huxham and Vangen, 2005). It is assumed that any innovative capacity to solve intergovernmental problems using networks is the outcome of social engineering – defined here as network management (Kickert et al., 1997a; Klijn and Teisman, 1997). The questions dealt with in this chapter are answered by combining insights gained from the intergovernmental relations literature and policy network studies, and using case study data on two Flemish intergovernmental networks (Voets, 2008).

Boundary-spanning, scanning and innovative management

The main hypothesis of this chapter is that management in an intergovernmental setting of (mainly) public organizations can only be innovative if the presumed managers are of the 'boundary-spanning type'. Five different management roles are presented below and those who play those roles are analysed. The analysis shows that these managers should combine some characteristics typical in persons who are in a boundary-spanning position and that these roles are variations on the boundary-spanning theme. First, though, the chapter elaborates on what boundary-spanning individuals are and what innovative management in an intergovernmental context means.

Features of boundary-spanning individuals

There is much in the management literature on the concept of boundary-spanning individuals (see for instance Leifer and Huber, 1977; Leifer and Delbecq, 1978; Tushman and Scalan, 1981; Jemison, 1984). Historically, the concept has been used mainly in relation to stakeholder management, especially in those situations where there is high environmental uncertainty. Under such conditions, Robbins and Coulter (2002, p. 77) have argued that managers should put more effort into managing their relations with stakeholders. They consider boundary-spanning to be crucial in such efforts, and stress that it concerns more specific forms of interactions with various external stakeholders, focused on information exchange (in order to reduce uncertainty). In doing so, boundary-spanners have their feet in multiple settings and go beyond simple scanning and monitoring of the environment. Empirical management studies have shown that boundary-spanners are 'strongly linked internally and externally, so that they can both gather and transfer information from outside their sub-unit' (Tushman and Scanlan, 1981, p. 84). This strand of research suggests that their competence is an important determinant of boundary role status: the combination of internal linkages (in their own unit or organization) and external linkages (with other units or other organizations) makes up their perceived competence and determines their boundary role status

(1981, pp. 94, 96). Boundary-spanning is regarded here as a role status based on perceived competences and the combination of both seems to be necessary in order to legitimize innovative management in the relations between organizations.

More recently, Sullivan and Skelcher (2002) have reviewed the empirical evidence on building individual, organizational and collaborative capacity in the public sector (see also the work of Agranoff, Bingham, Huxham, Keast, Mandell, McGuire, O'Leary, Vangen). The functioning of boundary-spanners or (in their words) 'reticulists' is part of the individual level (other individual-level features being trust and leadership). Boundary-spanners are individuals who exhibit the necessary combination of skills for collaboration. In this contemporary view, boundary-spanning is about much more than information exchange; achieving collaboration is the main goal. Sullivan and Skelcher have summarized the attributes of boundary-spanners as follows: boundary-scanning (i.e. permanent appreciation of the changing environment); the ability to play roles; communication; prescience; networking; negotiating; conflict resolution; risk-taking; problem-solving and self-management (2002, pp. 101–102). Boundary-spanners are trusted as persons in the network and building trust is one of the most important activities they engage in.

According to Baker (2006), the public policy literature has adopted the concept of boundary-spanners as relationship-makers and relationship managers. His critique is that scholars focus mainly on the attributes that these persons should possess in order to achieve this relational management capacity, but few attempts have been made to examine their activities throughout the development of organizational relationships using longitudinal case study evidence. In the few exceptions cited by Baker, the evidence suggests that boundary-spanners perform different activities at different stages (Lowndes and Skelcher, 1998; quoted by Baker, 2006). He has also stressed the need to link the individual and organizational levels, as the hybridity of boundaries between organizations is a result of the hybridity that emerges between key individuals representing those organizations: 'individual level hybridity is a necessary prerequisite of organizational hybridity' (2006, p. 17). This duality is also a finding in the research reported on in this chapter.

So far, there are some building blocks for an analysis of the boundary-spanners in the two case studies described below: boundary role status and power; perceived competence; the combination of skills; the importance of being trusted; the need to examine their activities; different roles at different stages and the focus on hybridity between persons and organizations. A definition of innovative management in an intergovernmental context and how it links up with boundary-spanning individuals is now provided.

Boundary-spanning individuals and innovative management

Innovative management is defined here as deliberate attempts by persons in the position of boundary-spanner to change (perceptions of) existing routines and established interactions between autonomous public organizations (in this case of different governmental tiers) towards reframing their existing relations and types of interactions, thereby creating policy windows for new forms of collaboration or at least creating new processes that are expected to lead to new forms of collaboration. The term 'management' implies that this reframing takes place without a change in the basic institutional setting of the legal or formal framework of intergovernmental relations. The term 'deliberate' implies that management is goal-oriented, rationally inspired and driven by strategic thinking, making use of changes in the environment (i.e. boundary-scanning). Thus, while institutions do matter, the focus here is on agency on the part of individuals and organizations within these settings, including the active use of environmental conditions.[1] In other words, boundary-spanners are innovative if they actively create or mediate new links between the changes in the environment and the behaviour of organizations – in this chapter in the context of intergovernmental relations in particular.

Boundary-spanning: Who is who?

In order to manage intergovernmental networks successfully, actors have to scan and span the boundaries of governmental tiers, politics and administration, the public and private sectors, different policy sectors and so on. In this regard, the way in which network management is at the crossroads of politics and administration has proved to be of particular interest in the cases studied. This is particularly the case as this aspect and the specific role of public officials has so far been underdeveloped in the literature on intergovernmental management (Agranoff, 2004).

Empirical studies in the private sector have demonstrated that under conditions of high task uncertainty, the number of boundary roles will increase to deal with the greater information-processing requirements (Tushman, 1977, pp. 594–600). There is often more than one boundary-spanner: 'The emergence of multiple boundary-spanners with multiple functions at different stages is consistent with existing literature' (Baker, 2006, pp. 15–16). Baker (2006) makes an additional useful distinction between the emergence of a policy entrepreneur (a leading politician) and the emergence of a collaborative entrepreneur (a public official). In his own study of a public–private partnership, he has demonstrated that both play important and alternate roles, although different ones at different stages.

Typically in intergovernmental networks, there is no single manager (Agranoff, 2007). Network management activities are deployed by both public and private actors, including executive/legislative politicians, civil servants from agencies/departments, technocrats/generalists, private actors, or a mix of such actors (Kickert et al., 1997b; Huxham and Vangen, 2005). Management is often a result of these joint efforts. The term 'joint', then, does not necessarily imply that this is the result of deliberate or rationally inspired cooperation or teamwork. More likely than not, management is the product of the loosely coupled activities of politicians and managers, acting individually at different levels and at different positions in the network. Hence, it is expected that more than one boundary-spanner would be found in the case studied, made up of both politicians and civil servants.

A semi-inductive qualitative approach

The authors opted for case study research, because it brings hidden proceedings and activities to the fore and allows for a dynamic analysis (Yin, 2003). In order to analyse the actual boundary-spanners and their features, and to assess their innovative capacity, a semi-inductive qualitative approach was taken.

Step one: Mapping management activities

First, management activities were mapped starting from the network management framework developed by Kickert et al. (1997b), which includes a wide range of network management strategies. Kickert et al. organized the strategies in clusters based on the level they are directed at (policy game or network), and on the points of intervention (interactions or ideas).

The first distinction they make is between more operational management activities and more institutional management activities. The first level is the game level, in which the 'game management' is aimed at influencing the interaction processes between actors in a policy game,[2] in a context where those that are managing consider the network structure as a constant. The second level is the network level, in which management is aimed at changing or altering features of the network itself. This 'network constitution' refers to all activities that are aimed at sustained changes in the network itself, as they redefine rules and change the distribution of resources, hence the 'meta-governance' of the network (Klijn, 1996). Network constitution strategies attempt to influence the context or the action arena in which games between actors are played, while management at the game level attempts to influence the ongoing processes within and throughout the network institution. The general intergovernmental setting is considered as an institutional framework in which both levels are situated.

The second distinction has to do with whether management is aimed at substance or at process, and so trying to work on the ideas and perceptions of actors or trying to influence the ways in which actors interact. Developing a new discourse or a common language is an illustration of the former, while deciding on new decision-making procedures is an example of the latter.

The strategies are expected to contribute to the quality of the policy processes (e.g. keeping the process going, improving discussions or the way in which decision-making or the interaction between participants is organized) and products (e.g. learning, changing discourses, planning documents and decisions, 'physical' achievements in the field) in and of the network. Table A.1 in the annex presents the complete set of management strategies, but these are not discussed in detail here.

The utilization and usefulness of these management strategies is context-dependent: 'Not all strategies are equally effective in every situation' (Kickert et al., 1997b, p. 169). Hence, the challenge for network managers is to use the right strategy or set of strategies at the right time.

Step two: Discerning management roles

Secondly, based on this mapping of management activities (developed in more detail in Voets, 2008), this study also forwarded a role typology. A grounded typology of roles was developed based on the actual management behaviour of actors in the case studies, but using the existing set of network management strategies discussed above. It is acknowledged that, like all role typologies, this particular one has it limits, but the authors feel that it is a basis for more systematic testing in a broader set of case studies or quantitative research.

The role typology is constructed by coding data in terms of the type of management strategies (game and/or network, ideas or interactions), level of activity (high/medium/low) and the dominant type of activity that the actors displayed (operational, vision, networking, leadership, creativity). The roles were ascribed by the researchers, based on the assessments made by the interviewees. Finally, these roles are assigned at the overall network level. The role analysis was not conducted at the game level (e.g. games played on specific topics, issues), although this would certainly result in the picture becoming more nuanced.

Case studies

Research notes

The two case studies were analysed using multiple methods, in three consecutive rounds of analysis: a quick scan of the case; an in-depth document analysis based on primary and secondary sources; and a series of semi-structured and open-ended face-to-face interviews. In the case of 'Project Gentse Kanaalzone', 27 actors were interviewed, and the analysis covers the network from its origins in 1993 until June 2004. In the case of 'Parkbos Gent', 25 actors were interviewed and the case covers the period between spring 1996 and July 2007.

The case of 'Project Gentse Kanaalzone'

'Project Gentse Kanaalzone' (PGK) is an ongoing strategic planning process (started in 1993) in the area surrounding the canal Ghent-Terneuzen. The issues are complex: there are intense economic activities in the maritime–industrial canal area, combined with considerable environmental nuisances. Historically, there are a number of residential areas here. The parallel and uncoordinated development of housing and economic activities has resulted in an entanglement of both, leading to increased pressure on the area.

The main objective of PGK is to reconcile both functions of the area through an integrated approach, with the participation of relevant actors. The PGK aims to improve the environmental quality and increase economic development prospects by reducing the pollution of soil, water and air, by increasing quality of life through infrastructural interventions (e.g. by developing buffer zones between housing and industry), by linking residential areas, by intervening in the flows of traffic in the area, by expropriating housing in uninhabitable areas, by developing and reorganizing water, road and railway systems, and by relocating companies. Such development should be coordinated through a joint vision on the development of the area.

The main members of the network are the three local governments, the provincial government, dozens of governmental units of the Flemish government, Dutch governments, citizens' groups, companies, interest groups, consultants and political parties. The policy sectors involved are economy, spatial planning, public infrastructure (roads and water) and the environment.

The case of 'Parkbos Gent'

'Parkbos Gent' (PBG) is an ongoing policy process (started in 1996) to develop a multifunctional park in the south of the urban region of Ghent. The issues and ambitions in the focus area are complex; it is an open landscape, pressured by urbanization in the greater Ghent region. There are different claims (heritage, science park, agriculture, recreation, housing, nature, etc.), and these claims need to be matched with the ambitions of a number of actors to achieve substantial forestation in the focus area (250 to 300 hectares as part of Flemish policy).

The network focused much of its energy on developing and implementing a legal spatial plan that could accommodate different interests, without diverging from the goal of a number of actors of substantial forestation. It currently faces the challenge of implementing the goals and ambitions set out in the spatial implementation plan.

The main members of the network are the three local governments, the provincial government, dozens of governmental units of the Flemish government, interest groups and consultants. The policy sectors involved include the economy, spatial planning, agriculture, recreation and the environment.

Discerning the management activities, managers and main attributes

Lessons from the network management activities framework

The framework put forward by Kickert, Klijn and Koppenjan proved to be a good anchor. There are some lessons that are useful for developing or using the framework in future research.

First, while strategies can be singled out (to some extent), they are very often combined in practice. These combinations can be deployed simultaneously or in a sequential mode. Sometimes parallel, sometimes at a later stage, arranging[3] and constitutional reform[4] are used as well. Constitutional reform, for instance, is used to achieve the network agenda, and network managers attempt to arrange a formal network structure. In order to do so, in each case, they also attempt to activate an actor to take up formal leadership of the network.

Secondly, the focus should not be solely on the network management strategies; otherwise, the analysis risks resulting in an overly instrumental view, perhaps typical for the early days of the Dutch network school. As Huxham and Vangen (2005) and other scholars have already argued, this study shows that the rationale behind instruments and techniques in most cases is inspired by 'political' motives, and it is the combination of both that gives instruments their real 'strategic' meaning. For this reason, analysis of the network management strategies should be linked to the strategic goals behind the strategies. Otherwise, it becomes very difficult to distinguish between network management and the complete array of actions taken by network participants. As network management is 'aimed at promoting joint problem solving or policy development' (Kickert et al., 1997a, p. 43), one needs to look at the concrete goals that network managers attempt to achieve when using a management strategy. The typology maps the management strategies according to their 'external' logic, while the 'internal' logic within the network and the logic of the network managers should be the first step in achieving a proper understanding of the motives behind their use. Network management should therefore include a political perspective, which can also result in adding a number of strategies to the typology.

For instance, one important, more political network management strategy is coalition building. In the PBG case, the proponents of forestation consciously built a coalition with other sectarian interests in order to isolate the farmers who were going to lose their farmland to (be transformed into) woods. This coalition building effort was successful because the network managers linked different policy games, grounding their forestation ambitions in a larger package deal that could no longer be opened up in the final stage of decision-making at the Flemish level. In doing so, the network managers consciously kept the agricultural administration out of the network, and only allowed another administration that was suspected of serving the farmers' interests to play a secondary role.

A second, parallel strategy used in the PBG case was to create pressure to ensure that politicians would not halt the planning process at some point (for instance, because of protests by farmers) by mobilizing the general public through various forms of communication. The general public was activated not only to create pressure, but also in an attempt to change the perceptions of decision-makers about the need to create more woods. Part of this strategy included the activation of non-governmental organization (NGO) with a mission to create more woods in Flanders.

By adding network management strategies like coalition building and pressure creation, network management analysis becomes more considerate of the political dimension of and within networks, and of the political strategy inspiring the network managers. This could lead to a broader and less instrumental interpretation of management strategies, based on an in-depth analysis of the rationales utilized in the network itself.

Thirdly, the focus on the actual goals of network management in the two cases also shows that many strategies are deployed covertly. Network managers face a dilemma. They are expected to embody the collaborative spirit of the network and to manage in the interests of the network agenda as a whole. However, in order to achieve success, some management activities require the managers to be manipulative, coercive, and rather sneaky (Huxham and Vangen, 2005, p. 66). In the cases studied, for instance, actors are activated and de-activated using coercive power (by using political influence to order a governmental unit to leave or to join in). Some actors are not allowed full play by the network managers, while others are kept out strategically. Some actors are activated only to avoid negative power play on the part of another actor. Network managers in both cases strictly control the meeting agenda, not only in terms of process but also in terms of substance. As such, the management activities are only partially open and collaborative; part of the activities is not, and remains backstage.

Individual excellence or team efforts?

This qualitative study confirms that there is more than one boundary-spanner, and that it is more fruitful to look at a set of boundary-spanners, playing different roles at different times and at different levels of the network.

In the cases studied here, network management is the work of informal network teams that bring together local, provincial and Flemish governmental actors, as well as consultants. Excepting the project coordinator in the PGK network and the consultants, in both networks the main network managers are self-appointed and gradually develop their management role.

In the PGK case, for instance, an official from the local port authority is very active in attempting to change the perceptions of a number of actors away from considering the whole project as simply being about their economic agenda, or that the port authority is not aiming to exercise influence beyond its jurisdiction via the network. There is also a provincial civil servant involved, who focuses more on the level of interactions, attempting to develop and utilize personal networks to activate the desired actors in the network. Later on, he also deploys the resources of his own organization to accommodate discussions.

One example from the PBG case is that the head of the Flemish woods administration starts off as the main initiator who works on both levels (ideas and interactions), with the formal mandate of the competent minister, but he gradually shares and delegates management activities. On the one hand, spatial planners and consultants join in and are more focused on the ideas and perceptions (e.g. by drawing up images and plans to arrange the focus area). On the other hand, also because he feels he misses out on the experience of managing the interactions from a network perspective, he brought in the network champion of the PGK case for the management of interactions.

Although both cases show that there is no 'master plan' for managing networks and that there are too many contingencies that cannot be controlled or foreseen (e.g. outcome of elections, budgetary situations), management is not simply a random set of actions. At times, actors managing the network clearly coordinate their strategies. For instance, they may have informal meetings, develop strategies on how each parent organization can be locked in to provide the required resources, discuss which actors pose problems and should be isolated and so on. It is clear that such close interactions that occur to manage the network require (or lead to) high levels of trust. The network managers develop good personal relations and argue that managing the network would have never succeeded without the building of these personal relationships.

Network managers coordinate informally, they play different roles (see below), producing innovative intergovernmental cocktails: one actor takes care of the activation of actors through social networks, another actor attempts to ensure that the content of the policy decisions matches the network agenda and so on. The analysis also shows what innovative capacity is often about: bridging structural holes, which are defined by Skelcher and Sullivan (2002) as 'the gaps between those clusters of activity that when linked produce synergy and added public value' (2002, p. 96). In both cases, they act within the constraints of the intergovernmental setting, but create substantive and process linkages to first develop and later achieve a joint agenda that requires resources from different tiers and sectors. The innovative intergovernmental cocktails, which consist of ingredients derived from different governmental tiers (e.g. local, provincial and Flemish resources), policy sectors (e.g. planning, forestation, economy, heritage, infrastructure) and policy instruments (e.g. construction, subsidies, legislation), are drawn from the political and administrative realm (including political parties) and across the public–private divide (e.g. interest groups, companies). Bridging these gaps, however, also involves battles about whose activities and resources are to be deployed for whose agenda – it is certainly not a unified regime.

Skills and a drive

The analysis of network managers and their activities also shows two crucial attributes, namely skills and a drive for the network agenda.

Skills

The right combination of skills and capacities is needed to create the required intergovernmental policy mix. Intergovernmental collaboration requires actors who can tolerate, but also utilize, high levels of complexity and uncertainty. Intergovernmental network managers seem to be able to navigate through the pea-soup that is made up of the amalgamation of policies, interests, actors, relations, tiers and contingencies.

They are not network super heroes with special powers, but rather, combine their institutional positions and drive to achieve success with their personal skills. Paraphrasing one of the interviewees, these actors play in the intergovernmental champions' league. Weberian bureaucrats are too dependent on features of a rational governing system, while networks demand that the capacity matches rational (long-term) and political views (short-term) on policy-making.

Interestingly, the network managers in both cases have different specialized skills to achieve their tasks, which is very similar to the list defined by Skelcher and Sullivan (2002). The difference is that it has been found here that certain network managers are linked more closely with certain skills, but not all share the same ones (or are on the same level), as the above authors suggest. While they are all able to scan boundaries, not all have the ability to play multiple roles. All have some varying capacity for networking and negotiating. Some are better at conflict resolution, risk-taking, problem-solving and self-management than others (2002, pp. 101–102). However, they are all able to acquire a certain level of trust as persons in the network, and building trust is one of the most important strategies they engage in.

Drive

Network managers have a drive, determination and passion for the network. They stress that it is not a nine-to-five job and it is impossible to achieve success without a personal conviction of the importance of the network agenda. The ownership of the main intergovernmental boundary-spanners is linked to mission-driven endeavours (Agranoff, 2005, p. 19) and fuelled by personal beliefs. In both cases studied here, they are (mainly) men with a mission.

This determination is also fuelled by the roots of the actors involved. Politicians in Flanders are known to have a special interest in their locality and in serving their local interests at the central level ('political localism'). However, civil servants at the provincial and Flemish levels are also driven by a local (in both cases 'Ghent') reflex, which is labelled administrative localism (Voets, 2008).

Hybrid politico-administrative relations

In both case studies, administrative officials (e.g. the project coordinator, the head of the provincial environmental administration, the provincial governor) are at the heart of the network management. Their actions represent the bulk of network management. Politicians seem to take up a more supportive role (most importantly to ensure that political decisions are made). In both cases, administrative officials take the initiative, but are silently backed by a number of politicians who do not want to commit themselves too publicly because of the sensitive nature of the issues involved.

The administrative officials actively co-produce policies and strategies to achieve them, including strategies towards political actors and the use of party political channels. Instead of politicians setting out the strategic policy objectives and putting administrative officials to work to implement them, the praxis in both cases seems to be the other way round. Administrative officials develop strategic policy objectives, and attempt to pull the strings of competent politicians in order to obtain the required decisions and resources. This strategy is relatively successful in both cases.

A number of politicians have no problem with the proactive behaviour of administrative officials, adhere to the processes and form alliances with civil servants. They also believe in the value of a long-term vision and action programme. The prominent position of administrative officials, however, can lead to conflicts with some politicians who feel threatened in their position, and in their ability to present themselves.

Some actors also feel that the main network managers sometimes deploy activities that are considered political and unfit for civil servants, such as pressure creation through civil actors. Some politicians feel that such strategic planning processes take away their autonomy to make political deals.

The network managers have developed a set of antennae that are 'politically sensitive' and they are aware of the risk that politicians might feel that they have been bypassed. Generally speaking, they are able to identify the boundaries between the political and administrative realm and have been very prudent in spanning both. The network managers do not discard or bypass the political processes/politicians in policy processes; they actively deal with these and also team up with political officials to get decisions made. Interestingly, such collaborations between civil servants and politicians cut across intergovernmental and sectarian divides. In the PGK, for instance, a local alderman competent in urban planning teamed up with a provincial civil servant of environmental administration, the provincial governor and a Flemish cabinet member competent in port affairs. The hybrid model of politico-administrative relations that Aberbach et al. (1981) already forecasted more than 25 years ago is now a reality in both intergovernmental networks.

While there is much intergovernmental boundary-scanning and spanning, such activities do not change the boundaries of the state; rather, they change the boundaries within the state. The networks become a world of their own within the government system: they bring actors together in a project and area-based logic, which gradually becomes a system with a proper agenda, a distinctive organization and culture, at the crossroads of the boundaries between the participating organizations.

Five roles of potential innovative management

Based on network management activities, a typology was developed that consists of five management roles. This is linked to the work on intergovernmental network management conducted by Agranoff (2003, 2007), who has also identified a number of roles but has not developed them systematically.

The five distinct roles are: network operator; network champion; network promoter; creative thinker and vision keeper. These roles are now developed in more detail and illustrated with empirical evidence. For each role, a discussion of what the role is, how the role takes shape, who plays it, the extent to which the role is similar or different in both cases and how this helps to build innovative capacity is provided.

Network operator

A 'network operator' is responsible for the daily management of the network: he functions as a secretariat that takes care of all the administrative tasks and the day-to-day management tasks. However, the network operator is not limited to administrative functions only; he is, for instance, also the main contact for and communicator between actors in and outside of the network. This role is important because it is a form of power (Huxham and Vangen, 2005), as the operator is 'most responsible for establishing, moving, and orchestrating the network' (Agranoff, 2007, p. 93).

In the case of the PGK, a civil servant was hired specifically to function as a full-time network operator. Hence, the network operator (officially called the 'project co ordinator') is a formal position and person in the network, who is jointly financed by the public partners in the network. Interestingly, he is a former representative of one of the network actors. His track record (having served in different positions both in and outside government) has equipped him with the attributes discussed earlier. In the PBG case, there are plans to hire a full-time network operator, but financial resources have not been committed to this purpose so far.

In both cases, the actors consider the role of the network operator to be an important one. While there was no real competition in the PGK case for who should take up this role, this is certainly an issue in the PBG case. In both cases, it is clear that the provincial environmental administration was keen on playing this role because this helps with legitimization (of the province as a political level actor) and control: the actor who plays the role of network operator has control over the operational side of the network, a source of power often neglected by scholars (Huxham and Vangen, 2005).

At first, the role of the network operator appears to be very similar to that of a traditional administrator. However, the innovative capacity is that such an administration of intergovernmental networks is not likely to exist otherwise; it is part of what can be called the regime performance of the network (Voets et al., 2008). The role of the network operator institutionalizes network capacity that was not present before. It also becomes a formal element that highlights the importance of the network: capacity is created and committed to operate an intergovernmental network.

Network champion

A 'network champion' is an actor who excels in networking in terms of building, maintaining and using connections with other actors at the personal, professional and party political levels. He is a spider in the arrangement's web. The collaborative network champion has a heart for the network agenda (as opposed to other highly networked actors who only strive for their own individual agenda).

The findings of Agranoff (2007, p. 93) are confirmed in this study, namely that the main network champion in both cases is not the convener or chairperson – but he does team up with the person holding that function. In the case of the PGK, the main network champion is in fact the right hand of the chairperson. In the case of the PBG, the position of the main network champion is unclear; at times, he is an informal chair, but most of the time the initiative (and hence, the position of chair) lies with other actors (such as the Flemish woods administration and Flemish planning administration).

In both cases, the main network champion is the same person, namely the head of the provincial environmental administration. He joined on the personal, professional and party political levels. Not only was he able to figure out the desired intergovernmental configuration, but he was also able to actively link actors together. The network champion is also very clearly targeted in accessing new networks by linking up to actors with a high centrality in other networks. Many interviewees argued that such networking is a bare necessity. According to the network managers, the governmental praxis in Flanders (i.e. a very crowded institutional and highly politicized, party-cratic, clientelist arena, imbued with political localism) demands that administrative officials take up a more active and 'political' role if they are to achieve results.

In both cases, actors consider the role of network champion to be an important one. Actors are expected to bring in their network sources, but it is clear that the network champion in both cases has both the 'largest' network and is the most able to use other actors' network access. In both cases, the head of the provincial environmental administration was keen on playing it – he clearly gets a kick out of doing so.

However, it is clear that the conditions for the network champion to achieve success were better in the PGK case than in the PBG case. One of the conditions that varied was the different actor constellation in each case, while another was the partly different time period in which he functioned – the political context during the period in which PGK was analysed was more convenient than the political context during the period in which PBG was analysed (e.g. different coalitions in the Flemish government).

The innovative capacity of the network champion lies in networking capabilities across tiers, sectors and the politico-administrative divide. Without many formal resources to do so, the creation of a network arena or intergovernmental web provides an intergovernmental coordination potential in its own right, in terms of relations. Compared to traditional intergovernmental relations, the formal-legalistic relations are explicitly combined with social relations in function of a joint agenda.

Network promoter

A 'network promoter' is defined here as an actor who is considered to be authoritative, accepted by all actors as a principal (in moral terms, not in terms of power or hierarchy). He holds a position of trust and is also the one to whom other actors direct their grievances or concerns. He tries to keep things together and is expected to manage conflicts. If necessary, this actor might even 'sanction' network members, mainly based on a moral authority, trust and informal acceptance. He is the active chair, accepted by most actors as authoritative, and is perceived to be neutral. In an intergovernmental network, he is also a go-between among the local, provincial and Flemish governments. As such, he promotes the network inter-governmentally.

In the PGK case, the provincial governor is the network promoter. He has no formal competencies regarding the focus area, although he functions at the crossroads of the local, provincial and central government. He holds substantial moral weight, has great moral authority and no identifiable interests. In the PBG case, the main flaw identified by the network managers is precisely the lack of such a network promoter who can 'control' the inner arena of the network and promote the network in the outer arena. While there were formal chairpersons in the PBG according to who had the lead in the project, no one was able to become the network promoter. Actors were too clearly identified with individual interests or were too young and inexperienced or not accepted to play this role.

The added value of the network promoter is to carry the weight of the network. The network promoter is able to transcend the different cultures and attitudes and keep the representatives in a workable mode. He is able to capture the conflict between governmental actors, acting as a guardian of the intergovernmental catchment area or border region that any intergovernmental network presents. In this respect, he helps to innovate intergovernmental relations by introducing a (new kind of) intergovernmental leadership that respects the equality of the various levels, mainly based on informal and personal characteristics.

Creative thinker

A 'creative thinker' is an actor who delivers impeachable expertise, develops concepts, models, and produces tools to build 'groupware',[5] and to induce consensus. He actively attempts to frame and reframe the mindsets of other actors, and to forward innovative and joint concepts in order to incorporate different interests. The creative thinker can also play a role on the level of interactions, and take up a 'network coaching' role, for instance in terms of quick wins, or identifying convenient formulas for meetings. Ideally, the creative thinker has no stake in the focus area or in the issues that are on the table, and hence is 'free' to give creative input.

As the cases are quite focused on issues of spatial planning, planning consultants are the main 'creative thinkers'. They introduced new spatial concepts of thinking and looking, and thereby influenced ideas (at the game and network levels). They were also able to present intergovernmental linkages, especially in terms of substance, as they conducted studies and projects for many actors involved in the network at different tiers (e.g. the city of Ghent, the Flemish planning administration). As a result, they created more substantive links between different policy processes. Moreover, they worked in interactions, for instance by suggesting ways to jointly manage the focus areas, such as the kind of network structure that should be put into legislation.

The creative thinkers helped to innovate in intergovernmental relations, in terms of ideas and interactions. The decision to bring in these creative thinkers itself is already a moment of innovation, while they in turn can activate the innovative potential of the intergovernmental network. They present an additional capacity for intergovernmental problem-solving that is not present in the participating organizations or at the individual tiers.

Vision keeper

In keeping with Agranoff's (2003) notion, a 'vision keeper' is an actor in or outside the network, public officials or a non-public actor, who is or becomes a strong 'believer' in the network's added value. These actors are concerned with the progress of the collective. Their concern with the overall performance of the network separates them from stakeholders or network participants, who focus mainly on their organizational goals. The vision keepers also function as 'risk managers' – detecting potential problems in the network but also in the network environment. These actors are also activated by the other network managers if their assistance is required.

In the PGK, there are two main vision keepers – the former representative of the port authority and a civil servant of the Ghent city administration (but also the former project co ordinator). Both have now taken a step back or have switched positions. In the PBG, the main vision keeper is a planning official from the Flemish administration.

Their innovative capacity is to transcend the tendency to focus on a single organization, sector or tier. They act as sounding boards for network managers. The vision keeper helps to ensure reflexivity and meta-governance potential.

Summing up the role analysis

Five management roles have been identified that can be played by one or more actors. In the PGK, all the roles were present. In the PBG, three roles were clearly present, but two are more ambiguous (network operator and network promoter). These five roles can be combined in single persons, but the analysis shows that actors are often 'specialized' in one or a set or cluster of these roles. The presence and successful combination of these roles contributes to intergovernmental capacity-building, offering better prospects for achieving coordination and overcoming governmental fragmentation (Agranoff, 2008, p. 11).

The five network roles are distinct, but also linked (Agranoff, 2003, p. 18). Without the right contacts and understanding of how to use them (the role of the network champion), the network is unlikely to gain a critical mass to move forward. Without someone taking up the role of organizing the actual operations of the network and taking up the administrative burden of the network, the network may not surpass the level of good intentions. The function of a network promoter is also important, as it helps to create leadership in the network, and also provides a spokesperson outside the network. The network promoter then builds on the administrative support of a network operator and the network relations managed and created by the network champion. The function of vision keeper is one that typically develops over time, but keeps the network in a reflexive mode and also helps to identify, assess and even address risks. Finally, the role of creative thinker proves to be a vital one. More often than not, excelling in networking does not mean that this brings in the required input to move networks ahead. In both cases, the creative input was crucial to developing the network agenda successfully, both in terms of ideas (e.g. new frames to discuss or to look at the area) and interactions (e.g. setting up workshops or ways to deal with stakeholders).

Based on our limited research, it cannot be claimed that the five roles are absolute requirements for successful networks, but they certainly seem to increase the chances for success in intergovernmental problem-solving.

Conclusions

This chapter has set out to analyse how network management can help build innovative capacity to solve intergovernmental problems. Using a two-step approach – building on the network management activities framework of Kickert et al., and developing a role typology – the study mapped network management activities, identified who the network managers actually are, outlined some key attributes and described how this helps to create innovative capacity for intergovernmental problem-solving.

In terms of the network management activities used, it is clear that the framework of Kickert et al. provides a very useful anchor for studying network management. In order to develop and use the framework in the future, the authors suggest looking at the ways in which these strategies are combined, analysing the motives behind the use of each strategy to add a stronger political perspective to it, and taking into account the dark side of network management. In terms of insights, the analysis of network management activities in both cases showed how innovative management is a mix of individual excellence but also of team efforts, how a certain set of skills and having a heart for the network agenda proves crucial to achieving success, and how the hybridity of politico-administrative relations in an intergovernmental setting is a reality that is actively created.

Based on the analysis of network management strategies, a role typology was able to be developed. Five distinct roles were identified, and it was argued that the mix of these roles creates the innovative capacity required to deal with contemporary intergovernmental challenges. The leitmotiv in these roles is the art of boundary-spanning and boundary-scanning. In doing so, the joint management activities of network operators, network champions, network promoters, vision keepers and creative thinkers create intergovernmental cocktails that are not likely to exist otherwise.

The innovative potential of network management in an intergovernmental context is clear. It helps to make intergovernmental relations multilateral, collaborative and to combine a wide range of policy issues (as opposed to bilateral intergovernmental transactions between governments). Network management offers better prospects for achieving coordination and overcoming governmental fragmentation, and stimulates more collaborative than competitive intergovernmental relations. It also contributes to intergovernmental capacity-building, for instance in terms of creating a web of social relations that can be used to exchange ideas or increase the availability of expertise across tiers. Through network management, an arena to 'capture' conflict between governmental actors is created (Loughlin, 2007; Agranoff, 2008, p. 11). This innovation can be developed in the boundary zone between autonomous governments that participate in networks. In other words, the existence of the grey zone of boundary-spanning and boundary-scanning stimulates innovation, as human creativity makes it possible to deal with the complexities of formulating issues and potential solutions.

Innovation, then, is related to the features of boundary work: the capacities of and for motivated network managers who can think and act strategically flourish when and where roles are mixed up, where actors develop in a new setting, and when the perceptions, goals and strategies of actors meet. It is this mix of institutional and personal features that increases the possibilities for introducing innovation into intergovernmental networks.

Notes

1. Changes in the environment that directly explain the reframing of the interactions are not considered as management.
2. Policy games are strategic interaction processes taking shape around issues (Kickert et al., 1997).
3. Arranging essentially refers to creating, sustaining and changing ad hoc provisions that suit groups of interactions in a policy game (Klijn and Teisman, 1997, p. 110).
4. A strategy aimed at changing the network conditions or the institutional context in which policy games are played.
5. Groupware is 'group development that reaches mutual understanding and transcends hierarchy-based communication/interaction that allows multiple cultures, procedures, and divisions of labor to come together' (Agranoff, 2007, p. 213).

9

Innovating Entrepreneurship in Health Care: How Health Care Executives Perceive Innovation and Retain Legitimacy

Wilma van der Scheer, Mirko Noordegraaf and Pauline Meurs

Introduction

This chapter focuses on the executive's role in innovating health care. A distinction is made between two types of innovations: entrepreneurial innovations and institutional innovations. The first type aims to find new ways to enlarge market share, size and the competitive position of organizations. The latter aims to find new ways of connecting 'old' and 'new' logics (ways of thinking and working) in health care in order to make a long-standing contribution to a new type of health care system. This study looks at how health care executives view and enact both types of innovations.

Both types of innovations are related to ongoing changes in health care systems, in which a new market logic, new policies and new technologies force executives to rationalize health care delivery, compete with others and upgrade and up-scale organizations. According to Osborne and Brown (2005), such changes imply a break with the past and require new innovative structures and techniques as well as new management skills. This requires entrepreneurial innovations at the organizational level. At the same time, executives cannot escape accepted professional and organizational logics based on professional ethics and administration, such as budgetary control and risk exclusion. Consequently, health care executives run the risk of being squeezed between politically driven reform policies on the one hand and resistance to change from, for example, professional staff on the other that are required to implement change (Goodwin, 2006). Neither direct government control nor new business-like organizational forms seem to provide executives with durable legitimacy anymore. Thus, not only are entrepreneurial innovations that are aimed at new products and business models required, but also institutional innovations, in order to find ground for new ways of thinking and working in health care and in order to retain legitimacy. The central questions are: *How do executives deal with opposing value systems? Do executives find innovative ways to combine innovations and legitimacy?*

The next few sections set the scene. After a brief explanation of the changes in health care (in the Netherlands) and the consequences for the position of executives, the chapter elaborates on the role of health care executives as 'institutionally active agents' and on the difference between entrepreneurial and institutional innovations in health care. Next, executive strategies are empirically explored by studying the outcomes of an extensive research survey, conducted in 2000 and repeated in 2005. At the end of the chapter, some conclusions are drawn.

Retaining legitimacy in times of change

In the Netherlands health care traditionally is a public/private/ professional affair. Health care professionals work for private organizations with a public task, predominantly funded by public means (Helderman et al., 2005). During decades the central government took direct responsibility for the development of the sector by means of elaborate planning, budgeting and tariff control of independent health professionals. Not-for-profit health care providers and insurers (sick funds) acted as quasi-governmental organizations, implementing governmental policy and regulations (Helderman, 2007; van der Scheer, 2007). Successful management of these organizations required public administration competencies. The Dutch health care sector, however, is a public sector in transformation. Like in other countries, technical and political ends, such as cost-containment and improved efficiency, have gained importance, in addition to traditional 'institutional' ends, reflecting professional values governing the provision of necessary and appropriate care, safety, accessibility and so on (Osborne and Gaebler, 1992; Pollitt, 2002; Kirby, 2006). At the beginning of the 1990s, the Dutch government stated three policy goals for the health care sector. It had to be innovative, cost-efficient and demand-driven (van der Grinten and Kasdorp, 1999; WRR, 2004). Existing political planning, budgeting and price control instruments were no longer considered to be adequate for realizing these aims. Markets were seen as new instruments to realize policy goals and government started to create market conditions in the health care sector (Putters, 2001; Helderman et al., 2005; Helderman, 2007). The intention was to limit the role of government and to control conditions for an optimal functioning of markets in the field of health care (Dijstelbloem et al., 2004).

This reorientation towards markets in the health care sector is a long-term endeavour. Initial steps were made 20 years ago, and today the Dutch health care sector is driven by a mix of market forces and governmental planning, budgeting and price control (Dijstelbloem et al., 2004; van der Scheer, 2007). It is not clear whether this mix will evolve towards more market elements, as this strongly depends on the colour of governmental coalitions. This creates substantial uncertainty about the ultimate importance of markets in Dutch health care. At the same time market conditions are becoming incorporated in the way the sector functions and develops. New logics of appropriate actions are disseminated through government guidelines, legislation, and practices of inspection and audit regimes (Noordegraaf et al., 2005; van der Scheer, 2007). Entrepreneurial risk is created for providers and insurers. Established market positions are breaking down. Price competition brings growing attention for cost management and productivity. Private payments are added to the traditional public funding of health services, etc. (Varkevisser et al., 2008). As a consequence, executives of health care organizations are facing a situation in which their management routines – the rules of the game that belong to the public administration management tradition – rapidly become obsolete in substantial parts of their work (Pollitt and Bouckaert, 2000; Grit and Meurs, 2005; Goodwin, 2006; Kirby, 2006; Noordegraaf, 2007). The emerging market conditions require other, more business-like knowledge and competencies of executives in health care (van der Scheer, 2007; Noordegraaf and van der Meulen, 2008). In order to retain legitimacy it makes sense for executives to adapt to the new logic and incorporate the new entrepreneurial way to go about things and engage entrepreneurial innovations (Clarke and Newman, 1997).

The strategy of adaptation may be perceived as legitimate from one perspective but abject from another perspective; it may be wise considering external claims and expectations, but wrong considering what traditionally is believed to be morally just in health care. Legitimacy is not only a matter of complying with law and state agencies (regulative legitimacy) but is also about what is perceived as morally just (normative legitimacy) and about respecting accepted, taken-for-granted scripts (cognitive legitimacy), especially in such an institutionalized field as health care (see Scott and Meyer, 1991; Ruef and Scott, 1998; Scott et al.,

2000; Scott, 2001). What may contribute to the external legitimacy of executives and organizations (from the point of view of politicians, policy-makers, insurers, etc.), may be at the expense of internal legitimacy (from professionals and clients). According to this institutionalist point of view, legitimacy and institutionalization are virtually synonymous (Suchmann, 1995). Organizations are likely to resist innovations that are inconsistent with performing known tasks. Some even belief revolutionary changes in public sector organizations are impossible to implement because of the many constraints (interdependencies, strong traditions, tied relationships, involved interest groups) that govern the activities of public agents (Terry, 1996; Mouwen, 2006). Putters (2001) calls this the 'institutional trap', referring to the pressure on executives of health care organizations to conform to the demands of the health care field. How to innovate in such a field?

The executive role in an institutionalized sector

According to Terry (1996) the very function of public managers, such as health care executives, is to be responsive to the demands of political elites, the courts, interest groups and the citizenry, and at the same time preserve the integrity of public organization. The word integrity refers to the reasons for existence of the organization, its desired social function and its collective institutional goals that legitimizes its actions. It refers to 'the completeness, wholeness, soundness, and persistence of cognitive, normative and regulative structures that provide meaning and stability to social behavior' (Terry, 1996, p. 27, see also Scott, 2001). In line with Selznick (1984), Terry (1990) argues that serving the public good is a task which is about preserving the organization's distinctive values, roles and competences. According to this point of view executives themselves should also be selective in adapting to external demands and should resist pressures and demands that weaken the organization's integrity because of erosion of its regulatory, normative and cognitive systems. This does not mean health care executives should have an antagonism toward change, on the contrary, controlled adaptation to changing circumstances is obviously an ongoing necessity. The thing is that change and innovation in such vital fields as health care should be guided by respect for existing belief systems and traditions and by loyalty to its values and unifying principles (the very reasons for their existence). What is more, innovative courses of action are required to preserve organizational integrity (see Friedrich, 1961 in Terry, 1990).

External events that threaten the organization's integrity may justify a radical break with the organization's established conduct, but they will also put executives for the difficult task to respect and simultaneously distance themselves from institutional pressures and to act strategically. It asks of executives to challenge and change the very same institutions that constrain them. This controversy is often referred to as the 'paradox of embedded agency', requiring of actors to alter institutional logics without disembedding from the institutional world (see e.g. Scott and Meyer, 1991; Suddaby and Greenwood, 2005; Battilana, 2006; Leca and Naccache, 2006; Slyke, 2006). It suggests executives can become 'institutionally active agents' and find new logics of legitimization that *bend*, rather than *break* with, traditional bases of legitimacy (also Terry, 1996; Newman, 2005; Battilana, 2006). Answers to how this can be done are sought in the enabling circumstances under which change is possible (see Koppenjan and Klijn, 2004; Dorado, 2005), in the enabling role of individuals' social position or the institutional awareness of individuals (see Battilana, 2006). Others believe we should focus on exploring meanings actors attribute to their roles, on exploring their beliefs, preferences and how they take on particular forms of identity (Newman, 2005; Suddaby and Greenwood, 2005; Leca and Naccache, 2006; Rhodes, 2007). In this chapter we follow the latter strategy, for we want to find out how the new entrepreneurial way of thinking has affected the perceptions and actions of health care executives and what sort of innovation strategies are undertaken. As mentioned in the introduction we distinguish between two sorts of innovations: entrepreneurial innovations and institutional innovations.

Entrepreneurial and institutional innovations

'Institutional innovations' are very different from 'entrepreneurial innovations' that – in response to external events – focus on new products, business models and a new 'entrepreneurial' language (see also the definition of private sector innovation from the OECD and Eurostat, 2005). Although product innovation is often seen as radical innovation, representing true discontinuity with the past (Osborne and Brown, 2005), the institutional impact – a real change in thinking and working in organizations – may be minor. As Exton (2008) found studying entrepreneurship in the UK National Health Service, the new entrepreneurial strategy and language may remain 'loosely coupled' to mainstream organizational practices due to the interplay of power relations and 'old' institutions. Institutional innovations, instead, are connecting old and new logics in health care: developing new values and meanings, and engaging in new relations and partnerships (e.g. Scott et al., 2000). Each type of innovation serves its own goals and is accompanied by its own beliefs, languages and practices, thus affecting *executive identities* as well as *organizational practices, executive perceptions* and *actions*.

Where entrepreneurial innovations focus on instruments and measurements, institutional innovations focus on people and values. The first form seeks the objective: the facts function as proof for organizational effectiveness, which is used to enhance and prove output legitimacy. Plans are concrete, feasible, and have a clear beginning and end. The aim is to ensure organizational continuity by strengthening the competitive position of the organization (see for further elaboration Drucker, 1985; Terry, 1990; Osborne and Brown, 2005; van der Scheer, 2007; Exton, 2008). In this *business model*, new services (products) are developed in order to attract more patients (customers). Executives are encouraged to reinvent themselves to become more entrepreneurial and business-like managers, to take on images of competitive behaviour as requiring hard, macho or 'cowboy' styles of working (Clarke and Newman, 1997) and to become risk-takers and produce radical changes like 'real' entrepreneurs do (Terry, 1996). Executives who advocate entrepreneurial innovations should do well to learn from their private sector counterparts, to enlarge their knowledge about finances, rationing mechanisms and other private sector technologies and practices. Moreover, in a more market-driven context with a rising emphasis on matters of efficiency and accountability, a call for yet another 'type' of manager can be heard: managers from 'outside' health care, who are supposed to run health care organizations more as 'normal' businesses (Grit and Meurs, 2005).

The second form of innovating seeks the subjective or the social: change is an outcome of social interaction between multiple parties (see e.g. Denis et al., 1996; Ruef and Scott, 1998; Scott et al., 2000; Kirkpatrick and Ackroyd, 2003). Institutional innovation seeks recognition and support for new ways of thinking and working. The aim is to preserve the institution's distinctive values, roles and competences by re-shaping social orders without losing legitimacy. Therefore, health care executives have to consider patients' and professionals' interests, as well as private and public interests. In addition to measurable results and rules, professional values and client wishes need to be respected; for health care remains a matter of 'people processing', which depends on human contacts and trust. Quality is influenced by whether clients feel at home, and whether they are listened to, which are important ways to build and enhance input legitimacy. It requires of executives to cultivate and maintain a variety of supportive relationships, both internal and external, and a continuous effort to maintain a favourable public image

(Terry, 1996). This calls for managers who not only manage *downward*, controlling organizational operations, nor *outward*, achieving measurable results, but who also manage *upward* and actively seek support from internal and external interest groups (Moore, 1995). The corresponding leadership role is that of an intermediate in between multiple parties and interests; a role which requires a good insight in and feeling with the specific field of action, as one develops through long-standing experience.

Both types of innovations are summarized in Table 9.1, as well as the expected consequences on *executives' competences, organizational characteristics, perceptions and actions.*

Table 9.1   Entrepreneurial innovations versus institutional innovations

	Entrepreneurial innovations	**Institutional innovations**
Aim	Organizational continuity by strengthening the competitive position of the organization (market share)	Preserve the institution's distinctive values, roles and competences by re-shaping social orders
Action	Investments in product development, organizational growth, new organizational structures and the adoption of a new entrepreneurial role, language and business-knowledge	Conscious reinterpretation of policy terms and seeking public support for it, an intermediary role for senior staff members who are strongly embedded in the organizational field of action, relations with different stakeholders
Indicators	*Executive competences*: Business experience and knowledge	*Executive competences*: Long-standing experience in health care
	Organizational characteristics: New products, new organizational structures/ business models, organizational growth/mergers	*Organizational characteristics*: Adjustments are made, but no radical break with existing ways of working
	Executive perceptions and actions: Adoption of new entrepreneurial roles and language for senior staff	*Executive perceptions and actions*: Adoption of an intermediary role for senior staff members, adaptation to the specific institutional field, new relations/partnerships, maintaining a favourable public image
Effects	Output legitimacy	Input-legitimacy

In the next section we explore the impact of emerging market conditions in health care on *executives' competences, organizational characteristics, perceptions and actions* empirically.

The empirical research

Empirical data come from a large-scale survey that was sent to all (approximately 800) members of the Dutch association of Health Care Executives (NVZD), in 2000 as well as in 2005. Between 2000 and 2005, competition became a core issue in health care policy and major legislative changes were implemented, changing the Dutch health care system. Purchaser and provider splits were formalized, health care insurers became decisive, and a new cost-driven financing system was established (Den Exter et al., 2004; Helderman et al., 2005; van der Scheer, 2007). For this study we wanted to explore how executive competences, organizational characteristics, actions and perceptions have changed during the years 2000–2005. Do executives follow policies and opt for entrepreneurial innovations, or do they find innovative ways to combine entrepreneurship and other health care logics, and opt for institutional innovations?

The survey

The survey we used was basically a self-assessment tool. The survey provides insight in meanings executives attribute to their role and actions. Executives were asked about their personal backgrounds, their organizations, their perceptions and actions. The 2000 and 2005 surveys were largely identical, although some questions were altered or added. The most important changes were caused by contextual changes. In 2005, for example, we asked respondents about (perceived) impacts of policy-induced innovations. This is especially relevant for understanding the strategies executives pursue. The majority of the questions were closed questions. Answer categories were derived from interviews with executives of different types of organizations. In 2005 answer categories were again checked in interviews with executives of different types of organizations.

Table 9.2 shows the survey data used to study executive competences, organizational characteristics, perceptions and actions.

In order to provide insight into sector-specific forces that 'drive' executive behaviour we studied both general trends in health care management and differences between (sub)sectors. Where a question was newly added in 2005, only cross-sectional outcomes are studied.

Table 9.2   Questionnaire: Relevant data

Type of data	Data	Operational measures
Executive competence	Education Management education (Management) experience	University/vocational schooling Management programmes/ training Management/ executive positions, inside/outside health care, in what types of organizations
Organizational characteristics	Size of organization	Budget, staff, number of professionals
	Structure	Organizational structures, management structures
	Product development	New services, commercial activities
Executive perceptions and actions	Role	Role importance and role strength
	Interpretation of policy terms	Entrepreneurship, effectiveness, required changes, accountability
	Relationships	Internal/external contacts, meetings, participation in public debate

Respondents

The respondents are all Dutch health care executives, with so-called 'end responsibility'. They are members of the strategic apexes of different types of health care organizations, such as hospitals, organizations for mentally ill people, organizations for disabled people, organizations for elderly care and home care. The survey was sent to all members of the NVZD, which can be considered a representative sample. In 2000 the overall response rate was 46 per cent, and in 2005 the overall response rate was 42 per cent (i.e. 17 per cent of all Dutch health care executives). Table 9.3 shows the response rate per sector for the 2005 survey. For the 2000 survey a division per (sub)sector was not available.

Methods

To answer our questions we explored correlations between the 2000 and 2005 outcomes, and between (sub)sector outcomes and the mean. To find associations, chi-square was used for nominal variables, Spearman's rho for ordinal variables, and Pearson's correlation

Table 9.3 Response, 2005

Type of organization (sub)sector	Population N	Sample n (members NVZD)	Response i.r.t population N	Response i.r.t. sample n
Hospital	312	200	22%	35%
Organization for mentally ill people	204	122	30%	51%
Organization for disabled people	305	134	19%	43%
Organizations for elderly care and home care	1030	271	9%	35%
Total	1851	727	17%	42%

coefficient for interval and ratio variables. The values of Pearson's correlations and Spearman's rho were tested against '0' by means of a t-test approximation. The differences between independent groups were tested by the chi-square test in cases of nominal variables. In cases of ordinal, interval and ratio variables a one-way analysis of variance (ANOVA) was used. When there were three or more independent groups and, subsequently, in cases of significant differences, post hoc tests for multiple comparisons were carried out using Bonferroni intervals. With t-tests, unequal variances were assumed. In all cases, only significant outcomes ($p \leq 0.05$) are mentioned.

When relevant, outcomes are illustrated with tables.

Results

Executives' competence

With respect to *education*, outcomes show that respondents (both in 2000 and 2005) are largely educated alike. 2005 respondents do *not* have increasingly more economic or business administration backgrounds, nor are they less likely to have been educated as medical doctors or nurses. Many respondents have combined studies: economics, medicine, nursing or sociology, as well as management and business administration; the latter also through many additional courses and training. The only difference is that:

- in 2005 more executives are educated in (other) social sciences (than economics) than in 2000.

Table 9.4 Work experience, in years and number of (management) positions

	2000	2005
Years since first managerial position	*19.3*	*21.2*
Number of management positions	*3.3*	*4.4*
Number of end-responsible positions	*1.9*	*2.2*
Positions in health care	*2.3*	*3.2*
Positions outside health care	*1.0*	*1.3*

Table 9.5 Work experience, in different types of health care organizations (percentage)

	2000	2005
Work experience in just one health care organization	15	12
Work experience in just one type of health care organization	37	31
Work experience in different types of health care organizations	*48*	*57*

In 2005 we also asked respondents what sort of additional training they had followed. Outcomes show much attention is paid to matters of finance and business administration.

With respect to *work experience,* respondents in 2005 appear to be more experienced health care managers than the respondents of 2000. Tables 9.4 and 9.5 show: they have been working as a manager for a longer period of time; they have had more management positions (with and without end responsibility); they have had more managerial positions in health care organizations; they have worked more often in different types of health care organizations.

Besides these general trends, some sector-specific trends can be found related to initial education and work experience.

- In hospitals and organizations for mentally ill people, executives are more likely to have a medical (or psychological) background than in other organizations.
- Executives of hospitals and organizations for mentally ill people are less experienced managers than the mean (in years and number of management positions).

- Executives of organizations for elderly care and home care are more experienced managers than the mean.

The latter outcomes are likely to be related. Executives with professional backgrounds only become managers after having worked as a professional for many years.

A major change between 2000 and 2005 is a 9 per cent rise in the number of executives who have work experience in *different types* of health care organizations. Apparently, opposed to the call for more business-like managers from 'outside' health care, more executives come from 'other' types of health care organizations. Mobility between health care sectors has increased. We can also conclude that becoming a health care executive is preceded by an extensive process of socialization and education in health care and much experience in health care management. Managing a health care organization seems to require a *specialization* in health care management.

Organizational characteristics

Between 2000 and 2005 health care organizations have changed in multiple ways.

With respect to *size*, outcomes show:

- organizations have become larger, in terms of budgets, numbers of employees, numbers of professionals and numbers of locations.

With respect to *structures*, outcomes show:

- organizations are more often organized in divisions and clusters, with units that are organized around client groups, medical specializations or geographical areas.

Management structures have also been adapted. Most organizations have changed from a board of 'directors', with a clear-cut jurisdiction, to a CEO structure, with an executive board with a broad jurisdiction and a broad set of responsibilities.

In this model a supervisory board supervises policy and the actions of the executive board that is formally and factually responsible for the functioning of the organization (a two-tier structure). In many cases there is a first-responsible executive.

With respect to *product development*, outcomes show:

- organizations increasingly invest in the extension of services and commercial activities.

Executives of organizations for elderly care and home care show a more than average interest in commercial activities and extension of services. Executives of organizations for disabled people show a less than average interest in commercial activities.

With respect to size, structures and product development the same trends can be found in all sectors, but some differences between sectors have decreased. All organizations have grown in size, but, due to mergers, organizations for elderly care and home care have grown the most. Differences regarding structure remain varied. Hospitals, for example, are more often organized around medical specializations; organizations for mentally ill people are more often organized around client groups; organizations for disabled people and for elderly care and home care are more often geographically organized. To conclude, during the years 2000–2005 health care organizations have become bigger and more complex. Executives of all types of health care organizations had to deal with organizational scaling-up and restructuring. Further, all organizations tend to invest in the extension of services and commercial activities, but organizations for disabled people the least, and organizations for elderly care and home care the most.

Executive perceptions

Two questions were related to the executives' *role perception*. They were asked: (1) to rank the importance of different roles on a scale from 1 to 5: strategist, figurehead, entrepreneur, process manager, intermediate and administrator; (2) to rank how well they put the different roles into effect on a scale from 1 to 5. The outcomes are presented in Table 9.6.

Table 9.6   Role: Importance and performance (scale 1–5)

Roles	Role importance		Role performance	
	2000	2005	2000	2005
Figurehead	4.2	4.2	4.0	4.1
Strategist	4.7	4.6	4.4	4.4
Administrator	3.1	3.2	3.0	3.2
Process manager	3.0	3.1	2.8	2.9
Intermediate	3.3	4.2	3.4	4.1
Entrepreneur	4.3	4.3	4.0	3.9

The outcomes show that executives in 2000 and 2005 value the *strategist* role the most, followed by the entrepreneurial role. The *intermediary* role has gained importance between 2000 and 2005, and executives are the least satisfied with how they perform the *entrepreneurial* role.

The same trends can be found in all sectors. Hospital executives, however, are the least satisfied with the way they perform.

We posed several questions with respect to the way executives interpret *policy terms,* such as *entrepreneurship, required change, effectiveness* and *accountability.* All questions were only posed in the 2005 survey, so only cross-sectional correlations could be analysed.

With respect to *entrepreneurship* we asked respondents how they realized or practised entrepreneurship. Answers show entrepreneurship can mean many things. Table 9.7 shows the outcomes per sector on a 1–5 scale.

It appears executives of organizations for elderly care and home care interpret entrepreneurship more *economically* than the others do. For them, entrepreneurship is not just an attitude or a way to improve performance but also a 'market strategy'. In elderly care and home

Table 9.7 The meaning of entrepreneurship

	Hospitals	Organizations for mentally ill people	Organizations for disabled people	Elderly and home care	Mean
Creative use of resources	3.8	3.6	3.7	*3.9*	*3.8*
Optimizing work processes	*3.8*	3.6	3.5	3.4	*3.5*
Initiating commercial activities	3.0	2.6	*2.3*	*3.2*	*2.8*
Stimulating professional innovations	*4.1*	3.8	*3.7*	3.8	*3.9*
Realizing cooperation in order to meet regional demands	*3.7*	4.1	3.8	4.1	*4.0*
Entering new markets	*3.1*	3.2	3.2	3.8	*3.4*

care, entrepreneurship is more about 'entering new markets', the 'introduction of commercial activities', as well as about 'creative use of resources'. Executives of hospitals interpret entrepreneurship more *professionally* in terms of 'stimulating professionals to innovate' and 'optimizing work processes'.

We also asked how important the following *changes* are for their organizations: a more business-like attitude which focuses on results, a more professional attitude with more attention for the professional development of employees, a more entrepreneurial attitude with more attention for realizing innovations, more attention for quality of care, more attention for broader public issues with respect to health care and a better price/quality ratio (answers could be given on a 1–3 scale). The outcomes show that, generally speaking:

- executives feel a more business-like, entrepreneurial attitude is the most important, together with more attention for price/quality ratios.

Priorities, however, differ between sectors. Hospital executives focus more on quality of care; executives of organizations for elderly care and home care focus more on broader public issues concerning health care and less on professional attitude; executives of organizations for disabled people believe more attention is necessary for professional development of employees.

With respect to *executive effectiveness*, we asked respondents what decisive criteria for success are: to be able to deal with tensions and dilemmas; to realize changes; to achieve good financial results; to formulate a binding vision; to stimulate employees; to adapt to the situation (only one answer was possible).

Respondents of different types of organizations appear almost unisonous in their answers.

- Executives believe 'realization of changes' is the most important criterion for success, followed by formulating a 'binding vision'.

With respect to *accountability*, we asked respondents what they feel most accountable for and would prefer to be judged upon: complying to political commissions; optimizing logistics; financial results; competitive position; quality of care; public responsibilities (a maximum of two answers could be given).

Again, respondents of different types of organizations mostly agreed.

- They feel most accountable for 'quality of care', followed by 'financial results' and 'public ends'.

Combining the outcomes regarding executive perceptions, we can draw several preliminary conclusions. First, executives strongly focus on entrepreneurship. Executives believe a more entrepreneurial attitude should be stimulated throughout the organization in order to realize change, and that they themselves should act more as 'entrepreneurs'. Yet entrepreneurship appears difficult to put into practice, especially in hospitals. Both the meaning of entrepreneurship and the opportunities to put entrepreneurship into practice differ per organizational field. Secondly, executives believe realizing change is an important criterion for success. The change they feel most necessary for their organization is a more entrepreneurial attitude. It suggests the entrepreneurial role is virtually synonymous to the role of change agent. Yet, thirdly, executives themselves are not mostly concerned with change or competitive position, but with quality of care and financial results. That is what they feel they should really be held accountable for. Fourthly, the intermediate role – acting in between different parties inside and outside the organization – has gained importance to executives. In addition, realizing a binding vision is believed to be important to succeed. Apparently, executives believe they need to have a binding function for people inside and outside the organization.

Executive actions

In order to gain more insight into what relationships executives maintain we asked respondents: what stakeholders and sort of meetings they attend to; and in what ways they participate in public debates.

With respect to *internal contacts*, outcomes show:

- internal managerial contacts with other executives, managers and the supervisory board have increased between 2000 and 2005.

With respect to *external contacts*, outcomes show a growing external orientation between 2000 and 2005. Respondents maintain a broad network of external contacts, but:

- time spent on field contacts (with insurers, interest groups, etc.) increased
- time spent on governmental contacts (with politicians and civil servants) also increased.

A rise in field contacts and governmental contacts can be found in all sectors. Yet, executives of hospitals spend more time with insurers and – together with executives of organizations for mentally ill people – less time with politicians and civil servants than the others do, while executives of organizations for elderly care and home care and of organizations for disabled people invest a lot in politicians and civil servants. Executives of hospitals spend more time with professionals than others do, but less time with clients and employees.

Executives might seek support for their position in the *public debate*, for example, through participation in political parties, direct contacts with politicians and civil servants, participation in the board or a committee of sector organizations, and by mobilizing colleague executives and by using the media (more than one answer was possible). This question was newly added to the 2005 survey. The outcomes show:

- executives mainly participate in public debates through direct contact with politicians and civil servants and mobilization of like-minded colleagues.

With respect to participation in public debates, hospital executives are the least active. Executives of organizations for elderly care and home care are the most active in public debates about health care.

Executives have to deal with multiple internal and external stakeholders with diverse interests and expectations. Outcomes suggest external parties have gained importance. Much time is spent on managing relations and participation in diverse networks. It also appears public opinion is no longer a factor that can be neglected, though a comparison with the 2000 data is not possible on this matter. Nevertheless, outcomes do show executives spent more time on governmental contacts than before and actively try to influence politicians and the public, suggesting the work of health care executives has become increasingly '*political*'.

Conclusions

In this chapter we wanted to explore how the new entrepreneurial way of thinking has affected the perceptions and actions of health care executives and what sort of strategies are undertaken to combine innovations and legitimacy. We distinguished between two sorts of innovations: entrepreneurial innovations and institutional innovations. The latter type of innovations is especially interesting because long-lasting changes in health care call for innovations that connect old and new logics and that can provide legitimacy to new ways of organizing and operating. This means executives will have to *bend* rather than *break* existing institutional frames, by building on existing values and belief systems. We also looked for changes in executives' competences.

We conclude executives engage in both entrepreneurial and institutional innovations, and that in practice both innovation strategies mingle. Changes in size, structure and products indicate that between 2000 and 2005 many entrepreneurial activities took place, but also that executives adapt strategies to the specific field of action (subsector). Local and sector-specific circumstances, habits and traditions influence executives' perceptions and actions considerably. For instance, when executives were asked what is meant by 'entrepreneurship', the executives of the different types of organizations answer differently. Executives in elderly care and home care interpret entrepreneurship the most *economically*, executives of hospitals more *professionally* – in terms of 'stimulating professionals to innovate' and 'optimizing work processes'. It shows how executives reinterpret an abstract policy term such as entrepreneurship, by seeing it from prevailing institutional logics, and by matching it to local settings. In that sense, the intentional and radical nature of innovation strategies must not be exaggerated. Even 'real' entrepreneurial innovations are institutionally biased – they flow from and are softened by existing institutional surroundings. Besides a pre-occupation with change and entrepreneurial activities, executives put considerable effort in realizing support for new ways of thinking and working from a variety of internal and external parties, and in maintaining a favourable public image. Executives aspire an entrepreneurial role, and feel that to realize change a more business-like, entrepreneurial attitude is necessary throughout the organization. At the same time executives aspire more and more an intermediary role that binds internal and external parties. This double loyalty also shows in the way they are educated and trained. Executives combine long-standing experience in health care management with new business knowledge. Becoming a health care executive is preceded by an extensive process of socialization and education in health care and ample experience in managing health care organizations. Health care executives are *specialized* managers. Nevertheless, executives continuously seek to extend their knowledge, especially on matters of finance and business management. Not only executives' background but also their loyalties appear to be strongly related to their institutional roots. Despite all efforts to realize a more entrepreneurial way of thinking and working, most respondents' main priority is quality of care.

Further, we conclude the strategic space to operate and realize changes is more limited in organizations with high complex work processes and self-employed professionals. Executives of organizations for elderly care and home care appear to be the most entrepreneurially minded and institutionally active, and executives of hospitals the least. The latter are the least satisfied about the way they perform. They have more attention for professional affairs and less for external/political affairs and public issues/debates. It seems strong professional logics cannot only prevent existing institutional frames to break, but also to bend. In elderly care and home care entrepreneurial changes are more easily realized, but a break with traditions too, including the risk of long-term loss of legitimacy. We conclude, therefore, that thoughtful innovating in an institutionalized field such as health care requires the necessary 'diplomacy', which is so typical for steering networks, or 'management by negotiations', as Rhodes (2007, p. 1248) calls it. In daily practice this means executives have to act as liaisons: balancing between new and old stakeholders and between politically driven ambitions such as entrepreneurship, on the one hand, and prevailing institutional logics, full of local and sector-specific habits and traditions, on the other hand. Innovating in health care requires support from and dealing with professionals, as well as politicians, the media and the 'public' in general. As a result, the work of health care executives has 'politicized' too. Executives have to deal with many perspectives, parties, interests and issues, and are held accountable for many things they do not directly control.

In a situation in which old legitimacy grounds are falling apart while new ones are not yet clear, a strategy seems to be required of *'and ... and'*. Executives need to respect both established and new ways of thinking and working. They need to conform to new, output-oriented 'rules of the game', but simultaneously need to be careful not to lose other grounds of legitimacy. In order not to frustrate necessary innovations nor to harm legitimacy, the most appropriate strategy for executives may not be to act as an 'innovation hero' or 'champion' themselves, but as an 'innovation sponsor'. He motivates people for innovation, brings parties together, seeks support for innovations, but is also selective in adapting to external demands. The rise of entrepreneurship in health care is no clear-cut phenomenon. Entrepreneurship itself should be innovated.

Part IV
Discussion

10
An Innovative Public Sector? Embarking on the Innovation Journey

Victor Bekkers, Jurian Edelenbos and Bram Steijn

Introduction

Innovation in the public sector can be described as a learning process in which governments attempt to meet specific societal challenges, such as the fight against crime, the fight against rising sea levels or the fight against traffic congestion. The way in which governments are able to develop and implement new services, technologies, organizational structures, management approaches, governance processes and policy concepts in order to deal with these challenges touches upon the legitimacy of government. In the introductory chapter to this book, it was argued that many public innovations are aimed at creating meaningful and trustworthy interactions between government and society. The plea for an innovative public sector can, therefore, be understood in terms of the desire to create new and meaningful connections between government and society, while the incentive to embark on an 'innovation journey' refers to the desire to bridge the disconnection between government and society – a disconnection that is often described in terms of a lack of efficiency, a lack of quality or a lack of representation and participation. Therefore, the first question that is asked in this concluding chapter is how the contributions of the authors in this book can be understood in terms of 'lost connections and connective capacities'. The next section deals with this question.

Public innovation – as was argued in the first chapter of this book – differs in a number of respects from innovation in the private sector. Hence, it is important to take into account how the specific characteristics of the public sector – such as a lack of competition and the multi-rationality of policy problems that generate complicated trade-offs between values – influence the nature of public innovations processes, which very often tend to have an incremental character. This need to contextualize can also be framed in terms of looking at the 'milieux of innovation', in which different interdependent actors attempt to frame the need to innovate as well as how to innovate. Hence, the second question to be asked is how the specific characteristics and functioning of this 'milieux of innovation' can be recognized in the contributions that are gathered in this book. This question is picked up in Section 3.

The need for public sector organizations to innovate does not simply refer to the achievement of efficiency gains that is dominant, for instance, in reform ideologies such as New Public Management (NPM). In the end, successful public innovation deals with the question of whether governments are able to develop new services, new ways of working or new concepts that enable them to deal with the questions that society as a political community is wrestling with (Stone, 2003). These services, ways of working and concepts should, therefore, also be appropriate. Due to the political dimension of public innovation, it is not only important to look at the allocation of costs and benefits (which is referred to as the logic of consequence by March and Olsen, 1989) but also at the feasibility of the proposed innovations, which goes further than sheer efficiency and efficacy and encompasses other values such as political support, trust and being in accordance with the rule of the law. Hence, it is important to recognize that public innovations, due to their institutional embeddedness, also have to address the logic of appropriateness (March and Olsen, 1989). Therefore, the ways in which these two logics play a role in the assessment of the innovations must also be analysed. These were discussed in the previous chapters, and Section 4 of this chapter deals with this analysis.

Based on these comparative findings, Section 5 provides an outline of a research agenda that academics, but also policy-makers, should take into account when they want to embark upon an 'innovation journey'.

Innovations between lost connections and connective capacities

Chapter 1 argued that the public sector innovation challenge refers to the need for public sector organizations to be engaged in meaningful interactions with all kinds of actors in society, such as citizens, companies, interest and issue groups, and non-governmental organizations. These interactions take place in the context of a number of societal challenges that have a rather 'wicked' character, such as the fight against crime, the social quality of urban regions in particular, or the ageing of the population. These meaningful interactions are not given, but they have to be established. However, the tragedy is that a number of societal developments (such as globalization and individualization) and several political developments (such as liberalization and Europeanization) have undermined the possibility of establishing these meaningful interactions. This has been described in the introductory chapter in terms of lost connections. Hence, the innovation challenge of the public sector is to restore these lost connections or to establish new meaningful connections. This implies that the linking capacities of public sector organizations are an important asset in assisting with the development and implementation of public innovations. Hence, the first research question that this book deals with is: *How can public innovations be understood in terms of the need for linking capacities in order to create meaningful interactions between the government, the market and society? What answers to this question can be formulated, after looking at the contributions in this book?*

Pollitt has stated that innovation as such is not new but that it can be seen as one of many 'magic concepts' that policy-makers continuously use to demonstrate that governments are in an almost permanent struggle to show that they are willing and capable – through reforms – to be responsive to the changing needs of society. At the same time, Pollitt argues that the innovation track record of the public sector is quite impressive, if the focus is not solely on 'transformative innovations', based on the Schumpeterian model of 'creative destruction'. The search to establish meaningful interactions between governments and society requires a continuous and often *incremental* process of adaptation, which in the end might improve the legitimacy of government even more than more radical forms of innovation.

Fuglsang and Pedersen attempted to relate the discussion about public sector innovation to the ongoing NPM reform movement, which also attempts to reconnect government with society. However, from an NPM perspective, innovation is perceived as attempts to enhance the efficiency of the public sector. From this point of view, meaningful interactions between the government and society are defined as interactions that produce efficient, reliable and productive outcomes, which meet regulatory compliance measures. However, Fuglsang and Pedersen argued that this way of looking at innovations might frustrate the establishment of meaningful interactions. Innovations in the public sector take place in different ways as a response to various problems.

These problems, however, are not only challenges in terms of efficiency, productivity and compliance. This also influences the way in which the outcomes of public sector innovation should be assessed, and this is discussed in Section 5 of this chapter.

In the chapter by Kattel, Randma-Liiv and Kalvet (Chapter 4), an important addition is made to the recent literature about innovation. They convincingly show that in contemporary society, the administrative capacity within small states has become more important in order for them to survive the global economic competition in which the innovative capacity of an economy is of added value. The innovative capacity of these smaller economies has traditionally been defined in terms of the Washington Consensus. The emphasis in this Consensus is on both macroeconomic stability and open markets. The idea is that increased foreign investments bring in foreign competencies, know-how, linkages and increased competition for domestic producers that create more pressure to innovate. However, although the policies were successful in destroying outdated industrial capacities, they were ineffective in creating new capabilities and opportunities, whereas at the same time, the dependence of small economies on the international markets, of international productions and financial networks is high and thus fragile. Hence, for smaller states, it has become vital to build up their administrative capacity in order to survive the waves of global competition, thereby connecting these smaller states and economies to global and sustainable economic growth. Administrative capacity is defined as a set of relationships that determine governance rather than as a set of attributes attached to the instruments of government. In order to build upon this administrative capacity, many small states have looked at NPM as a useful concept to help them establish new connections with society. Paradoxically, Kattel et al. argued that NPM reforms have led to the opposite effects that have been quite visible in smaller states. As a result, the administrative capacity of the small states has changed, because (a) the governance structure has become much too dispersed, (b) the location of these governance resources falls outside the traditional Weberian and Westphalian boundaries of the state and (c) governance is transformed into meta-governance that focuses on the creation of a set of relationships. Hence, the effects of NPM reforms that aimed to stimulate connective capacities have led to the opposite: they have contributed to the emergence of broken connections. Also, the EU policies regarding these new smaller states had similar contradictory effects. On the one hand, they expanded market possibilities and provided access to larger pools of human and technological resources.

On the other hand, the innovation model that lay behind these EU policies asks from these smaller states policy skills for networking and long-term planning, which are not available. Hence, Kattel et al. argued that in order to build up administrative capacity to stimulate the innovation capacity of small economies, it is important that the government takes an active role in setting up relationships and in linking up the relevant private and public partners and their resources. In doing so, smaller states have a competitive advantage, since, due to their size, informal networks and personalism play a more important role than in larger countries. Hence, smaller states can profit from these networks in the exploitation of this advantage.

Traditionally, open competition has been viewed as a necessary condition for innovation, as shown in the introductory chapter. In keeping with this argument, public procurement is often defined as a necessary condition for the development and implementation of new products, services, technologies and so on in the public sector. A special kind of procurement is 'innovation oriented procurement', as Lember, Kalvet and Kattel have argued. In contrast to 'off-the-shelf' products, procurement for innovation involves procuring products that require additional research and development, which influences the innovative capacity of the providers. Hence, such procurements can be used to solve existing as well as emerging economic and social challenges, thereby helping governments to create more meaningful interactions with society (in terms of connective capacities). In doing so, the government can act as a technologically demanding first buyer by absorbing (in most cases financial) risks for products that are socially and ecologically in demand as well as by promoting learning, diffusion and adoption of these innovations. After looking at three types of innovation procurement projects in five Baltic and Nordic cities (Copenhagen, Helsinki, Tallin, Malmö and Stockholm), Lember et al. concluded that local governments can act as market creators to call for products that meet social needs. However, the case studies also showed that procurements for innovative solutions often fail; in these cases, all the initial attempts to purchase new solutions failed. However, the experience gained was later turned into successful results, often in relation to other social and economic needs and policy goals due to unintended spillover effects. The latter can be interpreted in terms of a shift in the innovation strategy: originally the local governments opted for a radical innovation, while later on and due to the problems encountered they opted for a more incremental strategy. Furthermore, the authors argue that a more cooperative and catalytic role played by the government (in terms of connective capacities) is needed instead of the role of buyer, thereby facilitating the inclusion of specific know-how to ensure that the innovation is more tailor-made, facilitating additional measures and providing proper funding to assist with the diffusion of the innovation.

Public innovation has an internal and external dimension to it. The external dimension refers, for instance, to the development of new services for citizens and companies or to the development of new concepts that help to reframe policy problems so that new approaches are made possible. Public innovation also has an internal dimension, as Lewis, Considine and Alexander showed in their contribution, in which they analysed the structure of advice and strategic information networks for politicians and bureaucrats in 11 local governments in the state of Victoria, Australia. They focused on the relationship between the existence of networks and the innovation process that takes place within the government. The notion of broken connections and linking capacities in order to understand public innovation can also be applied to intra-governmental networks, because it tells us something about the nature, the amount, the direction, the centrality and the intensity of the relationships between the relevant actors and the expectations that these actors have of the added value of the innovation. In their contribution, Lewis et al. showed that successful innovation inside government depends on the ways in which actors are able to link to one another and able to become engaged in meaningful interactions, which also tells us something about the functioning of these 'milieux of innovation'. The linking of people, resources and ideas takes place in free, new and informational spaces; spaces that transform themselves in specific local cultures that facilitate and stimulate interactions for innovation between various actors from the government, the market and society.

In the chapter by Voets and De Rynck (Chapter 8), the perspective on innovation changes again, that is towards the handling of societal challenges. These challenges can only be dealt with when governments are able to build up an innovative capacity that is defined as the ability to link up human creativity. Voets and De Rynck analysed how network management can help build innovative capacity to solve intergovernmental problems. Two case studies were examined, 'Project Gentse Kanaalzone' and 'Parkbos Gent' in Flanders (Belgium), to illustrate this. Voets and De Rynck concluded that the existence of the grey interaction zone stimulates innovation, as human creativity makes it possible to deal with the complexities of formulating issues and working towards their potential solutions. Network management helps to make intergovernmental relations multilateral and collaborative, and also helps to combine a wide range of policy issues (as opposed to bilateral intergovernmental transactions between governments). However, the development of these connective capacities can only flourish in a specific milieu, as described in the next section. Moreover, these capacities come forward in two vital activities of network management, namely boundary-spanning and boundary-scanning. Voets and de Rynck showed that these activities are being picked up and are being combined in different leadership roles. This is also discussed in the next section.

Innovation is at the heart of a complex Dutch railway project, called the 'RandstadRail'. This was analysed by van der Voort, Koppenjan, Ten Heuvelhof, Leijten and Veeneman. In Chapter 7, it can be observed that railway innovation is closely linked to a complex societal problem with mixed aspects – as with the fight against traffic jams, the modernization of the railways, urban and rural planning, the environment and so on – which creates a complex network of interdependent actors with different interests, views, know-how and other resources. The way in which the need to innovate is picked up and solutions can be implemented depends on the ability to connect various parties to one another, which also influences the management of this kind of project. In essence, the successful management of complex public innovation projects must link different values, while at the same time it has to balance them continuously. These values refer to the two logics that are central in this book: the logic of consequence and the logic of appropriateness, which are discussed in Section 4.

van der Scheer, Noordegraaf and Meurs looked at entrepreneurial activities in innovating Dutch health care. These activities should be understood as an ongoing process of change in health care systems; changes that attempt to establish meaningful interactions between the hospitals and other health organizations through the introduction of more market-based conditions. However, the concept of 'meaningful' is defined by health care managers as the creation of a more business-like health care system, in which market share, size, rationalization, cost and performance management, competitive position (price and quality) and leadership are important elements on the one hand, and the creation of new ways of thinking and working in order to retain legitimacy are important on the other. In order to achieve this, these ways of thinking and working have to respect the values and roles of health care professionals and their clients. In addition, this chapter shows that the innovation is primarily based on the idea of establishing new and more meaningful interactions between public sector health organizations and society. However, in the creation of the interactions, health care managers are caught between the logic of consequence and the logic of appropriateness. This is elaborated upon in Section 5. In terms of lost connections and connective capacities, van der Scheer et al. argued that the ambiguous environment in which these health care executives operate forces them to bridge and link the values and demands that can be derived from the logic of consequence as well as the logic of appropriateness.

What conclusions can be drawn from this comparison of contributions? First, it can be seen that the need to innovate is closely linked to the idea of establishing meaningful connections between government and society, gathered around societal challenges, which in many cases go beyond the desire to establish a more efficient government. Secondly, in doing so, the contributions show that the ability to link people, resources, knowledge and creativity is an important factor. In short, it is about *linking*. This implies that in order to develop and implement successful innovations, actors need to have the ability and the freedom to link to other actors, and invite them to embark on a joint innovation journey. Thirdly, several contributions showed that NPM as a modernization strategy does not stimulate actors to build up this linking capacity. It could even be argued that one of the undesired side effects of NPM is that, to some extent, it frustrates public innovation. More positively formulated, it only accentuates specific forms of public innovation. Furthermore, NPM defines public innovation from a government-centric perspective, while at the same time the contributions show that successful public innovations emerge from the interactions between government and society. At the same time, public innovations can only be implemented successfully in close interaction with both society and the market.

Public innovation milieux

It was discussed in Chapter 1 that a number of issues play an important role in the possibility to develop, foster and implement linking capacities. These issues have been described in terms of the existence of 'public innovation milieux', the emergence of policy networks of collaboration, the openness of these networks and the variety of resources (knowledge, experiences, people, information and contacts) and actors in these networks. The chapter also mentioned the role of the social capital that is present in these 'innovation milieux', the boundary-spanning role of leadership within and across these networks as well as the diffusion and adoption of new practices across organizational borders. Furthermore, when assessing the process and outcomes of public innovations, it is important to re-conceptualize the factors that are normally put forward in the private sector innovation literature as being relevant to innovation. It has been argued that the nature of public sector innovation has a more evolutionary than revolutionary character. Besides, it was argued that although the bureaucratic character of the public sector frustrates innovations, the dynamic and complex character of the public sector challenges, in which different rationalities and values have to be balanced, can stimulate innovation. Hence, it is important to establish what the roles of *'milieux of innovation' have been in the development and implementation of innovations in the public sector, as has been described in the previous chapters. What have been the relevant mechanisms, and how did the specific institutional setting of the public sector influence the functioning of these milieux?*

Pollitt argued that it is important to see public innovations in their context and that one should be critical of studies that attempt to grasp general and decontextualized models of how to increase the innovative capacity of governments. These studies are often put forward in more private sector-based studies on innovation. He argued that it is important to take a long-term view. It makes sense to look back at major public sector innovations of the past and see whether it is possible to identify any reasonable common denominator conditions that appear to be conducive to organizational and individual creativity. A more historic perspective also opens up the possibility of studying the more gradual and incremental sequence of changes and adaption which in turn, and looking back in the mirror, might lead to substantial transformations. Furthermore, in the way local organizations and individuals have exploited their creativity, at least two considerations should be mentioned. The first is, what are the risks that are at stake? Because many innovations do not work well, and even those that do work turn out to have additional, undesirable and unforeseen consequences, what are acceptable innovations, when looking at their outcomes? Hence, it is important in these 'milieux of innovation' to ask what the risk perception of the local actors who were involved has been. In order to manage these risks – and also in relation to the amount of public money that is spent on sometimes radical innovation projects which might end in failure – an implicit plea is made by Pollitt to embrace rather incremental instead of radical innovations and ambitious transformation strategies. The second consideration, which relates to the earlier one, is who of these local actors benefit from this call that government should innovate, what have been the motives for them to embark on an 'innovation journey' and how did they persuade other actors to also embark? What does this tell us about the quality of the organizations that have been involved, the kind of leadership that is shown and the partnerships in which these organizations have been involved?

Fuglsang and Pedersen argued that, in studying public sector innovation, there should be a move away from top-down and closed innovation models towards interactive and situated innovations. Hence, it is important to recognize the importance of employees in these 'milieux of innovation' and to seek interactions with them. Public sector institutions are employee-based institutions. Many employees must be able to respond to concrete and local problems in their daily work in order to deliver services that work in a proper and reliable way. Innovation strategies in the public sector should take this into consideration. This is an idea that is also put forward in theories about 'open system innovation', in which innovation is seen as an open and interactive process where many internal and external sources and ideas are brought in by many actors. Hence, Fuglsang and Pedersen argued, in keeping with Pollitt, that a contextual approach to public innovation should be embraced. The next question, however, is that given the specific context of innovation in the public sector, does it really differ from the private sector? In their view there are differences, but what the private sector and public sector have in common is that employees are the main source of innovation.

How does the idea of an 'innovation milieu' return in the contribution by Kattel, Randma-Liiv and Kalvet? In their chapter (Chapter 4), the idea of a national innovation system – as the network of institutions in the public and private sectors whose activities and interaction initiate, import, modify and diffuse new technologies (Freeman, 1987) – is questioned, because it is primarily focused on the production of codified scientific and technical knowledge regarding especially high-technology elements. In this system, no attention is paid to two interlinked elements: the administrative capacity of states and the size of these states. Kattel et al. argued that size matters in two different ways. On the one hand, the larger the size of a country, the more resources are available in terms of administrative capacity. This capacity can be used by governments to fulfil a linking role in the creation of close and cooperative relations between public and private institutions. A relatively small administrative capacity may frustrate this linking role. On the other hand, in a smaller state, informal networks and personalism in terms of social capital and 'milieux of innovation' fulfil an important role. That is also one of the reasons why some smaller states have an interesting innovation track record. From this point of view, a small size can be defined as a competitive advantage. At the same time, Kattel et al. argued that the government and international reform policies, in which an NPM reform ideology has prevailed, have contributed to the destruction of these informal networks due to their emphasis on de-personalization, the emergence of private monopolies due to incomplete privatization and liberalization and the lack of a critical mass of professional leaders, which are needed due to a dispersed governance structure (decentralization and deregulation).

Lember, Kalvet and Kattel have shown how five Nordic-Baltic Sea cities have attempted to use public procurement to achieve public innovations that meet the social and economic needs of these cities. In doing so, these cities have attempted to establish local 'innovation milieux' in which market solutions, which compete with one another, and additional research and development, may lead to innovative solutions, thereby meeting specific policy goals. How did these five local milieux function, when they were compared to one another? First, it can be seen that in the end, a more incremental than radical strategy that generates spillover and learning effects towards other policy sectors and goals, prevailed. Secondly, there was no correlation between the number of competitors and the success of the procurement initiatives. Thirdly, and related to the previous factor, the success of the innovation depended much more on the ability of these local governments to introduce supportive measures as well as to promote the diffusion as procurement itself. Hence, it can be concluded that as a general measure, public procurement itself is not enough, but that additional local and thus contextual measures are required. This also changes the role of government: instead of being a buyer, a more cooperative and catalytic role is needed. The latter also points at the necessity for conceptualizing public innovations in relation to the need to develop linking capacities. Fourthly, direct political support at the highest level is needed to add to the legitimacy of the project and to the procurement process itself. Fifthly, it is inevitable for governments to involve the know-how of external experts and consultants, because the city administrations involved do not necessarily have the required market and technological knowledge.

The topic of the importance of informal networks for innovation capacity is returned to in several other chapters, especially in Chapters 6–8. It can be seen that innovation in the public sector takes place 'in the shadow of hierarchy'. Innovation takes place in the grey zone between formal structures, in informal settings where public managers of different governmental bodies, societal organizations and private actors meet, without the burden of formal structures and rules ('what rules do we have to follow?'), formal positions ('who is responsible/accountable?') and power play ('who is in charge?').

Lewis et al. explored the overall structure of these 'milieux of innovation' from a social network analysis perspective. They focused on how network configurations around particular actors differ among politicians, senior executives and middle managers, as well as across various municipalities. Based on their study, Lewis et al. concluded that although structural (formal) positions in the network are considered important, the most important predictors of innovation are the network relationships of actors. Moreover, they found that managerial procedures (formal plans and structures) do not stimulate innovation at all. More importantly, innovators are those who are adept at working through relationships outside formal structures, for example in informal networks, in order to innovate. This is what Lewis et al. mean by the claim that innovation occupies a particular free institutional space. The researchers' most important finding is that innovation and innovators inhabit a specific kind of institutional space, defined in part by their structural position, but even more so by their place in informal actor networks. Not only do these spaces have a specific (virtual) location, but they can also be defined in terms of cultures. Lewis, Considine and Alexander mentioned the importance of specific *local cultures* inside government in which interactions for innovation between various actors in the government, the market and society emerge. Innovation is stimulated by networking, through contact with politicians from other governments and through contact with community sector peak organizations. Thus, active networking as an element of this culture is important for interactions between actors in loosely coupled network arenas.

In addition, the chapter by Voets and De Rynck (Chapter 8) stressed the importance of 'milieux of innovation' as 'grey interaction zones' in which creativity can be expressed in a free way and can be linked to each other. However, this linking presupposes network management. Network management contributes to intergovernmental capacity-building, for instance in terms of creating a web of social relations that can be used to exchange ideas or the availability of expertise across tiers. Voets and De Rynck found that the boundary-scanning and boundary-spanning activities of network managers are important for creating inter-relations between different kinds of actors. Voets and De Rynck used the five distinct roles discerned by Agranoff (2007), and argued that a mix of these roles creates the innovative capacity that is required to deal with contemporary intergovernmental challenges. These roles are that of vision keeper, creative thinker, network promoter, network champion and network operator. Public leaders must combine these roles; however, this is often too much for the ability of just one person. Hence, it is stated that this kind of leadership is not an act, but often an interaction on the part of different formal (official) and informal (unofficial) leaders in the network who are from the government, the market and society. The presence and successful combination of these roles contributes to intergovernmental capacity-building. In doing so, the joint management activities of network operators, network champions, network promoters, vision keepers and creative thinkers create intergovernmental cocktails that are not likely to exist otherwise.

From Voets and De Rynck, it can also be concluded that linking capacity benefits from a mixture of different management roles and styles. This is a striking element in the functioning of innovation milieux. This conclusion was also stressed by van der Voort et al. They concluded that the management of innovative projects requires a double management approach based on predict-and-control as well as prepare-and-adapt in managing innovative projects. A predict-and-control style is oriented on detailed terms of reference and a narrow task and goal definition; the prepare-and-adapt style is oriented on the development of more functional terms of reference and broad task descriptions. Where a predict-and-control project management style values controllability and the realization of early fixed goals, a prepare-and-adapt project management style stresses the values of flexibility, trust and learning. van der Voort et al. found that managers in the RandstadRail project did not use one approach but rather, a refined mix. In fact, one of the three guiding choices was inspired by predict-and-control; that was the unbundling and commercialization of the relations in the project. The other two guiding choices were inspired by prepare-and-adapt. The choice of management approach is heavily determined by the political conditions at the initiation of the project and not by some thought to respect one of the two competing values in innovative projects. The political momentum provides incentives to adopt functional terms of reference (prepare-and-adapt). Hence, as discussed in the next section, one specific characteristic of the milieu of public innovation is its political institutional embeddedness, which also influences the assessment of the innovation process and its outcomes.

van der Scheer, Noordegraaf and Meurs showed that the executives in Dutch health care organizations have been engaged in both managerial and institutional innovations. Local and sector-specific habits and traditions influence the executives' perceptions and actions considerably, although the emphasis on the strategies that have been followed varies. Some are more focused on managerial and economic benefits, especially in elderly care and home care; others are more focused on professional innovation, in terms of stimulating professionals to innovate and optimizing work processes. Confronted with either a dominant managerial or professional logic, executives adapt their strategies to the local settings in which they operate. van der Scheer et al. concluded that intentional and 'radical' strategies must not be exaggerated. In many cases, these kinds of strategies flow from and are softened by existing institutional surroundings. This is also based on data showing that executives put considerable effort into realizing support for new ways of thinking and working that stem from a variety of internal and external parties. In doing so, these executives aspire more and more towards an intermediary role that binds internal and external parties. Hence, in their contribution, the authors stressed the importance of studying public innovations in relation to the milieu in which they emerge. Besides, health care executives favour an incremental rather than a radical perspective on the development and implementation of innovation and change. Furthermore, the authors found evidence that a particular type of leadership – a key factor in terms of bonding and linking – has been aspired towards.

What conclusions can be drawn from this comparison of the findings of the chapters described above? The first is that context really does matter, which stresses the importance of studying the local and socially and institutionally embedded relations and interactions within a specific milieu as well as the importance of the role of politics, the logic of appropriateness and the public values within this milieu. In all the contributions above, references to this idea are made. This implies the use of a more ecological (Bekkers and Homburg, 2004; Thaens, 2006) and a complexity theory-oriented approach (Van Buuren and Edelenbos, 2004; Gerrits, 2009; Teisman et al., 2009) to studying public innovations. Typically in these approaches, attention is paid to the interactions and co-evolution of different environments, the values that are important in these environments, and the stakeholders who are dominant in these environments, in the framing and shaping of new innovations. Innovation approaches which do not recognize the importance of this context, its institutionalization – especially in comparison with the private sector – might fail or might produce outcomes which in the end are considered as unwanted.

A second conclusion refers to the informal nature of the 'milieux of innovation', where public managers and representatives of societal and market organizations meet as 'humans' and not as 'officials' or 'defenders of stakes'. In these spheres, people are less focused on defence, but more focused on development and creation. This finding is in keeping with other research findings. The informal spheres are 'open networks' in which the number and intensity of the interactions increase and lead to trustworthy relationships. Trust then leads to more information, experience and knowledge exchange between actors in the network, which again provide input into new directions and discoveries and in the end lead to more innovation capacity (March, 1999; Nooteboom, 2006; Edelenbos and Klijn, 2007). In these informal spaces, as described by Lewis et al. and Voets and De Rynck, spontaneous meetings of people who have not met before, and who would probably not meet in formal settings, emerge. These fresh and unexpected 'confrontations' lead to reflection and unfreezing, creating the ground for exploration, novelty and variety. However, the threat of creating informal, free and creative spaces is that the innovation is locked inside this free space and is not diffused to other spaces that are of a more formal nature. The danger is that innovative ideas and concepts stay within the niche and are not interconnected and unlocked to other arenas and systems. Implementation and follow up of strands of innovative ideas may not occur without proper embedding of the informal niches of innovativeness in formal processes, structures and procedures (Edelenbos, 2005). Both exploration in niches and exploitation in formal structures and organizations is needed in order to get innovation going (March, 1999).

A third conclusion that can be drawn is that the existence of free creative spaces can also be seen as the expression of the presence of social capital. These spaces can only be shaped if social capital within a specific sector is present, or if it can be developed. The importance of social capital, of informal personal and trustworthy networks as a reservoir of innovative capacity, was put forward in the contributions of Kattel et al., Lewis et al. and Fuglsang and Pedersen. Lewis et al. mentioned the networks and relations between actors that are also culturally embedded. Kattel et al. showed how the size of a state influences the social capital that can be exploited in order to become an innovative state, while Fuglsang and Pedersen stressed the importance of defining the employees (and their needs) as the social capital to be exploited in order to become an innovative government. However, in the formation and exploitation of this social capital, leadership plays an important role, as is argued later on in this section. At the same time, it is important to be aware of factors that might destroy this social capital. For instance, Kattel et al. argued that an NPM-based modernization strategy may frustrate the exploitation of social capital, but also that the dominant EU vision on innovation that lies behind innovation policies adds to this. However, this statement could be opposed in that although social capital is important, it is also important to look at the quality of this social capital to be exploited. Too much and too tight personal relationships could hamper integrity and could lead to corruption, because certain legitimate views and interests of specific 'outsiders' are excluded from the tight network.

A fourth conclusion refers to the nature of the innovation strategy that is dominant in the description of the innovation milieux. What is seen is that a rather incremental and evolutionary strategy is preferred. This is in contrast to more top-down and more transformative strategies. There may be several reasons for this. First, the need for a more evolutionary approach refers to the nature of many societal challenges, which can be described as complex and rather wicked. They are complex because many different but interrelated aspects are involved as is shown, for instance, in the cases described by Lember et al., Voets and De Rynck, and van der Voort et al. They are wicked because it is not quite clear what the relevant causes are, what the possible effects of possible strategies are and what criteria should be used to assess the wanted and unwanted effects. Secondly, due to the multitude of aspects of a complex network of actors, sometimes conflicting and overlapping interests are mobilized, which challenges the degree of support for the innovative approach that is put forward – support that might change as a result of the duration of many public innovation projects. How can these various actors be seduced to embark and to stay on a shared innovation journey? March (1999) has made a distinction between innovation as the exploitation of an idea and as an exploration of an idea. It may be argued that exploration, with its emphasis on communication and trial and error in order to create a process of shared understanding, favours a more evolutionary and incremental innovation approach. Thirdly, successful innovation strategies seem to mix different styles of leadership and different logics, and thus different values – values that refer to the logic of consequence versus the logic of appropriateness.

A fifth conclusion refers to the linking nature of the leadership that is required to develop and implement public innovation. Several arguments can be found in the different chapters of this book that point in this direction. The first argument refers to the boundary-spanning and boundary-scanning nature of leadership, which is required to link people, ideas and resources. Connective capacity becomes an important feature of managers in developing and realizing innovation. What these roles bind is that they are focused on managing relations between different sorts of actors (Robbins and Coulter, 2002). From the perspective of the five different but supplementary roles (as described above and more extensively in the chapter by Voets and De Rynck), boundary-spanners have their feet in multiple settings and go beyond simply scanning and monitoring the environment. They are linked internally to their formal home organizations (units, sectors), and externally to temporarily informal network arenas, and channel information, experience and knowledge between these structures. Boundary-spanners develop, gather and transfer knowledge, experience and information (Tushman and Scanlan, 1981). In this way, innovative intergovernmental cocktails emerge out of ingredients derived from different governmental tiers (e.g. local, provincial and Flemish resources), policy sectors (e.g. planning, economy, heritage, infrastructure) and policy instruments (e.g. constructions, subsidies, legislation), are drawn from the political and administrative realm (including political parties) and across the public–private divide (e.g. interest groups, companies). In public innovation, it is thus important that different boundaries are spanned. Boundary-spanning leads to variation and to the forging of interconnections among different actors with different views, values, knowledge and information. Boundary-spanning activities are beneficial for creating innovation in the public sector. The interconnecting capacity of people forming the networks and systems in the public sector is important for the development of innovative ideas and the spread of those ideas past the informal niche.

The second argument refers to the linking of actors in order to build an innovation network, or to shape an innovation milieu and to stimulate the development or exploitation of social capital in a network or milieu. This also influences the role of government.

The third argument refers to the linking of the political realm with the innovation project. Particularly in the analysis put forward by Lewis et al. of innovation networks in the Australian government, in the description by Lember et al. of procurement strategies in Nordic-Baltic Sea cities, in the chapter by Voets and De Rynck on Flemish innovation projects and in the analysis put forward by van der Voort et al. of the Dutch RandstadRail project, it can be seen that it is important to include the political realm in the project in order to enhance the project's legitimacy, to obtain and to maintain political support, to stabilize the flow of necessary (financial and other) resources and to mobilize the necessary contacts.

The fourth argument refers to the linking and balancing act between the values that are important in the logic of consequence (such as efficiency, effectiveness and compliance) and the logic of appropriateness (such as trust, support and legitimacy). This was demonstrated in the chapter by Fuglsang and Pedersen on innovation in the Danish public sector, the chapter by van der Voort et al. on the Dutch RandstadRail project and in the chapter by van der Scheer et al. that looked at innovation in the Dutch health sector.

However, when analysing the role of leadership, it can be seen that leadership is not only an open invitation in terms of linking. It is also important that linking is combined with protection. In order to have intellectual and creative safe havens, grey interaction zones and so on, it is important that leaders protect these safe havens and grey zones against possible disturbing external influences. In doing so, leadership is made important as a block buster. Leadership does not simply refer to promotion and the diffusion of innovation, but also refers to protection. This is a role that has not been put forward in the boundary-scanning and boundary-spanning roles discussed by Voets and De Rynck.

Caught between consequentiality and appropriateness

In Chapter 1, it was argued that public innovations – in terms of new products, processes, concepts and techniques that imply a discontinuity with the past – are always driven by and attempting to reconcile different values that go beyond sheer economic values such as efficiency and efficacy. Hence, in assessing public innovations, it is important to focus not only on the logic of consequence (stressing efficient and effective consequences of these new products, services, processes, concepts and techniques), but also to look at the appropriateness of these public innovations, thereby contributing to a legitimate and trustworthy public sector (March and Olsen, 1989). How can the process and outcomes of innovation in the public sector be assessed, given the need for the government to act efficiently and appropriately?

When looking at the outcomes of more radical innovations, Pollitt has asked the question of whether these innovations have been worth pursuing, especially looking at the amount of money that has been involved in contrast to the results that have been accomplished. How can politicians and other public office holders persuade the media and the public that a mismatch is acceptable? Again, in Pollitt's contribution, the implicit assumption is that a more incremental innovation strategy may increase acceptance of public innovation. He concluded that the appropriateness of an innovation, in terms of acceptance and trust, benefits from a more incremental innovation strategy.

Fuglsang and Pedersen also argued that the outcomes of public sector innovations should not only be assessed in terms of gains in efficiency, productivity or compliance. Respondents in their survey linked public sector innovation more to the quality of public services rather than to the efficiency of public services. This is not only because market pressure to perform efficiently is absent in Denmark, but also because citizens as users have been provided with more rights in terms of receiving better and more trustworthy services that better reflect and are more responsive to their needs. Innovations in services that focus on efficiency gains have a rather weak legitimacy. Fuglsand and Pedersen also pointed at another aspect, which is important for the acceptance of public sector innovations and has also been put forward in Pollitts' contribution. In their research, they referred to the innovation needs of public sector employees who have to respond to the concrete need to improve on quality and delivery. In doing so, these employees pursue innovation strategies of bricolage and tinkering in order to properly adjust the services they provide. However, due to their emphasis on control and standardization, NPM-based innovation initiatives that often have a top-down character may frustrate these 'trial and error' practices. Again, the appropriateness of public sector (service) innovations may be said to benefit from more incremental innovation strategies in which the emphasis is on quality rather than efficiency gains. Furthermore, Fuglsang and Pedersen argued that for policy-makers who are inspired by NPM, it is important to get involved in more employee-based and interactive innovation processes in which there is a balance between quality and efficiency.

The chapter by Kattel, Randma-Liiv and Kalvet (Chapter 4) on the innovation capacities of smaller states provided a warning against one-sided NPM-based innovation policies. In these policies a neo-liberal, macroeconomic orientation on the innovation capacity of a state is combined with a reform of the national state in which the 'logic of consequence' prevails. They argued that, although these NPM reforms, with their emphasis on efficiency, freedom of choice and accountability, are attempting to build up an administrative capacity that is required in order to become an innovative economy, the danger is that the opposite occurs: the importance of local informal networks and personnel contacts is being reduced.

In the contribution by Lember et al. on innovation-oriented procurement, it was shown that the logic of consequence is presented in the policy theory that lies behind this kind of procurement. Innovation-oriented procurement is seen as a way of stimulating innovation through the introduction of free and transparent market conditions that enable providers to compete for specific public sector solutions that meet specific social and economic needs against a reasonable price and quality. At the same time, Lember et al. showed that the creation of these market conditions is not enough: the innovations did occur but in another way and often in other sectors than was originally expected. Hence, their research showed that the logic of appropriateness plays an interesting role, but that this logic enters innovation-oriented public procurement programmes through the back door: re-shaping, learning and adaption is necessary. This also demands that the local authorities who are involved play a more cooperative and catalytic role. Moreover, they argued that in the assessment of innovations, the way in which these innovations meet societal needs should be taken into account instead of only looking at the legal conditions that guarantee a free and transparent procurement market. The first is more important than the second.

Although Lewis et al. addressed the relationship between the characteristics of social networks and intra-governmental innovation, their study also contained data on the normative views of the various actors in these networks. These views can tell us something about the ways in which innovations are assessed. The data showed that different people in different positions construct their own cognitive understanding of innovation and the values that play a role. Some politicians, more likely than bureaucrats, view innovation as something that involves large value changes in the community. However, Lewis et al. argued that there is no specific correlation between different groups and the assessment of different values that are at stake when assessing the approach and procedures followed in pursuing these innovative changes. However, one qualification has to be made. The structural position of politicians is fundamentally different from that of other positions. Being a politician is a significant predictor of innovator status. Hence, it can be cautiously concluded that politicians play an important role, which indirectly points at the relevance of looking at innovations that go beyond efficiency and effectiveness.

Public innovations that are caught between consequentiality and appropriateness were returned to in the discussion of the hybrid politico-administrative relationships that Voets and De Rynck described in their contribution. First, they showed that administrative officials such as project coordinators are at the heart of network management. Politicians seem to be in a more supportive position in such a way that ensures that the necessary political decisions are made. This political backup is needed to safeguard political support as well as to guarantee enough political trust in the goals and course of the projects. However, the proactive role of these administrative officials may lead to conflicts because they deploy activities that are political by nature, but which are necessary to safeguard the project. In order to do so, network managers develop a set of antennae that are 'political sensitive' so that not only the administrative but also the political realm can be scanned. The scanning of the political realm can, therefore, be interpreted as a way of scanning the appropriateness of the innovation, which goes further than looking at the sheer costs and benefits that are at stake.

van der Voort et al. stressed that the management of innovation is heavily structured by policy and politics. They stated that the innovation of the RandstadRail project is multi-layered and multi-embedded. These different layers developed different design and assessment criteria for the innovation project. The innovative project is legally, institutionally and technically innovative, which requires different modes of management (see above). On the one hand, there are values of legal innovation and some institutional innovations, which imply the decentralization of project management, safety regulations and standard settings. These innovations have their origins outside the project – they are instigated by a national policy trend (political momentum) to make more room for decentralized governmental organizations and local stakeholders. This also counts for the aspect of technical innovation – that is new interfaces between a variation of new and old technical systems. These requirements, demands and values are served by a flexible and tailor-made approach in which learning and adaptation is required. The logic of appropriateness of the local context is leading. On the other hand, the financing of the project, including the combination of the lump-sum funding with the turnkey contract for The Hague, provides incentives to steer on time and money, stressing values such as efficiency, controllability and predictability.

The evidence that van der Scheer, Noordegraaf and Meurs presented in their contribution on the role of health care executives in the development of entrepreneurial/managerial and institutional/professional innovations perfectly illustrates how health care innovations are caught between the logic of consequence – in terms of becoming more efficient, more business-like and more managerial – and the logic of appropriateness – in terms of developing new ways of thinking and working that help to improve the professionalism of the health care system. The legitimacy of the innovation strategies that these executives have conducted depends on attempting to meet the demands and values of both logics; although the emphasis varies with the specific sector in which these executives operate. At the same time, the authors argue that these executives have become more aware of the fact – also in their training – that they have to address both logics in order to be considered as a legitimate organization; this is certainly the case if the institutional and policy environment in which these executives function is rather ambiguous.

What conclusions can be formulated when looking at this comparison of results? Some recurring analyses are made in the contributions to this book. First, most authors showed that the nature of public innovation is more than simply developing and implementing innovations that contribute to the efficiency and effectiveness of the public sector. The solutions and approaches that these innovations put forward should also be appropriate, in a way that they are acceptable in the political climate and to the general public.

Secondly, and consequently, it is important to be aware of the one-sidedness in value orientation in the innovations that are proposed. Some authors have argued that the one-sided emphasis in NPM-driven innovations on the value of efficiency pushes aside other value orientations, which also limits the scope of interesting public innovations. At the same time, the opposite might be true. Innovations that only focus on public and political appropriateness, and do not take into account the need to be efficient and effective, might have a legitimacy problem. In their value orientations, public innovations should take into account the logic of consequence as well as the logic of appropriateness. At the same time, it is important to recognize that this balancing act is always contextual and shaped by the actors in the local innovation milieu.

Thirdly, it is observed that one reason why this logic of appropriateness is important lies in the role of politics. To some extent, this is not surprising if the words of March and Olsen (1989, p. 160) are taken into account: that politics is organized around the logic of appropriateness. The support that politicians provide to an innovation reflects the perceived contribution of the innovation to the handling of societal challenges that are on the political agenda. Political involvement does tell us something about the status of an innovation, as Lewis et al., Voets and De Rynck, and van der Voort et al. have also demonstrated.

Fourthly, it can be seen that due to the influence of the logic of appropriateness and the need to carry out a balancing act between different public values and different interests, in many contributions a plea is made for a more incremental and evolutionary innovation strategy. The public and political appropriateness of an innovation seems to be best suited to an incremental innovation strategy. This has at least two consequences. First, it presupposes the need to formulate a long-term and adaptive innovation strategy, which might be in conflict with the short-term orientation that is sometimes dominant in more top-down and transformative innovation programmes. Thus, public innovations require personal and institutional-adaptive capacity for the context of innovation. At the same time, it presupposes that politicians and policy-makers are able and willing to safeguard the functioning of the innovation milieu for a long time. This illustrates an interesting dilemma: on the one hand, durable political support is necessary; on the other, the political horizons of politicians and policy-makers have a short-term nature. Hence, it is important for the type of linking leadership that is required to bridge these two time horizons. This brings us to the second consequence that needs to be addressed, which is the style of leadership that is required. An evolutionary, adaptive and incremental innovation strategy, which requires support in the long run, does not require a type of leadership in which muscle power is demonstrated in order to achieve short-term and centrally imposed policy changes. Thus, public innovation needs a certain type of leadership, namely connective leadership.

Towards a new research agenda

This book has demonstrated that public innovations can and perhaps should be studied from the perspective of developing connective or linking capacities, which refers to several aspects and can be elaborated upon in different ways. They are not recalled here, as these aspects have already been addressed extensively in the previous sections. However, based on these findings, a number of relevant issues are sketched out that may be pursued by scholars of public administration and public management and that elaborate on the findings that have been put forward.

First, it has been stated that informal grey zones are required in order to develop innovations. However, what is known about these public innovation milieux? It would be interesting to have a closer look at the dynamics of these innovation 'milieux of innovation' networks. Hence, from a social network analysis perspective, not just the (meso-)structure of the innovation milieux but also the interactions that take place at the micro level are interesting. Which actors play what roles? What do these actors drive? Related to the motives and operations of these actors, it might be interesting to see how these actors attempt to balance private or organization(unit)-specific and public interests. How are these linked? There is also another important reason why this linking act is important. On the one hand, scholars point out that the social embedding of the relations and interactions – in terms of informal and personalized networks – is important in setting up and implementing innovation. On the other hand, what does this tell us about the integrity and openness of the public innovation milieux? Given the importance of personal and informal networks, how does this influence the content of the public interest? How is the public interest safeguarded?

Secondly, it is interesting to see how these informal grey zones are linked to the formal zones within public administration. Due to the emphasis on the creation of these grey zones, in which new ideas can be expressed, discussed and in which there is room for trial and error, it can be easily forgotten that the formal and institutionalized part of public administration also plays a vital role. It plays a role not just in terms of contributing to the creation of the conditions that lead to the emergence of these zones but also in relation to the adoption and diffusion of the innovations that are explored in these zones. Hence, it is important to see how the interactions and crossover between these informal and formal zones take place and what the vital mechanisms are.

Thirdly, many of the contributions to this book state that the development of linking capacities is vital. However, the use of capacities presupposes that people are able to develop these capacities. Hence, in observing the human resource management aspect of public innovation, it is interesting to see what competencies are required to fulfil various linking roles in different phases of the innovation trajectory, and how these competencies can be acquired and maintained,

Fourthly, several of the contributions saw that several layers of government were involved in the development and implementation of public innovation. Not only have the local, regional and national levels been mentioned but also the European level. Hence, it would be interesting to analyse in depth how these various levels are linked to one another, what kinds of crossovers occur, how they limit one another's discretion or how they might even contribute to the creation of innovation milieux. Therefore, the multi-level aspect of public innovation is a field that can be explored much further.

Last, but not least, the financial crisis that broke out in 2008 and the massive support that governments have provided to the financial sector and other economic sectors of society in order for them to survive have meant that governments in many western countries are now being forced to settle their accounts. In many countries, the government is looking critically at its expenditure in relation to the tasks that it performs. Cutbacks on operations and scrutiny of programmes are being conducted. At the same time, many governments define this moment as an opportunity to modernize the government and the public sector itself. In doing so, they are embarking on a new innovation journey. It is hoped that the insights put forward in this book can help them navigate through the stormy weather that lies ahead. Although there may be political and public pressure to explore and exploit transformative, top-down and efficiency-based innovation and modernization strategies, it is important to take into account the insights that have been presented in this volume: develop a robust, and thus adaptive and evolutionary innovation strategy in which the need to create a more efficient government is balanced by a government that is perceived to be trustworthy and legitimate in relation to the social challenges that lie ahead.

Appendix

Annex

Table A.1   Strategies for network management

	Game level	Network level
Strategies aimed at ideas/perceptions of actors	Covenanting Influencing perceptions Bargaining Development of common language Prevention of/introduction of ideas Furtherance of reflection	Reframing Changing formal policy
Strategies aimed at the interactions between actors	Selective (de-)activating Arranging Organizing confrontations Development of procedures Furtherance of facilitation, brokerage, mediation and arbitration	Network (de-)activating Constitutional reform: changing rules and resources (de-)coupling games Changing incentives Changing internal structure and position of actors Changing relations Management by chaos

Source: Kickert et al. (1997b), p. 170.

References

Abbott, A. (1997) 'Of Time and Space: The Contemporary Relevance of the Chicago School', *Social Forces*, 75 (4), 1149–1182.

Aberbach, J.D., Putnam, R.D. and Rockman, B.A. (1981) *Bureaucrats and Politicians in Western Democracies* (Cambridge, MA: Harvard University Press).

Abernathy, W.J. and Utterback, J.M. (1978) 'Patterns of Innovation in Industry', *Technology Review*, 80 (7), 40–47.

Ades, A. and Di Tella, R. (1997) 'National Champions and Corruption: Some Unpleasant Interventionist Arithmetic', *The Economic Journal*, 107 (443), 1023–1042.

Adriaansens, H. (1985) *Algemene Sociologie* (Den Haag: VUGA).

Agranoff, R. (2003) *Leveraging Networks: A Guide to Public Managers Working Across Organizations* (Washington, D.C.: IBM Endowment for The Business of Government).

Agranoff, R. (2004) 'Researching Intergovernmental Relations', *Journal of Public Administration, Research and Theory*, 14 (4), 443–446.

Agranoff, R. (2005) 'Managing Collaborative Performance: Changing the Boundaries of the State?', *Public Performance and Management Review*, 29 (1), 18–45.

Agranoff, R. (2007) *Managing Within Networks: Adding Value to Public Organizations* (Washington, D.C.: Georgetown University Press).

Agranoff, R. (2008) Toward an Emergent Theory of IGR Governance at the Dawn of the Network Era (Paper presented at the ASPA–EGPA 4th Transatlantic Dialogue), http://www.4tad.org/ws/paper_wks1_agranoff.pdf, 12–14 June 2008.

Albury, D. (2005) 'Fostering Innovation in Public Services', *Public Money and Management*, 25 (1), 51–56.

Altshuler, A. (1997) 'Bureaucratic Innovation, Democratic Accountability, and Political Incentives', in A. Altshuler and R. Behn (eds) *Innovation in American Government: Challenges, Opportunities, and Dilemmas* (Washington, D.C.: Brookings Institution).

Altshuler, A. and Luberoff, D. (2003) *Megaprojects. The Changing Politics of Urban Public Investment* (Washington, D.C.: Brookings Institution Press).

Amsden, A. (1989) *Asia's Next Giant: South Korea and Late Industrialization* (Oxford: Oxford University Press).

Amsden, A. (2007) *Escape from Empire: The Developing World's Journey through Heaven and Hell* (Cambridge, MA: MIT Press).

Argyris, C. and Schön, D. (1978) *Organizational Learning: A Theory of Action Perspective* (Boston: McGraw Hill).

Armstrong, H.W. and Read, R. (2003) 'The Determinants of Economic Growth in Small States', *The Round Table*, 92 (368), 99–124.

Arthur, B.W. (1994) *Increasing Returns and Path Dependence in the Economy* (Ann Arbor: University of Michigan Press).

Australian Bureau of Statistics (2001) *Census Basic Community Profile* (Canberra: Common Wealth of Australia).

Baccarini, D. (1996) 'The Concept of Project Complexity – A Review', *International Journal of Project Management*, 14 (4), 201–204.

Baker, K. (2006) The Contribution of Boundary-Spanning Individuals to the Development of a Strategic Service Delivery Partnership: A longitudinal UK Case Study (Paper presented at the ASPA-EGPA 2nd Transatlantic Dialogue), http://soc.kuleuven.be/io/performance/paper/WS3/WS3_Keith%20Baker.pdf, 1–3 June 2006.

Barber, B. (1984) *Strong Democracy, Participatory Politics for a New Age* (Berkely: University of California Press).

Barlow, J. (2000) 'Innovation and Learning in Complex Offshore Construction Projects', *Research Policy*, 29 (7), 973–989.

Barry, A. (2001) *Political Machines: Governing a Technological Society* (London and New York: Athlone Press).

Barzeley, M. and Gallego, R. (2006) 'From "New Institutionalism" to "Institutional Processualism": Advancing Knowledge about Public Management Policy Change', *Governance*, 19 (4), 531–557.

Bason, C. (2007) *Velfærdsinnovation – ledelse af nytænkning i den offentlige sektor* (København: Børsens Forlag).

Bass, B.M. and Avolio, B.J. (1994) *Improving Organizational Effectiveness Through Transformational Leadership* (Thousand Oaks, CA: Sage Publications).

Battilana, J. (2006) 'Agency and Institutions: The Enabling Role of Individuals' Social Position', *Organization*, 13 (5), 653–676.

Baumgartner, F. and Jones, B. (2002) 'Positive and Negative Feedback', in F. Baumgartner and B. Jones (eds) *Policy Dynamics* (Chicago: University of Chicago Press).

Beetham, D. (1991) *The Legitimation of Power* (London: Macmillan).

Bekkers, V.J.J.M. and Homburg, V.M.F. (2005) *The Information Ecology of E-Government* (Amsterdam: IOS Press).

Bekkers, V. and Homburg, V. (2004) 'E-government as an Information Ecology: Backgrounds and Concepts', in V.J.J.M. Bekkers and V.M.F. Homburg (eds) *The Information Ecology of E-Government* (Amsterdam/Berlin/Oxford/Tokyo/Washington: IOS Press).

Bekkers, V.J.J.M., van Duivenboden, H. and Thaens, M. (2006) 'Public Innovation and Information and Communication Technology. Relevant Background and Concepts', in V.J.J.M. Bekkers, H. van Duivenboden and M. Thaens (eds) *Information and Communication Technology and Public Innovation: Assessing the ICT-Driven Modernization of Public Administration* (Amsterdam/Berlin/Oxford/Tokyo/Washington: IOS Press), pp. 3–21.

Bekkers, V.J.J.M., Fenger, M.J.H. and Korteland, E. (2007) 'Governance, Democracy and the European Modernization Agenda: A Comparison of Different Policy Initiatives', in V.J.J.M. Bekkers, G. Dijkstra, A. Edwards and M. Fenger (eds) *Governance and the Democratic Deficit: Assessing the Democratic Legitimacy of Governance Practices* (Aldershot: Ashgate).

Bekkers, V.J.J.M., Dijkstra, A.G., Edwards, A.R. and Fenger, H.J.M. (2007) 'Governance and the Democratic Deficit: An Evaluation', in V.J.J.M. Bekkers, G. Dijkstra, A. Edwards and M. Fenger (eds) *Governance and the Democratic Deficit: Assessing the Democratic Legitimacy of Governance Practices* (Aldershot: Ashgate).

Bell, R. (1998) *Worst Practise* (New York: EAI).

Benedict, B. (1996) 'Problems of Smaller Territories', in M. Banton (ed.) *The Social Anthropology of Complex Societies* (London: Tavistock Publications), pp. 23–36.

Bessant, J. (2003) *High-Involvement Innovation: Building and Sustaining Competitive Advantage through Continuous Change* (Chichester: Wiley).

Binks, J. (2006) Using Public Procurement to Drive Skills and Innovation (A Report for the Department of Trade and Industry. Local Futures), http://www.berr.gov.uk/files/file28573.pdf, 16 December 2007.

Booker, C. (2004) *The Seven Basic Plots: Why We Tell Stories* (London: Continuum).

Borins, S. (2000) 'Loose Cannons and Rule Breakers, or Enterprising Leaders? Some Evidence About Innovative Public Managers', *Public Administration Review*, 60 (6), 498–507.

Borins, S. (2001) 'Encouraging Innovation in the Public Sector', *Journal of Intellectual Capital*, 2 (3) 310–319.

Borins, S. (2008) *Innovations in Government: Research, Recognition and Replication* (Washington, D.C.: Brookings Institution).

Botero, G. (1590) *Delle cause della grandezza delle città* (Rome: Vincenzio Pellagallo).

Brammer, S. and Walker, H. (2007) Sustainable Procurement Practice in the Public Sector: An International Comparative Study, http://www.bath.ac.uk/management/research/papers.htm, 16 December 2007.

Brandson, T., Van de Donk, W.P. and Montgomery, J.D. (1986) 'Bureaucratic Politics in South Africa', *Public Administration Review*, 46 (5), 407–413.

Bray, M. and Packer, S. (1993) *Education in Small States: Concepts, Challenges, and Strategies* (Oxford, NY: Pergamon Press).

de Bruijn, J.A., ten Heuvelhof, E.F. and in 't Veld, R.J. (2002) *Process Management. Why Project Management Fails in Complex Decision Making Processes* (Dordrecht: Kluwer Academic).

Brunsson, N. and Jacobsson, B. (2002) *The World of Standards* (Oxford: Oxford University Press).

Burns, T. and Stalker, G. (1961) *The Management of Innovation* (London: Tavistock).

Burns, J.M. (1978), *Leadership* (New York: Harper & Row).

Burns, T. and Stalker, G.M. (1996) *The Management of Innovation*, 3nd edn (Oxford: Oxford University Press).

Burt, R. (1992) *Structural Holes: The Social Structure of Competition* (Cambridge, MA: Harvard University Press).

van Buuren, A. and Edelenbos, J. (2004) 'Conflicting Knowledge: Why is Knowledge Production Such a Problem?', *Science & Public Policy*, 31 (4), 289–299.

Cabral, L., Cozzi, G., Denicoló, V., Spagnolo, G. and Zanza, M. (2006) 'Procuring Innovations', in N. Dimitri, G. Piga and G. Spagnolo (eds) *Handbook of Procurement* (Cambridge: Cambridge University Press).

Carlile, P.R. (2002) 'A Pragmatic View of Knowledge and Boundaries: Boundary Objects in New Product Development', *Organization Science*, 13 (14), 442–455.

Castells, M. (1996), *The Rise of the Network Society* (Cambridge: Blackwell).

Cave, J. and Frinking, E. (2007) Public Procurement for R&D, http://www2.warwick.ac.uk/fac/soc/economics/staff/faculty/cave/publications/pp_for_rd.pdf, 16 December 2007.

Chandler, A.D. (1990) *Scale and Scope: The Dynamics of Industrial Capitalism* (Cambridge, MA: Harvard University Press).

Chang, H.J. (2007) *Bad Samaritans: Rich Nations, Poor Policies, and the Threat to the Developing World* (London: Random House).

Chesbrough, H.W. (2003) *Open Innovation: The New Imperative for Creating and Profiting from Technology* (Boston: Harvard Business School Press).

Cimoli, M. (2000) *Developing Innovation Systems: Mexico in the Global Context* (New York: Continuum-Pinter Publishers).

Cimoli, M., Ferraz, J.C. and Primi, A. (2005) *Science and Technology Policies in Open Economies: The Case of Latin America and the Caribbean* (Santiago ECLAC), www.cepal.org, 16 June 2008.

Clarke, J. and Newman, J. (1997) *The Managerial State: Power, Politics and Ideology in the Remaking of Social Welfare* (London: Routledge).

Coleman, J.S., Katz, E. and Menzel, H. (1966) *Medical Innovation: A Diffusion Study* (New York: Bobbs Merrill).

Compagnon, J. (2001) *The Normandy Landings: The Strategic Victory of World War II* (Rennes: Éditions Ouest-France).

Considine, M. and Lewis, J.M. (2005) 'Mapping the Normative Underpinnings of Local Governance', in P. Smyth, T. Reddel and A. Jones (eds) *Community and Local Governance in Australia* (Sydney: UNSW Press).

Considine, M. and Lewis, J.M. (2007) 'Innovation and Innovators Inside Government: From Institutions to Networks', *Governance*, 20 (4), 581–607.

Considine, M., Lewis, J.M. and Alexander, D. (2008) 'Governance, Networks and Civil Society: How Local Governments Connect to Local Organizations and Groups', in J. Barraket (ed.) *Strategic Issues in the Not-for Profit Sector* (Sydney: UNSW Press).

Considine, M., Lewis, J.M. and Alexander, D. (2009) *Networks, Innovation and Public Policy: Politicians, Bureaucrats and the Pathways to Change Inside Government* (Basingstoke: Palgrave Macmillan).

Cooke, P. (1992) 'Regional Innovation Systems: Competitive Regulation in the New Europe', *Geofonwi*, 23 (3), 365–382.

Damanpour, F. (1991) 'Organizational Innovation: A Meta-Analysis of Effects of Determinants and Moderators', *Academy of Management Journal*, 34 (3), 555–590.

Dansk Center for Forskningsanalyse (CFA) (2005) *Forskning og udviklingsarbejde i den offentlige sektor: Forskningsstatistik Metode og datagrundlag* (Aarhus: Aarhus Universitet).

Dansk Center for Forskningsanalyse (CFA) (2006a) *Dansk erhvervslivs innovation 2004: del af den fælleseuropæiske innovationsstatistik – tabelsamling* (Aarhus: Aarhus Universitet).

Dansk Center for Forskningsanalyse (CFA) (2006b) *Innovation i dansk erhvervsliv: Innovationsstatistik 2002–2004* (Aarhus: Aarhus Universitet).

Dempsey, P.S., Goetz, A.R. and Szyliowicz, J.S. (1997) *Denver International Airport: Lessons Learned* (New York: McGraw-Hill).

Den Exter, A., Hermans, H., Dosljak, M. and Busse, R. (2004) *Health Care Systems in Transition: Netherlands* (Copenhagen: WHO).

Denis, J., Langley, A. and Cazele, L. (1996) 'Leadership and Strategic Change under Ambiguity', *Organization Studies*, 17 (4), 677–699.

Deutsch, M. (1973) *The Resolution of Conflict: Constructive and Destructive Processes* (New Haven: Yale University Press).

Dijstelbloem, H., Meurs, P.L. and Schrijvers, E.K. (2004) *Maatschappelijke dienstverlening, een onderzoek naar vijf sectoren* (Amsterdan: Amsterdam University Press).

DiMaggio, P. and Powell, W. (1991) 'The Iron Cage Revisited: Institutional Isomorphism and Collective Rationality in Organizational Fields', in W. Powell and P. DiMaggio (eds) *The New Institutionalism in Organization Analysis* (Chicago: UCP).

Dodgson, M. and Bessant, J. (1996) *Effective Innovation Policy: A New Approach* (London: International Thomson Business Press).

Dolewitz, D. and Marsh, D. (2000) 'Learning from Abroad: The Role of Policy Transfer in Contemporary Policy-Making', *Governance*, 13 (41), 5–23.

Dorado, S. (2005) 'Institutional Entrepreneurship, Partaking, and Convening', *Organization Studies*, 16 (3), 383–413.

Drechsler, W., Backhaus, J.G., Burlamaqui, L., Chang, H.J., Kalvet, T., Kattel, R., Kregal, J. and Reinent, E.S. (2006) 'Creative Destruction Management in Central and Eastern Europe: Meeting the Challenges of the Techno-Economic Paradigm Shift', in T. Kalvet and R. Kattel (eds) *Creative Destruction Management: Meeting the Challenges of the Techno-Economic Paradigm Shift* (Tallinn: PRAXIS Centre for Policy Studies).

Drucker, P. (1985) *Innovation and Entrepreneurship: Practice and Principles* (New York: Harper & Row).

Dunleavy, P., Margetts, H., Bastow, S. and Tinkler, J. (2006) 'New Public Management is Dead – Long Live Digital-era Governance', *Journal of Public Administration Research and Theory*, 16 (3), 467–494.

Dvir, D. and Lechler, T. (2004) 'Plans Are Nothing, Changing Plans Is Everything: The Impact of Changes on Project Success', *Research Policy*, 33 (1), 1–15.

Earl, L. (2002) *Innovation and Change in the Public Sector: A Seeming Oxymoron – Survey of Electronic Commerce and Technology* (Ottawa: Statistics Canada).

Earl, L. (2004) *An Historical Comparison of Technological Change, 1998–2000 and 2000–2002, in the Private and Public Sectors* (Ottawa: Statistics Canada).

Easterly, W. and Kraay, A. (2000) 'Small States, Small Problems? Income, Growth, and Volatility in Small States', *World Development*, 28 (11), 2013–2027.

Easton, D. (1965) *A System Analysis of Political Life* (London: Wiley).

Edelenbos, J. (2005) 'Institutional Implications of Interactive Governance: Insights from Dutch Practice', *Governance*, 18 (1), 111–134.

Edelenbos, J. and Klijn, E.H. (2006) 'Managing Stakeholder Involvement in Decision Making: A Comparative Analysis of Six Interactive Processes in the Netherlands', *Journal of Public Administration Research and Theory*, 16 (3), 417–446.

Edelenbos, J. and Klijn, E.H. (2007) 'Trust in Complex Decision-Making Networks: A Theoretical and Empirical Exploration', *Administration and Society*, 39 (1), 25–50.

Edler, J., Rufland, S., Hafner, S., Rigby, J., Georghiou, G., Hommen, L., Rolfstam, M., Edquist, C., Tsipouri, L. and Papadakou, M. (2005) *Innovation and Public Procurement: Review of Issues at Stake. Study for the European Commission* (Fraunhofer Institute Systems and Innovation Research).

Edler, J. (2006) Demand Oriented Innovation Policy (Paper presented at the ProACT Conference), http://inderscience.metapress.com/app/home/

contribution.asp?referrer=parent&backto=issue,11,14;journal,5,121; linkingpublicationresults,1:110891,1, 15–17 March 2006.

Edler, J. and Georghiou, L. (2007) 'Public Procurement and Innovation: Resurrecting the Demand Side', *Research Policy,* 36 (7), 949–963.

Edquist, C. and Hommen, L. (2000) 'Public Technology Procurement and Innovation Theory', in C. Edquist, L. Hommen, and L. Tsipouri (eds) *Public Technology Procurement and Innovation* (Norwell: Kluwer Academic).

Edquist, C., Hommen, L. and Tsipouri, L. (2000) *Public Technology Procurement and Innovation* (Dordrecht: Kluwer Academic Publishers).

Edquist, C. (2005) 'Systems of Innovation: Perspectives and Challenges', in J. Fagerberg, D. Mowery, R.R. Nelson (eds) *Oxford Handbook of Innovation* (Oxford: Oxford University Press).

Edquist, C. and Hommen, L. (2008) *Small Economy Innovation Systems: Comparing Globalization, Change, and Policy in Asia and Europe* (Cheltenham: Edward Elgar).

European Commission Expert Group (ECEG) (2005) Public Procurement for Research and Innovation: Developing Procurement Practices Favourable to R&D and Innovation, http://europa.eu.int/invest-in-research/pdf/'report_public_procurement_research_innovation_en.pdf, 16 December 2007.

European Commission Working Group (ECWG) (2006) Pre-Commercial Procurement of Innovation: A Missing Link in the European Innovation Cycle, http://ec.europa.eu/information_society/research/key_docs/documents/procurement.pdf, 16 December 2007.

European Union (2000), Parliament Website, http://www.europarl.europa.eu/summits/lis1_en.htm, 23 March 2000.

European Union (2006–2007) Policy Trends and Appraisal Report, http://www.proinno-europe.eu/trendchart 2006–2007, 13 March 2008.

Evans, B., Ruschemeijer, D. and Skocpol, T. (1985) *Bringing the State Back In* (Cambridge: Cambridge University Press).

Evans, P.B. and Rauch, J. (1999) 'Bureaucracy and Growth: A Cross-National Analysis of the Effects of Weberian State Structures on Economic Growth', *American Sociological Review,* 64 (5), 748–765.

Exton, R. (2008) 'The Entrepreneur: A New Breed of Health Service Leader?', *Journal of Health Organization and Management,* 22 (3), 208–222.

Fagerberg, J., Mowerey, D. and Nelson, R. (2005) *The Oxford Handbook of Innovation* (Oxford: Oxford University Press).

Ferlie, E., Lynn L. Jr. and Pollitt, C. (2005) 'Afterword', in E. Ferlie, L. Lynn Jr. and C. Pollitt (eds) *The Oxford Handbook of Public Management* (Oxford: Oxford University Press).

Ferrand, A. (1997) *Arromanches: History of a Harbour: Mulberry Harbour* (Cully: OREP Publications).

Floricel, S. and Miler, R. (2001) 'Strategizing for Anticipated Risks and Turbulence in Large-Scale Engineering Projects', *International Journal of Project Management,* 19 (8), 445–455.

Flyvbjerg, B., Bruzelius, N. and Rothengatter, W. (2003) *Megaprojects and Risks. An Anatomy of Ambition* (Cambidge: Cambridge University Press).

Frederickson, H.G. (2005) 'Whatever Happened to Public Administration? Governance, Governance Everywhere', in E. Ferlie (ed.) *The Oxford Handbook of Public Management* (Oxford: Oxford University Press).

Freeman, C. (1987) *Technology, Policy, and Economic Performance: Lessons from Japan* (London: Pinter).

Freemna, C. (1991) 'Networks of Innovators', *Research Policy*, 20 (5), 499–514.

Frissen, P. (1999) *Politics, Governance and Technology* (Cheltenham: Edward Elgar).

Fuglsang, L. (2008a) 'Balancen mellem bricolage og innovation: ledelsesdilemmaer i bæredygtig offentlig innovation', *Paper read at Det Danske Ledelsesakademis 3. Konference* (Clarion Hotel: København).

Fuglsang, L. (2008b) *Innovation and the Creative Process: Towards Innovation with Care* (Cheltenham and Northampton, MA: Edward Elgar).

Fuglsang, L., Højland, J. and Pedersen, J.S. (2008) 'Public Innovation with Care: A Quantitative Approach', in L. Fuglsang (ed.) *Innovation and the Creative Process. Towards Innovation with Care* (Cheltenham and Northampton, MA: Edward Elgar).

Fukuyama, F. (1995) *Trust* (London: Hamish Hamilton).

Galbraith, J.R. (2004) 'Designing the Innovating Organization', in K. Starkey, S. Tempest and A. McKinlay (eds) *How Organizations Learn*, 2nd edn (London: Thomson).

Gallagher, K.P. and Zarsky, L. (2007) *The Enclave Economy: Foreign Investment and Sustainable Development in Mexico's Silicon Valley* (Cambridge, MA: MIT Press).

Gallouj, F. and Weinstein, O. (1997) 'Innovation in Services', *Research Policy*, 26 (4–5), 537–556.

Geroski, P.A. (1990) 'Procurement Policy as a Tool of Industrial Policy', *International Review of Applied Economics*, 4 (2), 182–198.

Gerrits, L.M. (2009) *The Gentle Art of Coevolution* (Rotterdam: Optima Grafische Communicatie).

Giuliani, E., Pietrobelli, C. and Rabellotti, R. (2005) 'Upgrading in Global Value Chains: Lessons from Latin American Clusters', *World Development*, 33 (4), 549–573.

Goodwin, N. (2006) *Leadership in Health Care: A European Perspective* (London: Routledge).

Granovetter, M. (1973) 'The Strength of Weak Ties', *American Journal of Sociology*, 78 (6), 1360–1380.

Greve, C. (2008) *Konkurrence – og offentlig service* (København: FTF Dokumentation, NR).

van der Grinten, T. and Kasdorp, J. (1999) *25 jaar sturing in de gezondheidszorg: van verstatelijking naar ondernemerschap* (Den Haag: SCP).

Grit, K. and Meurs, P. (2005) *Verschuivende verantwoordelijkheden: Dilemma's van zorgbestuurders* (Assen: Koninklijke Van Gorcum).

Habermas, J. (1987) *Theorie des kommunikativen Handels* (Frankfurt am. Main: Suhrkamp).

Hall, P. (1993) 'Policy Paradigms, Social Learning and the State', *Comparative Politics*, 25 (3), 275–296.

Hall, P. (1999) *Cities in Civilization: Culture, Innovation, and Urban Order* (London: Phoenix).

Hartley, J. (2005) 'Innovation in Governance and Public Services: Past and Present', *Public Money and Management*, 25 (1), 27–34.

Helderman, J.K., Schut, E., Van der Grinten, T. and Van de Ven, W. (2005) 'Market-Oriented Health Care Reforms and Policy Learning in the Netherlands', *Journal of Health Politics, Policy and Law*, 30 (1–2), 189–209.

Helderman, J.K. (2007) *Bringing the Market Back In? Institutional Complementarity and Hierarchy in Dutch Housing and Health-Care* (Rotterdam: Erasmus University Rotterdam).

ten Heuvelhof, E., Koppenjan, J.F.M., Broekhans, B., Leijten, M., Veeneman, W. and van der Voort, H. (2008) *Het RandstadRailproject: Lightrail, Zware Opgave. Onafhankelijk onderzoek Randstadrail Haagse Deel* (The Netherlands: Stadsgewest Haaglanden).

von Hippel, E. (1976) 'The Dominant Role of Users in the Scientific Instrument Innovation Process', *Research Policy*, 5 (3), 212–239.

von Hippel, E. (1988) *The Sources of Innovation* (Oxford: Oxford University Press).

von Hippel, E. (2005) *Democratizing Innovation* (Cambridge, MA: MIT Press).

Högselius, P. (2005) *The Dynamics of Innovation in Eastern Europe: Lessons from Estonia* (Cheltenham: Edward Elgar).

Hood, C.H. (1995) 'Contemporary Public Management: A New Global Paradigm', *Public Policy and Administration*, 10 (2), 104–117.

Huxham, C. and Vangen, S. (2005) *Managing to Collaborate: The Theory and Practice of Collaborative Advantage* (London: Routledge).

Ingebritsen, C., Neumann, I., Gstöhl, S. and Beyer, J. (2006) *Small States in International Relations* (Seattle: University of Washington Press).

Jayasuriya, K. (2005) 'Capacity Beyond the Boundary: New Regulatory State, Fragmentation, and Relational Capacity', in M. Pinter and J. Pierre (eds) *Challenges to State Policy Capacity: Global Trends and Comparative Perspectives* (Basingstoke: Palgrave Macmillan).

Jemison, D.B. (1984) 'The Importance of Boundary Spanning Roles in Strategic Decision-Making', *Journal of Management Studies*, 21 (2), 131–152.

Jensen, M.B., Johnson, B., Lorenz, E. and Lundvall, B.A. (2007) 'Forms of Knowledge and Modes of Innovation', *Research Policy*, 36 (5), 680–693.

Jones, O. and Beckinsale, M. (1999) Analyzing the Innovation Process: Networks, Micropolitics and Structural Change (Research *Paper 9919*), http://www.abs. aston.ac/UK, 16 December 2007.

Kalvet, T. (2004) 'The Estonian ICT Manufacturing and Software Industry: Current State and Future Outlook' (Seville: Institute for Prospective Technological Studies-Directorate General Joint Research Centre, European Commission).

Kanter, R. (1985) *The Change Makers* (London: Unwin).

Katzenstein, P.J. (1985) *Small States in World Markets: Industrial Policy in Europe* (Ithaca, NY: Cornell University Press).

Kay, A. (2006) *The Dynamics of Public Policy: Theory and Evidence* (Cheltenham: Edward Elgar).

Keegan, A. and Turner, J.R. (2002) 'The Management of Innovation in Project-Based Firms', *Long Range Planning*, 35 (4), 367–388.

Kelman, S. (2008) 'The "Kennedy School School" of Research on Innovation in Government', in S. Borins (ed.) *Innovations in Government: Research, Recognition and Replication* (Washington, D.C.: Brookings Institution).

van Kersbergen, K. and Van Waarden, F. (2001) *Shifts in Governance: Problems of Legitimacy and Accountability* (Den Haag: NOW).

van Kersbergen, K. and van Waarden, F. (2004) ' "Governance" as a Bridge Between Disciplines: Cross-Disciplinary Inspiration Regarding Shifts in

Governance and Problems of Governability, Accountability and Legitimacy', *European Journal of Political Research*, 43 (2), 143–171.

Kickert, W.J.M. and Koppenjan, J.F.M. (1997) 'Public Management and Network Management: An Overview', in W.J.M. Kickert, E.H. Klijn and J.F.M. Koppenjan (eds) *Managing Complex Networks* (London: Sage Publications).

Kickert, W.J.M., Klijn, E.H. and Koppenjan, J.F.M. (1997a) 'Managing Networks in the Public Sector: Findings and Reflections', in W.J.M. Kickert, E.H. Klijn and J.F.M. Koppenjan (eds) *Managing Complex Networks. Strategies for the Public Sector* (London: Sage Publications).

Kickert, W.J.M., Klijn, E.H. and Koppenjan, J.F.M. (1997b) *Managing Complex Networks: Strategies for the Public Sector* (London: Sage Publications), pp. 35–61.

Kingdon, J.W. (1995) *Agendas, Alternatives and Public Policies*, 2nd edn (New York: Harper).

Kirby, E. (2006) 'The Impact of Competition on the Importance of Conforming to Social Norms: Strategies for Managed Care Organizations', *Journal of Health Organization and Management*, 20 (2), 115–129.

Kirkpatrick, I. and Ackroyd, S. (2003) 'Transforming the Professional Archetype?', *Public Management Review*, 5 (4), 511–531.

Klijn, E.H. (1996) 'Analyzing and Managing Policy Processes in Complex Networks: A Theoretical Examination of the Concept Policy Networks and Its Problems', *Administration and Society*, 289 (1), 90–119.

Klijn, E.H. and Teisman, G.R. (1997) 'Strategies and Games in Networks', in W.J.M. Kickert, E.H. Klijn and J.F.M. Koppenjan (eds) *Managing Complex Networks. Strategies for the Public Sector* (London: Sage Publications).

Klijn, E.H., Edelenbos, J. and Steijn, B. (2010) 'Trust in Governance Networks; Its Impacts on Outcomes', *Administration and Society*, 42 (2), 193–221.

Kline, S.J. and Rosenberg, N. (1986) 'An Overview of Innovation', in R. Landau and N. Rosenberg (eds) *The Positive Sum Strategy: Harnessing Technology for Economic Growth* (Washington, D.C.: The National Academies Press).

Knoke, D. (1990) *Political Networks: The Structural Perspective* (New York: Cambridge).

Koch, P., Cunningham, P., Schwabsky, N. and Hauknes, J. (2005) *Innovation in the Public Sector: Summary and Policy Recommendations* (Oslo: Publin Report No. D24, NIFU STEP).

Kondratiev, N. (1998a) 'The Concepts of Economic Statics, Dynamics, and Conjuncture (1924)', in N. Makasheva, W. J. Samuels and V. Barnett (eds), S. Wilson (trans.) *The Works of Nikolai D. Kondratiev* (London: Pickering and Chatto).

Kondratiev, N. (1998b) 'Long Cycles of Economic Conjuncture (1926)', in N. Makasheva, W. J. Samuels and V. Barnett (eds), S. Wilson (trans.) *The Works of Nikolai D. Kondratiev* (London: Pickering and Chatto).

Koppenjan, J. and Klijn, E.H. (2004) *Managing Uncertainties in Networks: A Network Approach to Problem Solving and Decision Making* (London: Routledge).

Korteland, E.H. and Bekkers, V.J.J.M. (2007) 'Diffusion of E-government Innovations in the Dutch Public Sector: The Case of Digital Community Policing', *Information Polity*, 12 (3), 139–150.

Korteland, E. and Bekkers, V. (2008) 'Diffusion and Adoption of Electronic Service Delivery Innovations in Dutch E-policing', *Public Management Review*, 10 (1), 71–88.

Kregel, J.A. (2004) External Financing for Development and International Financial Instability (G-24 Discussion Paper United Nations Conference on Trade and Development), http://www.unctad.org/en/docs/gdsmdpbg2420048_en.pdf, 2004, 16 June 2008.

Kregel, J. and Burlamaqui, L. (2006) *Finance, Competition, Instability, and Development Microfoundations and Financial Scaffolding of the Economy* (Tallin: The Other Canon Foundation and Tallinn University of Technology Working Papers in Technology Governance and Economic Dynamics, TTU Institute of Humanities and Social Sciences).

Kregel, J.A. (2008a) The Discrete Charm of the Washington Consensus (The Levy Economics Institute of Bard College Working Paper), http://www.levy.org/pubs/wp_533.pdf, 16 June 2008.

Kregel, J.A. (2008b) Financial Flows and International Imbalances: The Role of Catching Up by Late-Industrializing Developing Countries (The Levy Economics Institute of Bard College Working Paper), http://www.levy.org/pubs/wp_528.pdf, 16 June 2008.

KREVI (2008) *Kommunale kontrakter i overblik. En kortlægning af intern kontraktstyringspraksis i kommunerne* (Århus: KREVI).

Krugman, P. (2008) Trade and Wage, Reconsidered (Woodrow Wilson School of Public and International Affairs), http://www.princeton.edu/~ pkrugman/pkbpea-draft.pdf, 16 June 2008.

Kundera, M. (2007) 'Die Weltliteratur', *New Yorker*, 8 (7), 28–35.

Kurki, M. (2008) *Causation in International Relations: Reclaiming Causal Analysis, Cambridge* (Cambridge: Cambridge University Press).

Kwak, Y. (2005) 'A Brief History of Project Management', in E.G. Carayannis, Y. Kwak and F.T. Anbari (eds) *The Story Of Managing Projects: An Interdisciplinary Approach* (Westport, Conn.: Praeger Publishers).

Landes, D.S. (1999) *The Wealth and Poverty of Nations: Why Some Are So Rich and Some So Poor?* (New York: Norton).

Laumann, E. and Knoke, D. (1987) *The Organizational State: Social Choice National Policy Domains* (Madison: University of Wisconsin Press).

Lawton, A. (2005) 'Public Service Ethics in a Changing World', *Futures*, 37 (2/3), 231–243.

Leca, B. and Naccache, P. (2006) 'A Critical Realist Approach to Institutional Entrepreneurship', *Organization*, 13 (5), 627–651.

Leifer, R. and Delbecq, A. (1978) 'Organizational/Environmental Interchange: A Model of Boundary Spanning Activity', *The Academy of Management Review*, 3 (1), 40–50.

Leife, R. and Huber, G.P. (1977) 'Relations among Perceived Environmental Uncertainty, Organization Structure, and Boundary-Spanning Behaviour', *Administrative Science Quarterly*, 22, 235–247.

Lewis, J.M. (2005) *Health Policy and Politics: Networks, Ideas and Power* (Melbourne: IP Communications).

Lewis, J.M. (2006) 'Being Around and Knowing the Players: Networks of Influence in Health Policy', *Social Science and Medicine*, 62 (9), 2125–2136.

Lin, N. (2001) *Social Capital: A Theory of Social Structure and Action* (Cambridge: Cambridge University Press).

Lindblom, C.H. (1959) 'The Science of Muddling Through', *Public Administration Review*, 19 (2), 79–88.

Loughlin, J. (2007) 'Reconfiguring the State: Trends in Territorial Governance in European States', *Regional and Federal Studies*, 17 (4), 385–404.

Loureiro, G. and Curran, R. (2007) *Complex Systems Concurrent Engineering; Collaboration, Technology Innovation and Sustainability* (London: Springer).

Lowenthal, D. (1987) 'Social Features', in C. Clarke and T. Payne (eds) *Politics, Security, and Development in Small States* (London: Allen & Unwin).

Lowndes, V. and Skelcher, C.K. (1998) 'The Dynamics of Multi-Organizational Partnerships: An Analysis of Changing Modes of Governance', *Public Administration*, 76 (2), 313–333.

Lubanski, N. (2007) 'Rammerne om og styringen af institutionerne', in J.S. Pedersen (ed.) *Ledelse i en refortid i velfærdsstatens maskinrum* (København: Danmarks Forvaltningshøjskoles Forlag).

Luhmann, N. (1984) *Soziale Systemen. Grundrisse einer algemeinen Theorie* (Frankfurt: Suhrkamp 4).

Lundin, R. and Söderholm, A. (1995) 'A Theory of the Temporary Organization', *Scandinavian Journal of Management*, 11 (4), 437–455.

Lundvall, B.A. (1988) 'Innovation As an Interactive Process: From User-Producer Interaction to the National System of Innovation', in G. Dosi, C. Freeman, R. Nelson, G. Silverberg and L. Soete (eds) *Technical Change and Economic Theory* (London: Pinter).

Lundvall, B.A. (1992) *National Innovation Systems: Towards a Theory of Innovation and Interactive Learning* (London: Pinter).

Lundvall, B.A. (1993) 'Explaining Interfirm Cooperation; Limits of the Transaction-Cost Approach', in R.F. Graebner (ed.) *The Embedded Firm; Understanding Networks Actors, Resources and Processes in Interfirm Cooperation* (London: Routledge).

Lundvall, B.A. (1995) 'Introduction', in B.A Lundvall (ed.) *National Systems of Innovation: Towards a Theory of Innovation and Interactive Learning*, 2nd edn (London: Pinter).

Luton, L. (2008) 'Beyond Empiricists versus Postmodernists', *Administration and Society*, 40 (2), 211–219.

Lynn, L. Jr., Heinrich, C. and Hill, C. (2008) 'The Empiricist Goose Has Not Been Cooked!', *Administration and Society*, 40 (1), 104–109.

Mannheim, K. (1980) *Man and Society in an Age of Reconstruction* (London: Routlege).

March, J.G. and Simon, H.A. (1958) *Organizations* (New York: John Wiley).

March, J.G. and Olsen, J.P. (1989) *Rediscovering Institutions* (New York: The Free Press).

March, J.G. (1999) *The Pursuit of Organizational Intelligence* (Oxford: Blackwell).

Martin, J. (2000) 'Economic and Community Development Through Innovative Local Government', *Sustaining Regions* 1 (1), 1–12.

Maskell, P. (2000) 'Social Capital, Innovation and Competiveness', in S. Baron, J. Field and T. Schuller (eds) *Social Capital: Critical Perspectives* (Oxford: Oxford University Press).

Mayntz, R. (1987) 'Politische Steuerung und gesellschaftliche Steuerungsprobleme', in T. Ellwein (ed.) *Jahrbuch zur Staats- und Verwaltungswissenschaft* (Band: Baden-Baden).

McDaniel, B. (2002) *Entrepreneurship and Innovation. An Economic Approach* (New York: Sharpe).

Miller, R. and Floricel, S. (2000) 'Building Governability Into Project Structures', in R. Miller and D. Lessard (eds) *The Strategic Management of Large Engineering Projects: Shaping Institutions, Risks and Governance* (Boston Mass: MIT Press).

Mintrom, M. and Vergari, S. (1998) 'Policy Networks and Innovation Diffusion: The Case of State Education Reform', *The Journal of Politics*, 60 (1), 126–148.

Mjoset, L. (2000) The Nordic Economies 1945–1980 (ARENA Working Paper Series Nr 6), http://www.arena.uio.no/publications/wp00_6.htm, 16 June 2008.

Moon, M.J. (2002) 'The Evolution of E-Government among Municipalities: Rhetoric or Reality?,' *Public Administration Review*, 62 (4), 424–433.

Moore, M. (1995) *Creating Public Value: Strategic Management in Government* (Cambridge, Massachusetts, London: Harvard University Press).

Moore, M. (2005) 'Break-Through Innovations and Continuous Improvement: Two Different Models of Innovative Processes in the Public Sector', *Public Money and Management*, 25 (1), 35–50

Moore, M. and Hartley, J. (2008) 'Innovations in Governance', *Public Management Review*, 10 (1), 3–20.

Morris, P.W.G. and Hough, G.H. (1987) *The Anatomy of Major Projects: A Study of Project Management* (Chichester: John Wiley & Sons), p. 218

Morris, C.W. (1998) *An Essay on the Modern State* (Cambridge: Cambridge University Press).

Mossberger, K. (2000) *The Politics of Ideas and the Spread of Enterprise Zones* (Washington, D.C.: Georgetown University Press).

Mouwen, C.A.M. (2006) *Strategie-Implementatie. Sturing En Governance in De Moderne Non-Profit Organisatie* (Assen: Van Gorcum).

Mulgan, G. and Albury, D. (2003) *Innovation in the Public Sector* (London: Strategy Unit Cabinet Office).

Mulgan, G. (2007) *Ready or Not? Taking Innovation in the Public Sector Seriously* (London: NESTA).

National Audit Office (2006a) *Achieving Innovation in Central Government Organizations: Detailed Research Findings, HC 1447–I* (London: The Stationary Office).

National Audit Office (2006b) *Achieving Innovation in Central Government Organizations, HC 1447–II* (London: The Stationary Office).

Nelson, R. and Winter, S. (1982) *An Evolutionary Theory of Economic Change* (Cambridge, MA: Harvard University Press).

Newman, J., Raine, J. and Skelcher, C. (2001) 'Transforming Local Government: Innovation and Modernization', *Public Money and Management*, 21 (2), 61–68.

Newman, J. (2005) 'Bending Bureaucracy: Leadership and Multi-Level Governance', in P. Du Gay (ed.) *The Values of Bureaucracy* (Oxford: Oxford University Press).

Noordegraaf, M., Meurs, P. and Stoopendaal, A. (2005) 'Pushed Organizational Pulls', *Public Management Review*, 7 (1), 25–43.

Noordegraaf, M. (2007) 'From Pure to Hybrid Professionalism: Present-Day Professionalism in Ambiguous Public Domains', *Administration & Society*, 39 (6), 761–785.

Noordegraaf, M. and Van der Meulen, M. (2008) 'Professional Power Play: Organizing Management in Health Care', *Public Administration*, 86 (3), 1–15.

Nooteboom, B. (2002) *Trust: Forms, Foundations, Functions, Failures and Figures* (Cheltenham: Edward Elgar).

Nooteboom, S. (2006) *Adaptive Networks: The Governance for Sustainable Development* (Delft: Eburon).

Nyiri, L., Osimo, D., Özcivelek, R., Centeno, C. and Cabrera, M. (2007). *Public Procurement for the Promotion of R&D and Innovation in ICT* (Luxembourg: Office for Official Publications of the European Communities, Institute for Prospective Technological Studies).

OECD (2003) *The E-Government Imperative* (Paris: OECD).

OECD (2005) *Modernising Government: The Way Forward* (Paris: OECD).

OECD and Eurostat (2005) *Guidelines for Collecting and Interpreting Innovation Data, Oslo Manual*, 3rd edn (Paris: OECD).

OECD (2006) *Government R&D Funding and Company Behaviour: Measuring Behavioural Additionality* (Paris: OECD).

OECD (2007) *Globalization and Regional Economies: Can OECD Regions Compete in Global Industries?* (Paris: OECD).

Ó Riain, S. (2004) *The Politics of High-Tech Growth: Developmental Network States in Global Economy* (Cambridge: Cambridge University Press).

Osborne, D. and Gaebler, T. (1992) *Reinventing Government* (Reading, MA: Addison-Wesley).

Osborne, S.P. and Brown, K. (2005) *Managing Change and Innovation in Public Service Organizations* (London: Routledge).

Osborne, S., Chew, C. and McLaughlin, K. (2008) 'The Once and Future Pioneers? The Innovative Capacity of Voluntary Organizations and the Provision of Public Services: A Longitudinal Approach', *Public Management Review*, 10 (1), 51–70.

Palma, H.G. (2005) 'The Seven Main "Stylized Facts" of the Mexican Economy since Trade Liberalization and NAFTA', *Industrial and Corporate Change*, 14 (6), 941–991.

Parsons, T. (1951) *The Social System* (London: Tavistock-Routledge).

Pedersen, J.S. (2004) *Nye Rammer – Offentlig opgaveløsning under og efter strukturreformen* (København: Børsens Forlag).

Pedersen, J.S. (2007) *Ledelse i en reformtid i velfærdsstatens maskinrum* (København: Danmarks Forvaltningshøjskoles Forlag).

Pedersen, J.S. (2008) 'Changing Success Criteria for Public Sector Institutions: Squaring the Circle?', in S. Scheuer and J.D. Scheuer (eds) *In the Anatomy of Change – A neo-Institutionalist Perspective* (Copenhagen: Copenhagen Business School Press).

Pedersen, J.S. (2009) *Den offentlige sektor efter reformerne (The public sector after the reforms)* (Copenhagen: Jurist- og Økonomforbundets Forlag).

Perez, C. (1983) 'Structural Change and the Assimilation of New Technologies in the Economic and Social System', *Futures*, 15 (5), 357–375.

Perez, C. (2002) *Technological Revolutions and Financial Capital: The Dynamics of Bubbles and Golden Ages* (Cheltenham: Edward Elgar).

Perez, C. (2006) 'Respecialization and the Deployment of the ICT Paradigm: An Essay on the Present Challenges of Globalization', in R. Compañó, C. Pascu, A. Bianchi, J.C. Burgelman, S. Barrios, M. Ulbrich and I. Maghiros (eds) *The Future of the Information Society in Europe: Contributions to the Debate* (Seville, Spain: European Commission, Directorate General Joint Research Centre).

Perrow, C. (1999) *Normal Accidents; Living with High-Risk Technology* (Princeton: Princeton University Press).

Phillips, A. (1971) *Technology and Market Structure: A Study of the Aircraft Industry* (Lexington, KY: Lexington Books).

Pich, M.T., Loch, C.H. and de Meyer, A. (2002), 'On Uncertainty, Ambiguity, and Complexity in Project Management', *Management Science*, 48 (8), 1008–1023.

Pinto, J.K. (1986) *Project Implementation: A Determination of Its Critical Success Factors, Moderators and Their Relative Importance across the Project Life Cycle* (Pittsburgh: University of Pittsburgh).

Pisani-Ferry, J., Aghion, P., Belka, M., von Hagen, J., Heikensten, L. and Sapir, A. (2008) Coming of Age: Report on the Euro Area (Bruegel Blueprint Series 4), http://www.bruegel.org/6062, 16 June 2009.

Pohl, H. and Sandberg, T. (2005) *Clean Vehicle Procurement: A Rear View and Guideline. Trendsetter Report nr 24* (City of Stockholm: Environment and Health Administration).

Pollitt, C. and Bouckaert, G. (2000) *Public Management Reform* (Oxford: Oxford University Press).

Pollitt, C. (2002) 'The New Public Management in International Perspective; An Analysis of Impacts and Effects', in K. McLaughin, K.S. Osborne and E. Ferlie (eds) *New Public Management: Current Trends and Future Prospects* (London: Routledge).

Pollitt, C. (2003) *The Essential Public Manager, Public Policy and Management* (Maidenhead: Open University Press).

Pollitt, C. and Bouckaert, G. (2004) *Public Management Reform: A Comparative Analysis*, 2nd edn (Oxford: Oxford University Press).

Pollitt, C. (2007) 'New Labour's Re-Disorganization: Hyper-Modernism and the Costs of Reform – A Cautionary Tale', *Public Management Review*, 9 (4), 529–543.

Pollitt, C. (2008) *Time, Policy, Management: Governing with the Past* (Oxford: Oxford University Press).

Pollitt, C. and Bouckaert, G. (2009) *Continuity and Change in Policy and Public Management* (Cheltenham: Edward Elgar).

Pollitt, C. and Hupe, P. (2009) 'Talking Governance: The Role of Magic Concepts in Public Administration,' *Paper in Preparation for Publication*, Public Management Center, Leuven University, 2010.

Pollitt, C. (2009) *Innovation in the Public Sector: An Introductory Overview* (Oxford: Oxford University).

Porter, M. (1990) *Competitive Advantage of Nations* (New York: Free Press).

Prahalad, C.K. (2006) 'The Innovation Sandbox', *Strategy+Business*, http://www.strategy-business.com/press/freearticle/06306, 16 June 2008.

Putnam, R. (1993) *Making Democracy Work* (Princeton: Princeton University Press).

Putnam, R. (2000) *Bowling Alone* (New York: Simon & Schuster).

Putters, K. (2001) *Geboeid ondernemen: een studie naar het management in de Nederlandse ziekenhuiszorg* (Assem: Koninklijke Van Gorcum).

Randma, T. (2001) 'A Small Civil Service in Transition: The Case of Estonia', *Public Administration and Development*, 21 (1), 41–51.

Randma-Liiv, T. (2002) 'Small States and Bureaucracy: Challenges for Public Administration', *Trames*, 6 (4), 374–389.

Radoševic, S. and Reid, A. (2006) 'Innovation Policy for a Knowledge-based Economy in Central and Eastern Europe: Driver of Growth or New Layer of Bureaucracy?', in K. Piech and S. Radoševic (eds) *Knowledge-Based Economy in*

Central and East European Countries: Countries and Industries in a Process of Change (Basingstoke: Palgrave Macmillan).

Rhodes, R.A.W. (1997) *Understanding Governance* (Maidenhead: Open University Press).

Rhodes, R. (2007) 'Understanding Governance: Ten Years On', *Organization Studies*, 28 (8), 1243–1264.

Reinert, E.S. (2007) *How Rich Countries Got Rich and Why Poor Countries Stay Poor* (London: Constable & Robinson).

Richards, J. (1982) 'Politics in Small Independent Communities: Conflict or Consensus?', *Journal of Commonwealth and Comparative Politics*, 20 (2), 155–171.

Ringeling, A. (1993) *Het imago van de overheid* (Den Haag: VUGA).

Robbins, S.P. and Coulter, M. (2002) *Management*, 7th edn (Prentice Hall: Pearson Education).

Robinson, E.A.G. (1963) *Economic Consequences of the Size of Nations* (London: Macmillan).

Rodrik, D. (2007) *One Economics, Many Recipes: Globalization, Institutions, and Economic Growth* (Princeton: Princeton University Press).

Rodrik, D. and Subramanian, A. (2008) Why Did Financial Globalization Disappoint? (John F. Kennedy School of Government), http://ksghome.harvard.edu/~drodrik/Why_Did_FG_Disappoint_March_24_2008.pdf, 16 June 2008.

Rogers, E.M. and Kincaid, D.L. (1981) *Communication Networks: A New Paradigm for Research* (New York: Free Press).

Rogers, E.M. (2003) *Diffusion of Innovations*, 5th edn (New York: Free Press).

Rothwell, R. and Zegveld, W. (1981) *Industrial Innovation and Public Policy* (London: Frances Pinter).

Rothwell, R. (1984) 'Creating a Regional Innovation-Oriented Infrastructure: The Role of Public Procurement', *Annals of Public & Cooperative Economics*, 55 (2), 159–172.

Ruef, M. and Scott, W.R. (1998) 'A Multidimensial Model of Organization Legitimacy: Hospital Survival in Changing Institutional Environments', *Administrative Science Quarterly*, 43 (4), 877–904.

Samuelson, P.A. (2004) 'Where Ricardo and Mill Rebut and Confirm Arguments of Mainstream Economists Supporting Globalization', *Journal of Economic Perspectives*, 18 (3), 135–146.

Sanders, R.P. (1998) 'Heroes of the Revolution', in P.W. Ingraham, J.R. Thompson and R.P. Sanders (eds) *Transforming Government: Lessons from the Reinvention Laboratories* (San Francisco: Jossey-Bass).

Scharpf, F.W. (1997) *Games Real Actors Play. Actor-Centered Institutionalism in Policy Research* (Boulder, CO: Westview Press).

van der Scheer, W. (2007) 'Is the New Health-Care Executive an Entrepreneur?', *Public Management Review*, 9 (1), 49–65.

Schuller, T., Baron, S. and Field, J. (2000) 'Social Capital: A Review and Critique', in S. Baron, J. Field and T. Schuller (eds) *Social Capital: Critical Perspectives* (Oxford: Oxford University Press).

Schumpeter, J.A. (1912) *Theorie der wirtschaftlichen Entwicklung* (München und Leipzig: Duncker and Humblot).

Schumpeter, J.A. (1934) *Theory of Economic Development: An Inquiry into Profits, Capital, Credit, Interest, and the Business Cycle* (Cambridge, MA: Harvard University Press).

Schumpeter, J.A. (1942) *Capitalism, Socialism, and Democracy* (New York: Harper).

Schumpeter, J.A. (1947) *Capitalism, Socialism, and Democracy*, 1st edn (London: Allen & Unwin).

Schumpeter, J. (1969) *The Theory of Economic Development. An Inquiry into Profits, Capital, Credit, Interest and the Business Cycle* (Oxford: Oxford University Press).

Schut, F.T. and Van de Ven, W.P.M.M. (2005) 'Rationing and Competition in the Dutch Health-Care System', *Health Economics*, 14, 59–74.

Scott, W.R. and Meyer, J.W. (1991) 'The Organization of Societal Sectors', in W.W. Powel and P.J. DiMaggio (eds) *The New Institutionalism in Organizational Analysis* (Chicago: University of Chicago Press).

Scott, J.C. (1998) *Seeing Like a State* (New Haven/London: Yale University Press).

Scott, J.C. (2000) *Social Network Analysis: A Handbook,* 2nd edn (Thousand Oaks, CA: Sage Publications).

Scott, W., Ruef, M., Mendel, P. and Carona, C. (2000) *Institutional Change and Health Care Organizations: From Professional Dominance to Managed Care* (Chicago: University Press of Chicago).

Scott, W. (2001) *Institutions and Organizations,* 2nd edn (Thousand Oaks, CA, London, and New Delhi: Sage Publications).

Selznick, P. (1984) *Leadership in Administration: A Sociological Interpretation* (Berkeley: University of California Press).

Serra, A. (1613) *Breve trattato delle cause che possono far abbondare l'oro e l'argento dove non sono miniere* (Naples: Lazzaro Scorriggio).

Sharif, N. (2006) 'Emergence and Development of the National Innovation Systems Approach', *Research Policy*, 35 (5), 745–766.

Shenhar, A.J., Dvir, D., Levy, O. and Maltz, A.C. (2001) 'Project Success: A Multidimensional Strategic Concept', *Long Range Planning*, 34, 699–725.

van Slyke, D.M. (2006) 'Agents or Stewards: Using Theory to Understand the Government-Nonprofit Social Service Contracting Relationship', *Journal of Public Administration Research and Theory*, 17 (2), 157–187.

Snellen, I.Th.M. (1987) *Boeiend en geboeid* (Alphen aan de Rijn: Samsom H.D. Tjeenk Willink).

Spohrer, J.S., Vargo, L., Caswell, N. and Maglio, P.P. (2008) 'The Service System is the Basic Abstraction of Service Science', *Proceedings of the 41st Hawaii International Conference on System Sciences.*

von Stamm, B. (2003) 'Managing Innovation, Design and Creativity', *Long Range Planning*, 34, 699–725.

Star, S.L. and Griesemer, J.R. (1989) 'Institutional Ecology, "Translations," and Boundary Objects: Amateurs and Professionals in Berkeley's Museum of Vertebrate Zoology', *Social Studies of Science*, 19 (3), 387–420.

Steinmetz, R., Thorhallsson, B. and Wivel, A. (2009) *Small States Inside and Outside the European Union: The Lisbon Treaty and Beyond* (Aldershot: Ashgate).

Stone, D. (2003) *The Policy Paradox* (New York: Norton & Co).

Suchmann, M.C. (1995) 'Managing Legitimacy: Strategic and Institutional Approaches', *The Academy of Management Review*, 20 (3), 571–610.

Suddaby, R. and Greenwood, R. (2005) 'Rhetorical Strategies of Legitimacy', *Administrative Science Quarterly*, 50 (1), 35–67.

Sullivan, H. and Skelcher, C.K. (2002) *Working Across Boundaries. Collaboration in Public Services* (Basingstoke: Palgrave Macmillan).

Sundbo, J. (1998) *The Theory of Innovation: Entrepreneurs, Technology and Strategy* (Cheltenham: Edward Elgar).

Sundbo, J. and Fuglsang, L. (2002) *Innovation as Strategic Reflexivity* (London: Routledge).

Sutton, P. (1987) 'Political Aspects', in C. Clarke and T. Payne (eds) *Politics, Security, and Development in Small States* (London: Allen and Unwin).

Swift, F. (1993) *Strategic Management in the Public Service – The Changing Role of the Deputy Minister* (Canada: Canadian Centre for Management Development).

Teisman, G.R., van Buuren, M.W. and Gerrits, L.M. (2009) *Managing Complex Governance Systems: Dynamics, Self-Organization and Coevolution in Public Investments* (London: Routledge), pp. 193–212.

Terry, L. (1990) 'Leadership in the Administrative State. The Concept of Administrative Conservatorship', *Administration & Society*, 21 (4), 395–412.

Terry, L. (1996) *Leadership of Public Bureaucracies: The Administrator as Conservator* (Thousand Oaks, CA: Sage Publications).

Teske, P. and Schneider, M. (1994) 'The Bureaucratic Entrepreneur: The Case of City Managers', *Public Administration Review*, 54 (4), 331–340.

Thaens, M. (2006) *Verbroken verbindingen herstelt* (Lemma: Den Haag).

Thorallsson, B. and Wivel, A. (2006) 'Small States in the European Union: What Do We Know and What Would We Like to Know?', *Cambridge Review of International Affairs*, 19 (4), 651–668.

Tijdelijke Commissie Infrastructuurprojecten (2004–2005) *Onderzoek naar infrastructuurprojecten. Tweede Kamer (29283 – nrs. 1–10)* (The Hague: Sdu Uitgevers).

Toivonen, M., Touminen, T. and Brax, S. (2007) 'Innovation Process Interlinked with the Process of Service Delivery: A Management Challenge in KIBS', *Économies et Sociétés*, 8 (3), 355–384.

Turner, J.R. and Keegan, A. (1999) 'The Versatile Project-Based Organization: Governance and Operational Control', *European Management Journal*, 17 (3), 296–309.

Tushman, M.L. (1977) 'Special Boundary Roles in the Innovation Process', *Administrative Science Quarterly*, 22 (4), 587–605.

Tushman, M.L. and Scanlan, T.J. (1981) 'Characteristics and External Orientations of Boundary Spanning Individuals', *The Academy of Management Journal*, 24 (1), 83–98.

van Twist, M. (1994) *Verbale vernieuwing* (Den Haag: VUGA).

Valente, T. (1998) *Network Models of the Diffusion of Innovations* (Creskill, NJ: Hampton Press).

Varkevisser, M., Capps, C.S. and Schut, F.T. (2008) 'Defining Hospital Markets for Antitrust Enforcement: New Approaches and Their Applicability TOT The Netherlands', *Health Economics Policy and Law*, 3 (23), 7–29.

Veenswijk, M. (2006) 'Cultural Change in the Public Sector: Innovating Frontstage and Backstage', in M. Veenswijk (ed.) *Organizing Innovation* (Amsterdam/Berlin/Oxford/Tokyo/Washington, D.C.: IOS Press).

van de Ven, A.H. and Rogers, E.M. (1988) 'Innovations and Organizations – Critical Perspectives', *Communication Research*, 15 (5), 632–651.

van de Ven, A., Polly, D., Garud, R. and Venkataraman, S. (1999) *The Innovation Journey* (Oxford: Oxford University Press).

van Gunsteren, H.R. (1976) *The Quest for Control: A Critique of the Rational-Central-Rule Approach in Public Affairs* (London: Wiley).

Voets, J. (2008) *Intergovernmental Relations in Multi-Level Arrangements: Collaborative Public Management in Flanders* (Leuven: KU Leuven).

Voets, J., Van Dooren, W. and De Rynck, F. (2008) 'A Framework for Assessing the Performance of Policy Networks', *Public Management Review*, 10 (6), 773–790.

Wade, R. (1990) *Governing the Market: Economic Theory and the Role of the Government in East Asian Industrialization* (Princeton: Princeton University Press).

Wade, R. (2004) *Governing the Market: Economic Theory and the Role of Government in East Asian Industrialization*, 2nd edn (Princeton: Princeton University Press).

Walker, R.M. and Enticott, G. (2004) 'Using Multiple-Informants in Public Administration: Revisiting the Managerial Values and Actions Debate', *Journal of Public Administration Research and Theory*, 14 (3), 417–434.

Walker, R.M. (2006) 'Innovation Type and Diffusion: An Empirical Analysis of Local Government', *Public Administration*, 84 (2), 311–335.

Walsh, V. (1988) 'Technology and Competitiveness of Small Countries: A Review' in C. Freeman and B.Å. Lundvall (eds) *Small Countries Facing Technological Revolution* (London: Pinter).

Walters, J. (2001) *Understanding Innovation: What Inspires It? What Makes It successful?* (Arlington: PricewaterhouseCoopers Endowment for the Business of Government), www.endowment.pwcglobal.com, 17 December 2007.

Warrington, E. (1997) 'Introduction', *Public Administration and Development* (special issue), 17 (1), 3–12.

Wasserman, S. and Faust, K. (1994) *Social Network Analysis: Methods and Applications* (New York: Cambridge University Press).

Weber, M., Roth, G. and Wittich, C. (1978) *Economy and Society* (Berkeley, CA: University of California Press).

Wetenschappelijke Raad voor het Regeringsbeleid (WRR) (2001) *Het borgen van het publieke belang* (Den Haag: Sdu).

Wetenschappelijke Raad voor het Regeringsbeleid (WRR) (2004) *Bewijzen van goede dienstverlening: Rapporten aan de regering nr. 70* (Amsterdam: Amsterdam University Press).

Williams, T.M. (1999) 'The Need for New Paradigms for Complex Projects', *International Journal of Project Management*, 17 (5), 296–273.

Williamson, J. (1990) 'What Washington Means by Policy Reform', in J. Williamson (ed.) *Latin American Adjustment: How Much Has Happened?* (Washington, D.C.: Institute for International Economics).

Winch, G.M. (2002) *Managing Construction Projects* (Oxford: Blackwell Science).

World Bank (2006) *Economic Growth in the 1990s: Learning from a Decade of Reform* (Washington, D.C.: World Bank).

Willke, H. (1991) *Systemtheorie*, 3rd edn (Stuttgart/New York: Fisher).

Windrum, P. (2008) 'Innovation and Entrepreneurship in Public Services', in P. Windrum and P. Koch (eds) *Innovation in Public Sector Services. Enterpreneurship, Creativity and Management* (Cheltenham: Edward Elgar).

Windrum, P. and Koch, P. (2008) *Innovation in Public Sector Services. Enterpreneurship, Creativity and Management* (Cheltenham: Edward Elgar).

Yin, R.K. (2003) *Case Study Research: Design and Methods,* 3rd edn (London: Sage Publications).

Young Foundation (2006) *Social Silicon Valleys: A Manifesto for Social Innovation, What It Is, Why It Matters and How It Can Be Accelerated* (London: Young Foundation).

Zand, D.E. (1972) 'Trust and Managerial Problem Solving', *Administrative Science Quaterly*, 17 (2), 229–239.

Zouridis, S. and Termeer, K. (2006) 'Never the Twain Shall Meet. Een oxymoron: innovatie in het openbaar bestuur', *Bestuurskunde*, 14 (7/8), 13–23.

Index